T0185173

# Human–Computer Interaction Series

**Editors-in-chief**

John Karat

Jean Vanderdonckt
Université catholique de Louvain, Louvain-la-Neuve, Belgium

**Editorial Board**

Ravin Balakrishnan, University of Toronto, Toronto, ON, Canada

Simone Barbosa, PUC-Rio, Rio de Janeiro, RJ, Brazil

Regina Bernhaupt, Ruwido, Salzburg, Austria

John Carroll, The Pennsylvania State University, University Park, PA, USA

Adrian Cheok, Keio University, Tokyo, Japan

Gilbert Cockton, Northumbria University, Newcastle upon Tyne, UK

Henry Been-Lirn Duh, University of Tasmania, Sandy Bay, TAS, Australia

Peter Forbrig, Universität Rostock, Rostock, Germany

Carla Freitas, Federal University of Rio Grande do Sul, Porto Alegre, RS, Brazil

Hans Gellersen, Lancaster University, Lancaster, UK

Robert Jacob, Tufts University, Medford, MA, USA

Panos Markopoulos, Eindhoven University of Technology, Eindhoven, The Netherlands

Gerrit Meixner, Heilbronn University, Heilbronn, Germany

Dianne Murray, Putting People Before Computers, London, UK

Brad A. Myers, Carnegie Mellon University, Pittsburgh, PA, USA

Philippe Palanque, Université Paul Sabatier, Toulouse, France

Oscar Pastor, University of Valencia, Valencia, Spain

Beryl Plimmer, University of Auckland, Auckland, New Zealand

Desney Tan, Microsoft Research, Redmond, WA, USA

Manfred Tscheligi, Center for Usability Research and Engineering, Vienna, Austria

Gerrit van der Veer, Vrije Universiteit Amsterdam, Amsterdam, The Netherlands

Shumin Zhai, IBM Almaden Research Center, San Jose, CA, USA

HCI is a multidisciplinary field focused on human aspects of the development of computer technology. As computer-based technology becomes increasingly pervasive—not just in developed countries, but worldwide—the need to take a human-centered approach in the design and development of this technology becomes ever more important. For roughly 30 years now, researchers and practitioners in computational and behavioral sciences have worked to identify theory and practice that influences the direction of these technologies, and this diverse work makes up the field of human-computer interaction. Broadly speaking it includes the study of what technology might be able to do for people and how people might interact with the technology. The HCI series publishes books that advance the science and technology of developing systems which are both effective and satisfying for people in a wide variety of contexts. Titles focus on theoretical perspectives (such as formal approaches drawn from a variety of behavioral sciences), practical approaches (such as the techniques for effectively integrating user needs in system development), and social issues (such as the determinants of utility, usability and acceptability).

For further volumes:
http://www.springer.com/series/6033

Tim Hussein • Heiko Paulheim •
Stephan Lukosch • Jürgen Ziegler • Gaëlle Calvary

Editors

# Semantic Models
# for Adaptive
# Interactive Systems

Springer

*Editors*

Tim Hussein
Interactive Systems Group
University of Duisburg-Essen
Duisburg, Germany

Heiko Paulheim
Data and Web Science Group
University of Mannheim
Mannheim, Germany

Stephan Lukosch
Faculty of Technology, Policy & Manageme
Delft University of Technology
Delft, The Netherlands

Jürgen Ziegler
Interactive Systems Group
University of Duisburg-Essen
Duisburg, Germany

Gaëlle Calvary
Grenoble Informatics Laboratory
Grenoble Institute of Technology
Grenoble, France

ISSN 1571-5035    Human–Computer Interaction Series
ISBN 978-1-4471-6238-4              ISBN 978-1-4471-5301-6 (eBook)
DOI 10.1007/978-1-4471-5301-6
Springer London Heidelberg New York Dordrecht

© Springer-Verlag London 2013
Softcover re-print of the Hardcover 1st edition 2013
This work is subject to copyright. All rights are reserved by the Publisher, whether the whole or part of
the material is concerned, specifically the rights of translation, reprinting, reuse of illustrations, recitation,
broadcasting, reproduction on microfilms or in any other physical way, and transmission or information
storage and retrieval, electronic adaptation, computer software, or by similar or dissimilar methodology
now known or hereafter developed. Exempted from this legal reservation are brief excerpts in connection
with reviews or scholarly analysis or material supplied specifically for the purpose of being entered
and executed on a computer system, for exclusive use by the purchaser of the work. Duplication of
this publication or parts thereof is permitted only under the provisions of the Copyright Law of the
Publisher's location, in its current version, and permission for use must always be obtained from Springer.
Permissions for use may be obtained through RightsLink at the Copyright Clearance Center. Violations
are liable to prosecution under the respective Copyright Law.
The use of general descriptive names, registered names, trademarks, service marks, etc. in this publication
does not imply, even in the absence of a specific statement, that such names are exempt from the relevant
protective laws and regulations and therefore free for general use.
While the advice and information in this book are believed to be true and accurate at the date of publication, neither the authors nor the editors nor the publisher can accept any legal responsibility for any
errors or omissions that may be made. The publisher makes no warranty, express or implied, with respect
to the material contained herein.

Printed on acid-free paper

Springer is part of Springer Science+Business Media (www.springer.com)

# Preface

Semantic technologies and, in particular, ontologies as formal and shareable representations of a domain play an increasingly important role in computer science, especially for the design, development and execution of interactive systems. Semantic models can serve a number of different purposes in this context. They can be used as functional core or user interface models in model-driven analysis, design, generation, and adaptation of user interfaces.

Ontologies may enhance the functional coverage of an interactive system as well as its visualization and interaction capabilities in various ways, e.g., by providing input assistance, intelligently clustering information, guiding collaborative interaction, or adapting the user interface according to the user's context. Especially in the latter case, ontologies can be applied for representing the various kinds of context information for context-aware and adaptive systems. In particular, they have promised to provide a technique for representing external physical context factors such as location, time or technical parameters, as well as "internal" context such as user interest profiles or interaction context in a consistent, generalized manner. Owing to these properties, semantic models can also contribute to bridging gaps, e.g., between user models, context-aware interfaces and model-driven UI generation.

There is, therefore, a considerable potential for using semantic models as a basis for adaptive interactive systems. The range of potential adaptations is wide comprising, for example, context- and user-dependent recommendations, interactive assistance when performing application-specific tasks, adaptation of the application functionality, adaptation of the collaboration process, or adaptive retrieval support. Furthermore, a variety of reasoning and machine learning techniques exist, that can be employed to achieve adaptive system behavior. Last, but not least, the advent and rapid growth of Linked Open Data as a large-scale collection of semantic data has paved the way for a new breed of intelligent, knowledge-intensive applications.

To explore that potential, we have established a workshop series called *Semantic Models for Adaptive Interactive Systems (SEMAIS)*. The workshop had its debut at the ACM Intelligent User Interfaces conference in Hong Kong in 2010, and was followed by two subsequent editions in Palo Alto in 2011, and in Lisbon in 2012. At the workshop, we have seen cutting edge research spanning from the employment of semantic models in the development and generation of interactive systems to novel interaction paradigms and applications for semantic data.

This book collects enhanced, revised, and updated versions of the best papers submitted to the three workshops editions, as well as additional original contributions. It provides insights into methodologies for designing adaptive systems based on semantic data, introduces models that can be used for building interactive systems, and showcases applications made possible by the use of semantic models.

## Book Outline

*UI²Ont—A Formal Ontology on User Interfaces and Interactions* by Heiko Paulheim and Florian Probst discusses the potentials of an encompassing ontology for describing user interfaces and the way humans interact with them. The authors show how such an ontology can be constructed from existing user interface description languages and describe how it can be employed for application integration.

*Generating Models of Recommendation Processes out of Annotated Ontologies* by Hermann Kaindl et al. shows how the development of interactive systems—in that case recommendation systems—can be automated to a certain extent by the use of ontologies. They discuss a methodology for turning a product ontology into a discourse system in which users can interactively choose products. The system was tested in active online stores, showing that the semi-automatically generated discourses were competitive with manually designed ones.

*Cognitive Semantic Categories as a Basis for a Prototype Adaptive Information System* by Evangelos Kapros and Simon McGinnes introduces a methodology for generating applications offering basic general operations on a dynamic data structure. They leverage findings from neurology and cognitive semantics to derive a set of archetypal categories, which is used as a top level for automatically generating intuitive visual designs for adaptive information systems.

*A Semantic Model for Adaptive Collaboration Support Systems* by Stefan W. Knoll et al. discusses an encompassing framework for fostering elastic collaboration processes, i.e., collaboration processes that are not statically predefined, but may be adapted to dynamic requirements and situational changes. Their approach is based on a semantic model that can be used to express information about process steps as well as the participants and their contexts, thus allowing for the implementation of dynamic applications.

*A Semantics-Based, End-User-Centered Information Visualization Process for Semantic Web Data* by Martin Voigt et al. introduces the *VizBoard* workbench, a system which allows end users without specific Semantic Web skills to create informative visualizations of Semantic Web data. By using semantic description of all visualization components, complex adaptive and interactive views can be generated.

*PASTREM: Proactive Ontology Based Recommendations for Information Workers* by Benedikt Schmidt et al. addresses the needs of information workers dealing with multiple diverse resources in various processes. The chapter discusses a recommender system that detects the user's current context and work process and identifies relevant items in the user's system. The system was evaluated using data collected from different work stations at an IT company, and is shown to provide more meaningful recommendations than common recommendation algorithms.

*Visualizing Search Results of Linked Open Data* by Christian Stab et al. introduces an approach for making search on Linked Open Data more intuitive for end users. Their approach provides a means to translate natural language keyword searches to formal queries on Linked Data, and gives the users visual feedback on both the system's understanding of the user's query and the search results. The authors show that users searching for information with their system are both faster as well as more satisfied than with traditional approaches.

*A Context-Aware Shopping Portal Based on Semantic Models* by Tim Hussein et al. illustrates how semantic models can be used as backend data source for both exploration and adaption of interactive systems. They show how semantic models can be used to provide faceted browsing as well as user adaption and recommendation, using spreading activitation on semantic data to make the system adapt to a user's preferences.

*Semantic Models for Interactive Systems: The Case of Tagging and Folksonomies* by Steffen Lohmann is concerned with a specific interaction technique that has become popular in the Web 2.0, i.e., tagging. User generated tags are used as a basis for finding and recommending content in large-scale platforms such as Flickr or YouTube. The chapter introduces a formal ontology for describing tagging interactions and the relations between individual tags, which can be used for novel graphical visualizations.

*User Interaction Templates for the Design of Lifelogging Systems* by Frank Hopfgartner et al. shows how semantics can help organizing and analyzing the abundance of data generated by lifelogging systems, i.e., systems that constantly track their users. They discuss use cases, interaction techniques, and information visualization approaches that are made possible by using semantic representations of the data collected by lifelogging systems.

## Acknowledgements

The editors would like to thank all the authors contributing chapters to this volume and participating in the peer reviewing process, as well as Beverley Ford and Ben Bishop at Springer for making this volume possible. Furthermore, we would like to thank the organizers of the ACM Intelligent User Interfaces conferences 2010–2012 for providing the frame for the SEMAIS workshop series, and all the participants at those workshops for their interesting submissions and stimulating discussions.

Duisburg, Mannheim, Delft, Grenoble                                    Tim Hussein
March 2013                                                                        Heiko Paulheim
                                                                                    Stephan Lukosch
                                                                                    Jürgen Ziegler
                                                                                    Gaëlle Calvary

# Contents

# Contents

# Contributors

**Edin Arnautovic** Vienna, Austria

**Matthias Breyer** Fraunhofer Institute for Computer Graphics Research (IGD), Darmstadt, Germany

**Dirk Burkhardt** Fraunhofer Institute for Computer Graphics Research (IGD), Darmstadt, Germany

**Dominik Ertl** Vienna University of Technology, Vienna, Austria

**Jürgen Falb** Vienna University of Technology, Vienna, Austria

**Eicke Godehardt** SAP Research, Darmstadt, Germany

**Cathal Gurrin** Dublin City University, Dublin, Ireland

**Ralph Hoch** Vienna University of Technology, Vienna, Austria

**Frank Hopfgartner** TU Berlin, Berlin, Germany

**Tim Hussein** University of Duisburg-Essen, Duisburg, Germany

**Jordan Janeiro** Delft University of Technology, Delft, The Netherlands

**Hermann Kaindl** Vienna University of Technology, Vienna, Austria

**Evangelos Kapros** The University of Dublin, Dublin, Ireland

**Stefan W. Knoll** Delft University of Technology, Delft, The Netherlands

**Gwendolyn L. Kolfschoten** Delft University of Technology, Delft, The Netherlands

**Timm Linder** University of Duisburg-Essen, Duisburg, Germany

**Steffen Lohmann** University of Stuttgart, Stuttgart, Germany

**Stephan G. Lukosch** Delft University of Technology, Delft, The Netherlands

**Simon McGinnes** The University of Dublin, Dublin, Ireland

**Klaus Meißner** TU Dresden, Dresden, Germany

**Kawa Nazemi** Fraunhofer Institute for Computer Graphics Research (IGD), Darmstadt, Germany

**Ada Okoli** Smart Information Systems GmbH, Viena, Austria

**Heiko Paulheim** University of Mannheim, Mannheim, Germany

**Stefan Pietschmann** TU Dresden, Dresden, Germany

**Roman Popp** Vienna University of Technology, Vienna, Austria

**Florian Probst** SAP Research, Darmstadt, Germany

**Martin Schliefnig** Smart Information Systems GmbH, Viena, Austria

**Benedikt Schmidt** SAP Research, Darmstadt, Germany

**Christian Stab** Fraunhofer Institute for Computer Graphics Research (IGD), Darmstadt, Germany

**Martin Voigt** TU Dresden, Dresden, Germany

**Yang Yang** Dublin City University, Dublin, Ireland

**Lijuan Marissa Zhou** Dublin City University, Dublin, Ireland

**Jürgen Ziegler** University of Duisburg-Essen, Duisburg, Germany

# Chapter 1
# UI²Ont—A Formal Ontology on User Interfaces and Interactions

**Heiko Paulheim and Florian Probst**

**Abstract** Formal models of user interfaces are widely popular in the literature, and various user interface description languages exist. For several use cases, the use of *ontologies* as models for user interfaces has been discussed, leveraging the advantages of a machine-interpretable semantics of user interface components. However, a comprehensive ontology of user interfaces and interactions is not available. In this chapter, we discuss the *UI²Ont* ontology, an ontology of user interfaces and interactions, which reuses many concepts defined in different user interface description languages and grounds them in the formal top level ontology DOLCE. We discuss the rationales of developing the ontology, give an overview of its basic concepts, and show its application in a framework for application integration on the user interface level.

## 1.1 Introduction

Software systems are complex. This holds in particular for the user interfaces of those software systems, which contribute about 50 % to the overall complexity of a software system (Myers and Rosson 1992). To deal with that complexity, models as abstractions of user interfaces are helpful.

To create such models, a variety of user interface description languages has been proposed (Guerrero-Garcia et al. 2009; Paternò et al. 2008; Souchon and Vanderdonckt 2003). These languages, most of which are XML-based, allow for describing user interfaces on an abstract level. The goal is, most often, to generate user interface code from them in a model-driven approach.

While most of those UI description languages are useful for their purpose, some use cases require a stronger formalization than that given by a UML diagram or

H. Paulheim (✉)
University of Mannheim, Mannheim, Germany
e-mail: heiko@informatik.uni-mannheim.de

F. Probst
SAP Research, Darmstadt, Germany
e-mail: f.probst@sap.com

T. Hussein et al. (eds.), *Semantic Models for Adaptive Interactive Systems*,
Human–Computer Interaction Series, DOI 10.1007/978-1-4471-5301-6_1,
© Springer-Verlag London 2013

an XML schema. A more formal approach is to use *ontologies* for describing the categories of things that exist in the domain of user interfaces, and their possible relations. An ontology is "a formal, shared conceptualization of a domain" (Gruber 1995), i.e., it captures the categories of things that exist in a domain, and their possible relations, in a formal manner.

Although ontologies have been widely adopted in other software engineering fields, e.g., in the domain of web services (Studer et al. 2007), their employment for user interface development is still rare. Although some first work is done, e.g., in the course of W3C's WAI ARIA initiative (W3C 2011a), a universal ontology of user interfaces is still missing.

This chapter discusses the development of $UI^2Ont$,[1] a formal ontology of user interfaces, split into a top level and a detail level. The former describes the general concepts that exist in the user interface domain (such as components and activities), the latter contains detailed taxonomies of those concepts, i.e., a categorization of component types etc. We have designed the $UI^2$Ont ontology by examining existing user interface description languages and formalizing the concepts contained therein in a rigid ontology, based on the formal top level ontology DOLCE (Masolo et al. 2003).

The rest of this chapter is structured as follows. Section 1.2 motivates the development of a formal ontology of user interfaces and interactions. and Sect. 1.3 discusses a number of potential use cases for such an ontology. Section 1.4 gives an overview on existing ontologies of the domain. Section 1.5 discusses design decisions and the building process of the $UI^2$Ont ontology, while Sect. 1.6 depicts the resulting ontology itself. A sample application using the ontology is discussed in Sect. 1.7. We conclude with a summary and an outlook on future work in Sect. 1.8.

## 1.2 Ontologies vs. UI Models

Although ontologies and software models are related, they are not essentially the same. Software models and ontologies are different by nature. An ontology claims to be a *generic*, commonly agreed upon specification of a conceptualization of a domain (Gruber 1993), with a focus on precisely capturing and formalizing the semantics of terms used in a domain. A software model in turn is *task-specific*, with the focus on an efficient implementation of an application for solving tasks in the modeled domain (Atkinson et al. 2006; Ruiz and Hilera 2006; Spyns et al. 2002). Thus, a software engineer would rather trade off precision for a simple, efficient model, with the possibility of code generation, while an ontology engineer would trade off simplicity for a precise representation (Paulheim et al. 2011). Another difference is that in software engineering, models are most often *prescriptive* models, which are used to specify how a system is *supposed* to behave, while ontologies are rather *descriptive* models, which describe how the world *is* (Aßmann et al. 2006). Figure 1.1 illustrates those differences.

---

[1] http://www.ke.tu-darmstadt.de/resources/ui2-ontology.

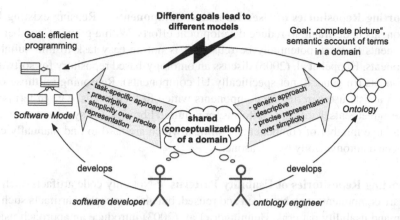

**Fig. 1.1** Ontologies and modeling languages serve different purposes (reprinted from Paulheim and Probst 2011)

Taking this thought to the domain of user interfaces and interactions, models are used to define particular user interfaces (e.g. with the goal of generating code implementing those interfaces), while a formal ontology would capture the nature of things that exist in the domain, e.g., which types of user interfaces exist, and how they are related.

Due to those differences, we argue that developing a formal ontology on user interfaces will not lead to yet another user interface description language, but to a highly formal model with different intentions and usages.

## 1.3  Use Cases

The literature discusses several use cases for employing ontologies in the field of engineering user interfaces, e.g. the position paper by Rauschmayer (2005) and our more recent survey (Paulheim and Probst 2010b). In the latter, we have identified a number of use cases where an ontological representation of the domain of user interfaces and interactions is required or at least beneficial. Those use cases address improving both the development process as well as the user interface itself.

**Automatic Generation of UI Code**    The classic use case for user interface models is generating user interface code from an abstract model, typically in an MDA based setting. An example for using ontologies as input models to a code generator is shown by Liu et al. (2005). The authors argue that employing background knowledge from a richly axiomized ontology can improve the quality of the generated user interfaces, e.g., by identifying useless interaction paths or illegal combinations of interaction components (e.g., foreseeing a mouse-triggered interaction on a device without a mouse). Furthermore, domain ontologies may already be used for other purposes in a software engineering project; they can be reused for creating the description of UI components.

**Supporting Repositories of User Interface Components**    Reusing existing UI components is desirable to reduce development efforts. With a growing number of components that can potentially be reused, it is not an easy task to find suitable components. Happel et al. (2006) discuss an ontology-based repository for software components (in general, not specifically UI components). Reasoning on those ontologies assists users in finding components which fit their needs, e.g., in terms of license agreements, hardware platforms, or required libraries. For systems to be built from a large number of components, conflicts which are hard to find manually can be detected automatically by a reasoner.

**Supporting Repositories of Usability Patterns**    Not only code artifacts such as software components may be stored and reused, but also conceptual artifacts such as design and usability patterns. Henninger et al. (2003) introduce an approach using ontologies for classifying and annotating usability patterns. The authors propose the use of ontologies for managing a repository of patterns. By representing those properties using formal ontologies, more sophisticated approaches could also validate those patterns, find inconsistencies and incompatibilities between different patterns, and identifying commonalities between different usability patterns.

**Integration of UI Components**    Ontologies may not only be used for *identifying*, but also for *integrating* user interface components. We have introduced an approach which uses ontologies for annotating user interface components and messages exchanged by those components (Paulheim and Probst 2010a). A reasoner acts as a central message processor which coordinates the interactions between the different components, based on formalized rules, thus facilitating run-time integration of user interface components. This example is discussed in more detail in Sect. 1.7.

**UI Adaptation**    Different users have different expectations and needs towards an application's user interface. Therefore, making user interfaces *adaptive* is a significant improvement regarding usability. Different approaches have been discussed to employ ontologies for building adaptive user interface have been discussed. The W3C's WAI ARIA initiative (W3C 2011a), for example, suggests the use of ontologies for annotating web based interfaces. Based on a user's profile and semantic annotations of the interface, a reasoner can decide on a optimal realizations for users with impairments, such as color-blindness.

**Self-explanatory User Interfaces**    User interfaces for complex systems are often difficult to understand. Therefore, users may need assistance in finding out how to achieve their goals, how particular user interface components work, and how they are related to each other. Kohlhase and Kohlhase (2009) discuss different approaches which use ontologies for automatically generating explanations in user interfaces, both textually and graphically: ontology-based formalizations of user interfaces are used to create help texts and visual hints at run-time.

## 1.4 Related Work

In the previous section, we have discussed a number of use cases for a formal ontology of the domain of user interfaces and interactions. Although there are some prototypes for those use cases, most of them are built on top of only small, pragmatic ontologies that fit the requirements of those use cases, but to the best of our knowledge, there has not been an attempt to build a concise and comprehensive ontology of the domain.

The *WAI ARIA* ontology (W3C 2011a), whose contents have been used as an input for our ontology, provides a taxonomy of *roles* that elements in a web based application can play, and a set of attributes of those elements. Annotations based on that ontology can be used to make web pages accessible for people with different impairments. The WAI ARIA ontology is not general, but has a strong bias towards web based user interfaces, which makes it difficult to transfer it to other types of user interfaces. The hardware parts of user interfaces are not contained in WAI ARIA, neither are user interactions. Furthermore, it is does not follow a rigid ontology engineering approach, but contains some questionable subclass relations. The top level consists of the three categories WINDOW, WIDGET, and STRUCTURE, but there are many categories which are sub-categories of more than one of those. For example, ALERT DIALOG is at the same time a sub-category of WINDOW and of REGION (a sub-category of STRUCTURE), where the latter is explained to be "a large perceivable section of a web page or document", while the former follows the notion of being a browser displaying such web pages and documents. Such contradicting axioms may cause some difficulties when reasoning on the ontology.

The *GLOSS ontology* (Coutaz et al. 2003) defines categories for *multi surface interactions*, i.e., interactions with tangible user interface components, user interfaces consisting of interactive surfaces (e.g., touch screens), and combinations thereof. The ontology has a strong focus on the hardware aspects of interactive devices and their relations. It contains a formalization of the top level, but omits a detail level laying out different types of devices and their attributes, nor does it contain further categorizations of interactions or user interface components.

The *FIPA device ontology* (Foundation for Intelligent Physical Agents 2002) is also an ontology of user interface devices, which focuses on mobile devices, such as smart phones. It provides means to describe the technical capabilities of such devices, e.g., audio input and output, memory, and screen resolution. While being suitable for certain use cases, such as comparing devices and their capabilities and defining requirements of software for such devices, the ontology is not expressive and detailed enough to be used for other scenarios in the user interface area.

A similar approach is taken by the W3C's *CC/PP* (Composite Capability/ Preference Profiles) recommendation (W3C 2004a), where capabilities and preferences of mobile devices are represented in RDF. While the recommendation contains an informative example vocabulary for displays and printers, CC/PP, like the GLOSS ontology, only defines the top level and leaves the specification of the detail level open. Another (meanwhile discontinued) attempt was made by the W3C in the course of the *Delivery Context Ontology* (W3C 2010), which focuses on mobile,

Java based application front ends to web services and provides means to formalize both mobile hardware and Java software. Although its scope is rather limited, it provides a reasonable degree of formalization.

Another aspect of user interfaces and interactions is addressed by the Computer Work Ontology (CWO) (Schmidt et al. 2011). The ontology formalizes the way people work with computers, the goals they pursue, and the actions they perform to achieve these goals. While this ontology provides a concise formal description of the activities, reusing top level ontologies such as DOLCE, it is not capable of capturing interactions with the components and those components as such.

All of the ontologies discussed are rather narrow in scope and do not cover the whole area of user interfaces. Furthermore, many of them are only weakly formalized and do not leverage extensive formalizations of top level ontologies. In contrast, UI$^2$Ont is the first ontology covering the entire spectrum of user interfaces and interactions, allowing for concise descriptions of interactions with classical interfaces as well as the formalization of multi-modal interactions.

## 1.5 Building the Ontology

Most ontology engineering approaches start from collecting concepts from the domain (Fernández et al. 1997; Uschold and King 1995). To that end, we have first reviewed a number of user interface description languages and extracted a list of concepts. Furthermore, we have re-used a number of top-level ontologies and aligned the concepts identified in the first step to those ontologies in order to facilitate a rich axiomatization.

### 1.5.1 Reuse of UI Description Languages

As discussed above, a number of user interface description languages already exists. From the large variety presented in the surveys (Paternò et al. 2008; Souchon and Vanderdonckt 2003), we picked a subset based on criteria such as popularity in the literature, relevance with respect to the modeling goals of the ontology, availability of detailed documentation (as the exact set of tags or keywords is needed for identifying key concepts), and expressiveness.

Figure 1.2 depicts the chosen subset, organized along the three levels of the Cameleon reference framework, i.e., the *concepts and tasks* level, the *abstract user interface* level, and the *concrete user interface* level (Calvary et al. 2003).$^2$

The set of languages taken into account for the development of the UI$^2$Ont ontology consists of UIML (OASIS 2009), XIML (RedWhale Software 2000), the

---

$^2$The fourth level, the *final user interface* level, consists of the interface as such, i.e., binary code, and therefore usually does not involve any model.

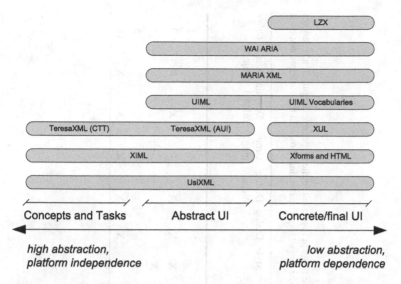

**Fig. 1.2** User interface description languages that have been used as input for our ontology (reprinted from Paulheim 2011)

abstract roles defined in *WAI ARIA* (W3C 2011a), and the abstract user interface parts of *UsiXML* (UsiXML Consortium 2007), *TeresaXML* (Paternò et al. 2008) and its successor *MARIA XML* (Paternò et al. 2009). For the detail level, we have used *LZX* (Laszlo Systems 2006), *XUL* (Mozilla 2011), *XForms* (W3C 2009) and *HTML5* (W3C 2011b), the *MONA UIML vocabulary* (Simon et al. 2004), the concrete user interface part of *UsiXML*, and the concrete roles defined in *WAI ARIA*.

Table 1.1 lists the key concepts from the different UI description languages that we have examined on the abstract UI level. In addition to those 52 concepts, we have identified 26 relations between those concepts. These collections have served as input for building the ontology.

The table shows that there are some differences between the different UI definition languages. Besides different modeling scopes, one reason is that the border between abstract and concrete user interface (Calvary et al. 2003) is not sharply defined: e.g., *Condition* belongs to the abstract user interface part of MARIA, but to the concrete user interface part of UsiXML. Since the table only depicts the languages' respective abstract user interface parts, such deviations occurred.

For the detail level, we have collected definitions of user interface components and user and system activities (which are often expressed as system events notifying about those activities). Figure 1.3 exemplarily shows the distribution of user interface component definitions across the concrete user interface languages examined. The figure shows that there is a "long tail" of components that are only defined in one or two languages. Therefore, it makes sense to unify the input of several languages when collecting concepts.

**Table 1.1** Key concepts identified from examined UI description languages. An X denotes that the concept is present in the respective language, a * denotes that it is present, but expressed as a relation. The table lists all the concepts that exist in at least two of the languages. The last line shows all the concepts that exist in only one language

| Language | User interface component | User interface | Inter-action | Input | Range | Output | Control | Condi-tion | Event | Navi-gation | Style | Dialog | Dialog element | Grou-ping | Domain model | Data object | Other |
|---|---|---|---|---|---|---|---|---|---|---|---|---|---|---|---|---|---|
| UsiXML | X | X | X | X | X | X | X |  |  | X |  |  |  | * |  |  | 1 |
| XIML | X | X | X |  | X | X | * | X |  |  | X | X | X |  | X | X | 9 |
| UIML | X | X | X |  |  |  |  | X | X |  | X |  |  |  |  |  | 3 |
| WAI ARIA | X |  |  | X |  |  |  |  |  |  |  | X |  |  |  |  | 5 |
| MARIA XML | X | X | X | X | X | X | X | X | X | X | X | X | X | X | X | X | 18 |

**Fig. 1.3** Distribution of UI component definitions across different UI description languages (reprinted from Paulheim 2011)

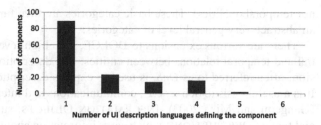

Number of UI description languages defining the component

## 1.5.2 Reuse of Top Level Ontologies

We have reused a number of foundational and upper level ontologies for several reasons. First of all, those ontologies already contain definitions for a larger number of concepts, so they reduce the initial efforts of developing the ontology. Second, using foundational level ontologies eases the interoperability with applications based on ontologies using the same foundational level ontologies. Third, foundational level ontologies provide a certain guidance which simplify the definition of useful categories and prevent typical modeling mistakes (Guarino and Welty 2009). Figure 1.4 shows the stack of ontologies that we have reused.

The scope of the UI description languages examined was in most cases limited to or at least focused on the software part of user interfaces. Therefore, we have reused the ontologies of software and of software components described by Oberle et al. (2009). These two ontologies define categories such as SOFTWARE, SOFTWARE COMPONENT, DATA, COMPUTATIONAL TASK, etc., and their relations, which form a useful basis for ontological modeling of software related things. The core software ontology defines software and software objects in general, while the core ontology of software components can be used to describe properties of actual software components, such as states and parameters.

These ontologies in turn build upon a set of top level ontologies: DOLCE (Masolo et al. 2003) divides the top level of PARTICULARS into ENDURANTS (i.e., entities that *are* in time, such as physical objects), PERDURANTS (i.e., entities that *happen* in time, such as events), QUALITIES inherent to other particulars (such as color or spatial position), and ABSTRACTS (i.e., entities that have neither spatial

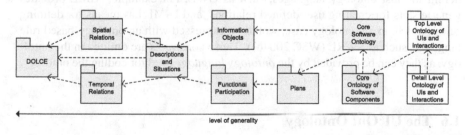

**Fig. 1.4** Stack of the ontologies that have been reused. The top and detail level ontologies of the user interfaces and interactions domain are located on the right hand side (reprinted from Paulheim 2011)

nor temporal qualities). These basic categories are then further subdivided to form an abstract, very general level of categories.

There are various extensions to DOLCE. Two high-level extensions define spatial and temporal relations between entities. The descriptions and situations extension, often referred to as *DnS*, is used to express descriptions *about* other entities. It is a useful basis to define, e.g., communications and interpretations of utterances (Gangemi and Mika 2003). INFORMATION OBJECTS, such as books, are a special type of DESCRIPTIONS, which carry information about other entities (Gangemi et al. 2005). Digital data objects in an information system are also considered information objects, therefore, information objects are the basic entities for defining software.

When software is executed, tasks are performed by an information system. Such tasks are defined by a plan, which is expressed by the software. Therefore, the ontology of plans (Bottazzi et al. 2006) is also reused by the ontology of software. It in turn builds upon the ontology of *functional participation* (Masolo et al. 2003), which defines relations between the execution of tasks and the entities involved in those executions, such as an object serving as an INSTRUMENT or a RESOURCE in a task execution process.

The basic categories and relations defined by the reused ontologies divide the ontology of user interfaces and interactions along two axis, as depicted in Fig. 1.5:

- At *design time*, there are only instances of the DESCRIPTIONS of user interfaces, such as the software specifications and the task descriptions. At *run time*, USER INTERFACE DESCRIPTIONS are realized by COMPUTATIONAL OBJECTS and TANGIBLE OBJECTS, and task descriptions are carried out as ACTIVITIES.
- TASKS and ACTIVITIES describe the interactions possible with user interfaces, while USER INTERFACE COMPONENTS and their realizations describe the COMPONENTS that are involved.

Some of the concepts and relations identified in the first step are already contained in the stack of reused ontologies. For example, tasks and events are already defined in the DOLCE ontologies, and data types (e.g., of data entered in input fields) are already defined in the ontology of software components.

Furthermore, there are constructs in some UI description languages that are inherent to most ontology languages, such as OWL. For example, XIML provides generic slots for creating user defined relations, and UIML has means for defining rules (which, in an ontology case, would be expressed with an ontology-based rule language, such as SWRL (W3C 2004b)). Those constructs are omitted in the ontology, as they can be provided by the *ontology language* used for coding the ontology.

## 1.6 The UI²Ont Ontology

The UI²Ont ontology consists of two levels: the top level ontology defines the elementary categories such as user interface components and interactions, and the basic

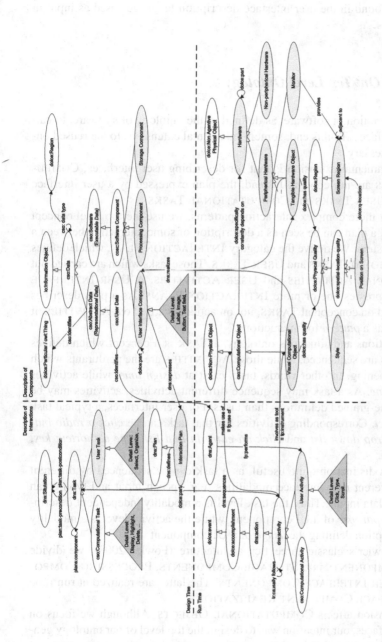

**Fig. 1.5** The top level of the ontology of the user interfaces and interactions domain. In *the upper part*, the design time concepts are shown, the *lower part* contains the run time concepts. The *left part* deals with interactions, the *right part* with components. The *white ellipses* denote concepts from the reused ontologies (with the following namespace conventions: DOLCE (dolce), Information Objects (io), Temporal Relations (tr), Functional Participation (fp), Plans (plan), Descriptions and Situations (dns), Core Software Ontology (cso), Core Ontology of Software Components (cosc)), the *grey ellipses* denote concepts from the top level ontology of the user interfaces and interactions domain. The *gray triangles* denote concepts carried out in the detail ontology (reprinted from Paulheim 2011)

relations that can hold between objects of those categories. The detail level ontology defines the sub-categories and actual types of components and interactions, based on the concepts found in the user interface description languages used as input in the design process.

### 1.6.1 The UI²Ont Top Level Ontology

We use the basic notion of software, as defined in the ontology of software, to categorize user interfaces. To this end, some fundamental extensions to the reused ontologies were necessary.

The first fundamental extension is that for describing user interfaces, COMPUTATIONAL TASKS are not enough. Instead, the plan expressed by a user interface consists of both USER TASKS and COMPUTATIONAL TASKS.

For describing more complex interaction patterns, we use the top level concept PLAN. Generally, a plan can be seen as a description of some interaction between a user and an IT system. We derive the category INTERACTION PLAN, which defines both COMPUTATIONAL TASKS and USER TASKS. Those tasks which are carried out as COMPUTATIONAL ACTIVITIES and USER ACTIVITIES. A USER INTERFACE COMPONENT expresses one or more INTERACTION PLANS. As a plan describes interactions based on conceptual TASKS, not on actually carried out ACTIVITIES, it can also be seen as a *pattern* for interactions.

In the descriptions and situations ontology, a TASK is a concept which defines how ACTIVITIES are sequenced, while those ACTIVITIES are the perdurants which are actually happening. In other words, tasks exist at *design time*, while activities happen at *run-time*. As a task may sequence different activities, activities may be used for more fine-grained definitions than tasks. For user interfaces, a typical task is *select an object*. Corresponding activities for that task can be *click a radio button*, *click on a drop down list* and *click an entry in that list*, *type a shortcut key*, etc.

We found this distinction quite useful, as a task can be sequenced by different activities for different user interface modalities (e.g. speech input and typing can be activities for data input). Thus, the task level is a modality independent description defining the *purpose* of a UI component, while the activity level is a modality dependent description defining the *usage* of a UI component.

Following Fowler's classic three tier architecture (Fowler 2003), we divide SOFTWARE COMPONENTS into STORAGE COMPONENTS, PROCESSING COMPONENTS, and USER INTERFACE COMPONENTS. The latter are realized at run time by USER INTERFACE COMPONENT REALIZATIONS.

The last extension affects COMPUTATIONAL OBJECTS. Although we focus on WIMP user interfaces, our intention was to design the top level of our ontology general enough to cover other forms of user interfaces, such as tangible components, as well. Therefore, we defined the category PERIPHERICAL HARDWARE, where TANGIBLE HARDWARE OBJECTS, as well as non-physical VISUAL COMPUTATIONAL

OBJECTS, can realized USER INTERFACE COMPONENTS. This construction allows our top level ontology to cover both WIMP based as well as tangible user interfaces.

Some of the UI description languages contain classes that have been modeled as relations in the ontology, e.g., `Abstract Adjacency` in UsiXML, which has been turned into the ADJACENT TO relation. Also, by aligning our ontology with the respective top levels, the domain and range of relations has sometimes been changed. The ADJACENT TO relation, for example, has been changed from a relation between user interface components to a relation between the SCREEN REGIONS they occupy.

The most specific categories in our top level ontology are at the level of USER INTERFACE COMPONENTS and USER TASKS. The definition of the subtypes of components and tasks is done in the detail level ontology.

Figure 1.5 shows the top level ontology. The size of the OWL implementation of the top level ontology is depicted in Table 1.2. Although we defined a number of additional classes, we have mostly reused existing relations. Therefore, the number of relations is comparatively low.

While the top level contains definitions of generic categories and relations used to describe user interfaces and interactions, the detail level aims at providing a categorization of user interface components and tasks which is as complete as possible.

As discussed above, we have followed the distinctions imposed by the reused upper level ontologies, which encourage the separation of information objects and their realizations, as well as of description of tasks and actually carried out activities. Transferred to our domain, this results in separating the design time level from the run time level.

Due to this distinction, there are various points where the detail level ontology enhances the top level ontology: on the design time level, taxonomies of USER INTERFACE COMPONENTS, USER TASKS, and COMPUTATIONAL TASKS, are defined. On the run time level, hierarchies of USER ACTIVITIES are defined, as well as HARDWARE ITEMS with which those activities are performed. We have intentionally *not* defined any axioms restricting the allocation of activities to tasks, in order not to exclude any forms of interaction. Furthermore, user interface components are realized at run time by computational objects (i.e., software) and tangible objects (i.e., hardware), as shown in Fig. 1.6, or mixtures of both.

## 1.6.2  The UI²Ont Detail Level Ontology

On the other hand, COMPUTATIONAL TASKS and COMPUTATIONAL OBJECTS are not further specified. Such as a specification is not necessary from a user interface perspective: for describing a user interface, it may be beneficial to describe how a user performs a selection task in a certain modality, but it is not relevant *how* the computer performs a certain computational task.

Due to this distinction, two possibilities of locating the detail level layer are possible: defining the details of TASKS and USER INTERFACE COMPONENTS on the

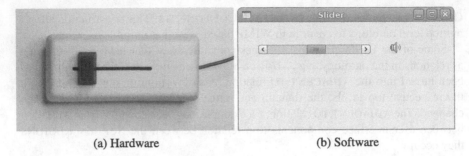

(a) Hardware                                    (b) Software

**Fig. 1.6** Different realizations of a slider user interface component[3]

**Table 1.2** Size of the OWL version of the top and the detail level ontology, as well as the reused ontologies

|                              | Classes | Relations | Axioms |
|------------------------------|---------|-----------|--------|
| Reused ontologies            | 169     | 331       | 2039   |
| UI$^2$Ont Top level ontology | 15      | 2         | 75     |
| UI$^2$Ont Detail level ontology | 179  | 11        | 448    |

design time level, or defining the details of ACTIVITIES and USER INTERFACE COMPONENT REALIZATIONS on the run time level. We decided for the former, since in some of the use cases discussed above, the run time level does not exist. In a repository of UI components, for example, those components are not instantiated and executed when the ontology is used, e.g., for querying the repository. Thus, only instances of categories of the description level exist. Therefore, it is useful to put as much detail as possible on that level.

In our analysis of user interface definition languages, we have identified 80 different types of user interface components, as shown in Fig. 1.7. Using a bottom-up clustering approach, we have grouped them in seven central categories:

- DATA INPUT COMPONENTS are used by the user to manipulate data. Examples are text input fields and radio buttons.
- PRESENTATION MANIPULATION COMPONENTS change the appearance of a user interface component, which is usually another one than the presentation manipulation component itself. Examples are scroll bars and window resizers.
- OPERATION TRIGGERING COMPONENTS are used to invoke system functionalities. Examples are buttons in a tool bar, and menu items.
- DECORATIVE ELEMENTS improve the appearance of user interfaces, are neither interactive nor informative. Examples are separation bars and empty spaces.
- OUTPUTS provide a human consumable representation of data. Examples are text and speech output.

---

[3]Image sources: http://www.flickr.com/photos/anachrocomputer/2574918867/, http://zetcode. com/tutorials/javaswttutorial/widgets/, accessed April 20th, 2011.

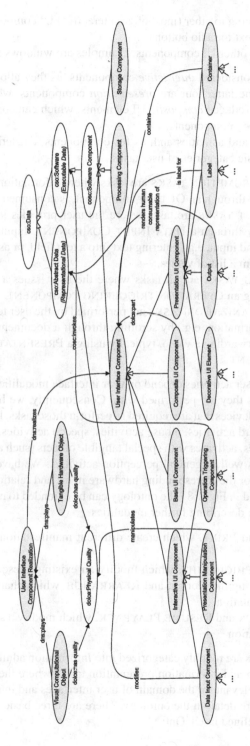

**Fig. 1.7** Top categories for UI components (reprinted from Paulheim 2011)

- LABELS assign meaning to other (most often interactive) UI components. Examples are text labels next to radio buttons.
- CONTAINERS group other UI components. Examples are windows and tool bars.

The first three are considered *interactive* components, as they allow the user to act with them, while the latter four are *presentation* components, which are non-interactive. We also introduced *composite* UI elements, which can contain both interactive and presentation components.

By collecting tasks and activities and, as for components, clustering them, we have identified four basic categories of user tasks:

- INFORMATION CONSUMPTION TASKS are tasks where information provided by the system, typically through an OUTPUT component, is consumed by user.
- INFORMATION INPUT TASKS are tasks where the user provides information to the system, typically through a DATA INPUT COMPONENT. Input tasks can be performed as unbound input, e.g., entering text into a text field, or as bound input, e.g., by selecting from a list of values.
- COMMAND ISSUING TASKS are all tasks where the user issues a system command, typically using an OPERATION TRIGGERING COMPONENT.
- INFORMATION ORGANIZATION TASKS are performed by the user to organize the consumption of information, e.g., by scrolling through a document, following a hyperlink, or fast-forwarding a video, typically using a PRESENTATION MANIPULATION COMPONENT.

Unlike user tasks, user activities depend on user interface modalities, i.e., the actual interactive devices they are performed with. Consequently, we have clustered them according to the devices that are required to perform those tasks, leading to categories such as keyboard activities, mouse activities, speech activities, touch activities, pen based activities, activities with special tangible objects (such as a *reacTable* (Jordà et al. 2007)), as well as general perception activities. We have furthermore defined 11 categories for the corresponding hardware items and relation axioms between those, as depicted in Fig. 1.8. The ontology can be extended to more activities and hardware items for describing further modalities.

- DISPLAY, PLAY, and PRINT, which create different manifestations of an information.
- HIGHLIGHT and DEHIGHLIGHT, which modify an existing presentation of objects, without changing there order, and REARRANGE, which changes the order of an existing presentation.
- SUSPEND PLAYBACK and RESUME PLAYBACK, which modify a streaming presentation of information.

Computational tasks are roughly categorized into information administration, information modification and information presentation tasks, where the latter are the ones which are most relevant for the domain of user interfaces and interactions, and are thus defined in more detail in the ontology. There are three basic categories for computational tasks defined in UI$^2$Ont:

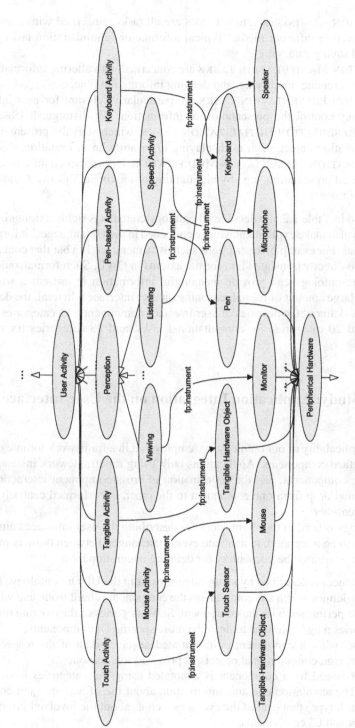

**Fig. 1.8** User activities and their mapping to hardware devices, as defined in UI²Ont (reprinted from Paulheim 2011)

INFORMATION ADMINISTRATION TASKS are all tasks concerned with managing data stored in different media. Typical information administration tasks are loading and saving data.

INFORMATION MANIPULATION TASKS are concerned with altering information objects, e.g., creating, modifying, and deleting information objects.

INFORMATION PRESENTATION TASKS are particularly relevant for user interfaces, as they control the presentation of information. We distinguish INFORMATION PRESENTATION INITIALIZATION TASKS, which start the presentation of an information object, such as displaying or printing an information object, and INFORMATION PRESENTATION MODIFICATION TASKS, which influence an already started presentation, e.g., by highlighting or moving a VISUAL COMPUTATIONAL OBJECT.

As depicted in Table 1.2, the detail level ontology contains is richly axiomatized. Those axioms also make explicit knowledge contained in the UI languages' informal documentations. For example, descriptions such as "a menu bar is a bar that contains menus" can be directly translated into formal axioms in OWL. Such formalizations assure that the ontology can provide meaningful information in use cases which demand for a large amount of formal reasoning on user interfaces. In total, the detail level ontology defines 80 categories of user interface components, 15 categories for user tasks and 20 categories for computational tasks, and 38 categories for user activities.

## 1.7 Case Study: Application Integration on the User Interface Level

To test the applicability of our ontology, we employed it in a framework for integrating user interface components. Applications built using this framework instantiate user interface components, and the coordination of cross-component interactions, such as drag and drop from one component to the other, is performed centrally by an ontology reasoner.

The ontology is used in that framework for describing the user interface components that are to be integrated, to annotate events exchanged between those components, and for providing the vocabulary for defining integration rules:

- Each component is described by using categories from the UI$^2$Ont ontology. This description defines which sub components the component is built from, and which tasks can be performed with the component. Sub-categories of the existing ontology categories may be defined to describe more specific UI components.
- At run-time, when a component is instantiated, instance data of the respective realizations, e.g., computational objects, is provided to a reasoner.
- Each event issued by a component is annotated using the categories from the ontology. The annotation contains information about the of activity (and corresponding task type) that caused the event, as well as about the involved information objects and UI components.

- Integration rules are defined that determine which (computational) activities are triggered by events. Those rules are defined using the vocabulary from the ontology.

The UI²Ont ontology alone is not enough to fulfill those functions. An additional ontology of the *real world domain* that the application is built for is required. For example, when annotating an event, the annotation may state that the user has selected an object in a table which identifies a bank account. While concepts such as SELECT ACTION, MOUSE, and TABLE are defined in the UI ontology, concepts like BANK ACCOUNT or CUSTOMER are concepts from the real world domain ontology.

Since different applications may use incompatible programming models for representing real world objects, but an exchange of that data is necessary in order to facilitate seamless interaction (such as dragging and dropping and object from one application to another), a rule-based mechanism is employed which supports a transformation between the different programming models, using the domain ontology as an interlingua (Paulheim et al. 2011).

A central event processor, based on an ontology reasoner and rule engine, processes the events, based on the integration rules and the axioms encoded in the ontology, determines how to react to an event, and notifies the respective components about the activities they are supposed to perform as a reaction. Those notifications are again annotated using the ontology. The event processor thus acts as a central coordinator facilitating the integration at run-time. Details about the framework can be found in Paulheim and Probst (2010a).

The integration framework completely decouples the interactions between the applications, which only communicate using the ontologies as an interlingua, forming a comprehensive layer of abstraction over the actual implementation. This allows the integration even of user interfaces developed with different technologies, such as Java and Flex, while still supporting deep integration such as drag and drop (Paulheim and Erdogan 2010).

We have applied the framework in the SoKNOS project for building an integrated emergency management system (Babitski et al. 2011), comprised of 24 applications (see Fig. 1.9). The respective integrated applications use 99 different annotated component types (only those components had to be annotated that are used in some cross-application interaction), and 189 different event types. For the prototype, we have used an additional domain ontology of emergency management (Babitski et al. 2009), which consists of 214 classes, 330 relations, and 1514 axioms.

In the SoKNOS project, different types of interactions with multiple modalities and user interface components have been combined, including desktop computers and laptops, large touch screens, and speech interaction devices. With the narrower scoped ontologies discussed in Sect. 1.4, that spectrum of interactions could not have been covered. Furthermore, the use of a reasoner for the automatic computation of possible interactions at run-time was only possible through the rich axiomatization of the UI²Ont ontology. Although a reasoner is run every time an event is processed, the event processing times are still below one second (Paulheim 2010).

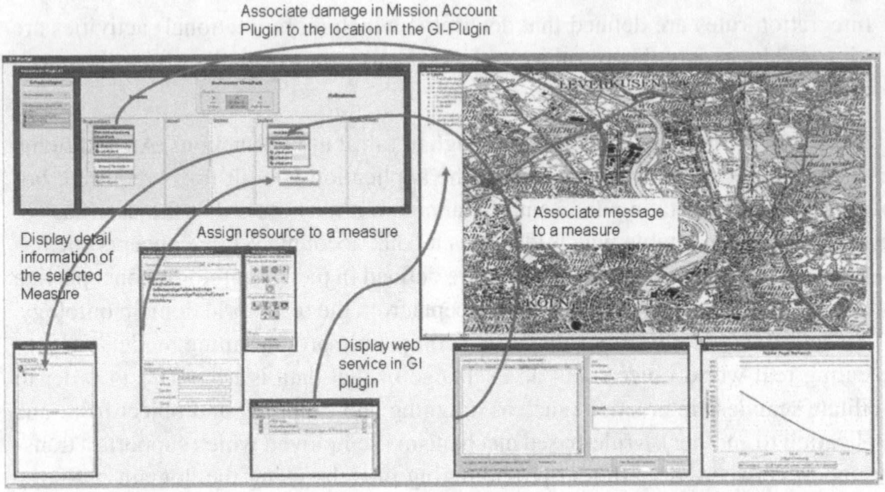

**Fig. 1.9** Screenshot of the SoKNOS project depicting the user interfaces of integrated applications (reprinted from Paulheim et al. 2009). The *arrows* indicate examples for possible interactions

## 1.8 Conclusion

In this chapter, we have laid out a number of use cases in which an ontology of the user interfaces and interactions domain can improve either the development process of user interfaces, or the user interfaces themselves. Motivated by those use cases, we have discussed the construction of a rigid, richly axiomized ontology of the domain, divided into a top level and a detail level ontology. The former contains modality-independent descriptions of tasks and components at design time, while the latter contains modality-dependent descriptions of activities and components at run time. The ontologies are based on a set of foundational ontologies, especially the generic top level ontology DOLCE.

For identifying the relevant concepts, we have used a number of existing user interface description languages. We have clustered the concepts identified and categorized them using the top level categories given by the reused higher level ontologies. Our analysis has shown that there is a "long tail" of concepts that are only covered by a few user interface description languages. This shows that it is beneficial to use the input of several of those languages.

From the use cases discussed as a motivation, we picked the use case of integration of user interface components to show how our ontology has been applied in a real world scenario. Based on the case a large-scale emergency management system, we have shown a real world application of the ontology discussed in this chapter.

Besides the use cases discussed in this paper, having an embracing and formal ontology of the domain of user interfaces and interactions has a number of additional advantages. As discussed above, several user interface description languages exist. During the process of building the ontology, we have observed a number of semantic ambiguities between those languages, e.g. the use of elements called *Dialog* with different meanings in different languages (a set of interactions following each other, a window on a screen blocking an application, etc.). Another example is the *List* element, which is sometimes used for static lists in texts (such as in HTML), sometimes for interactive selections (such as combo boxes). Such ambiguities make it difficult to work with different languages in parallel, especially without extensively consulting the respective documentations. Annotating user interface descriptions in different languages with a formal ontology can help identifying and resolving those ambiguities and foster an easier understanding of user interface models.

In their classical paper from 1996, Uschold and Gruninger discussed the vision of an ontology being used as an *inter-lingua* bridging different languages (Uschold and Grüninger 1996). Transferred to the domain of user interfaces and interactions, this vision could be embodied by a system able to translate between arbitrary user interface description languages and automatically convert models from one language to another, resulting in the ultimate portability of user interfaces across systems, platforms, and modalities. Although this vision is still distant, we believe that we have taken an important step in that direction by developing a unifying formal and comprehensive ontology of the domain.

# References

Aßmann, U., Zschaler, S., & Wagner, G. (2006). Ontologies, meta-models, and the model-driven paradigm. In *Ontologies for software engineering and software technology* (pp. 249–273). Chap. 9.

Atkinson, C., Gutheil, M., & Kiko, K. (2006). On the relationship of ontologies and models. In S. Brockmans, J. Jung & Y. Sure (Eds.), *LNI: Vol. 96. Workshop on meta-modelling (WoMM)* (pp. 47–60). Bonn: GI.

Babitski, G., Probst, F., Hoffmann, J., & Oberle, D. (2009). Ontology design for information integration in catastrophy management. In *Proceedings of the 4th international workshop on applications of semantic technologies (AST'09)*.

Babitski, G., Bergweiler, S., Grebner, O., Oberle, D., Paulheim, H., & Probst, F. (2011). SoKNOS—using semantic technologies in disaster management software. In *The semantic web: research and applications (ESWC 2011), Part II* (pp. 183–197).

Bottazzi, E., Catenacci, C., Gangemi, A., & Lehmann, J. (2006). From collective intentionality to intentional collectives: an ontological perspective. *Cognitive Systems Research, 7*(2–3), 192–208.

Calvary, G., Coutaz, J., Thevenin, D., Limbourg, Q., Bouillon, L., & Vanderdonckt, J. (2003). A unifying reference framework for multi-target user interfaces. *Interacting With Computers, 15*(3), 289–308.

Coutaz, J., Lachenal, C., & Dupuy-Chessa, S. (2003). Ontology for multi-surface interaction. In *Proceedings of IFIP INTERACT03: human–computer interaction* (pp. 447–454). IFIP Technical Committee No 13 on Human-Computer Interaction.

Fernández, M., Gómez-Pérez, A., & Juristo, N. (1997). METHONTOLOGY: from ontological art towards ontological engineering. In *Proceedings of the AAAI97 spring symposium* (pp. 33–40).

Foundation for Intelligent Physical Agents (2002). *FIPA device ontology specification*. http://www.fipa.org/specs/fipa00091/index.html.

Fowler, M. (2003). *Patterns of enterprise application architecture*. Reading: Addison-Wesley.

Gangemi, A., & Mika, P. (2003). Understanding the semantic web through descriptions and situations. In *LNCS: Vol. 2888. On the move to meaningful internet systems 2003: CoopIS, DOA, and ODBASE* (pp. 689–706). Berlin: Springer.

Gangemi, A., Borgo, S., Catenacci, C., & Lehmann, J. (2005). *Task taxonomies for knowledge content*. http://www.loa-cnr.it/Papers/D07_v21a.pdf.

Gruber, T. R. (1993). A translation approach to portable ontology specifications. *Knowledge Acquisition, 5*(2), 199–220.

Gruber, T. R. (1995). Toward principles for the design of ontologies used for knowledge sharing. *International Journal of Human-Computer Studies, 43*(5–6), 907–928.

Guarino, N., & Welty, C. A. (2009). An overview of OntoClean. In *Handbook on ontologies* (pp. 201–220). Chap. 10.

Guerrero-Garcia, J., Gonzalez-Calleros, J. M., Vanderdonckt, J., & Munoz-Arteaga, J. (2009). A theoretical survey of user interface description languages: preliminary results. In *LA-WEB '09: Proceedings of the 2009 Latin American web congress (LA-WEB 2009)* (pp. 36–43). Los Alamitos: IEEE Comput. Soc.

Happel, H.-J., Korthaus, A., Seedorf, S., & Tomczyk, P. (2006). KOntoR: an ontology-enabled approach to software reuse. In K. Zhang, G. Spanoudakis & G. Visaggio (Eds.), *Proceedings of the eighteenth international conference on software engineering & knowledge engineering (SEKE)* (pp. 349–354).

Henninger, S., Keshk, M., & Kinworthy, R. (2003). Capturing and disseminating usability patterns with semantic web technology. In *CHI 2003 workshop: concepts and perspectives on HCI patterns*.

Jordà, S., Geiger, G., Alonso, M., & Kaltenbrunner, M. (2007). The reacTable: exploring the synergy between live music performance and tabletop tangible interfaces. In *Proceedings of the 1st international conference on tangible and embedded interaction* (pp. 139–146). New York: ACM.

Kohlhase, A., & Kohlhase, M. (2009). Semantic transparency in user assistance systems. In *Proceedings of the 27th annual ACM international conference on design of communication. Special interest group on design of communication (SIGDOC-09)*, Bloomingtion, IN, United States (pp. 89–96). New York: ACM Special Interest Group for Design of Communication, ACM.

Laszlo Systems (2006). *OpenLaszlo—an open architecture framework for advanced Ajax applications*. http://www.openlaszlo.org/whitepaper/LaszloWhitePaper.pdf.

Liu, B., Chen, H., & He, W. (2005). Deriving user interface from ontologies: a model-based approach. In *ICTAI '05: Proceedings of the 17th IEEE international conference on tools with artificial intelligence* (pp. 254–259). Los Alamitos: IEEE Comput. Soc.

Masolo, C., Borgo, S., Gangemi, A., Guarino, N., & Oltramari, A. (2003). *WonderWeb deliverable D18—ontology library (final)*. http://wonderweb.semanticweb.org/deliverables/documents/D18.pdf.

Mozilla (2011). XUL. https://developer.mozilla.org/en/XUL.

Myers, B. A., & Rosson, M. B. (1992). Survey on user interface programming. In *CHI '92: Proceedings of the SIGCHI conference on human factors in computing systems* (pp. 195–202). New York: ACM.

OASIS (2009). *User Interface Markup Language (UIML) version 4.0*. http://docs.oasis-open.org/uiml/v4.0/uiml-4.0.html.

Oberle, D., Grimm, S., & Staab, S. (2009). An ontology for software. In *Handbook on ontologies* (pp. 383–402). Chap. 18.

Paternò, F., Santoro, C., & Spano, L. D. (2008). *XML languages for user interface models—deliverable D2.1 of the ServFace project*. http://www.servface.org/index.php?option=com_docman&task=doc_download&gid=5&Itemid=61.

Paternò, F., Santoro, C., & Spano, L. D. (2009). MARIA: a universal, declarative, multiple abstraction-level language for service-oriented applications in ubiquitous environments. *ACM Transactions on Computer-Human Interaction, 16*(4), 1–30.

Paternò, F., Santoro, C., Mäntyjärvi, J., Mori, G., & Sansone, S. (2008). Authoring pervasive multimodal user interfaces. *International Journal on Web Engineering & Technology, 4*(2), 235–261.

Paulheim, H. (2010). Efficient semantic event processing: lessons learned in user interface integration. In *The semantic web: research and applications (ESWC 2010), Part II* (pp. 60–74).

Paulheim, H. (2011). *Ontology-based application integration*. Berlin: Springer.

Paulheim, H., & Erdogan, A. (2010). Seamless integration of heterogeneous UI components. In *Proceedings of the 2nd ACM SIGCHI symposium on engineering interactive computing systems (EICS 2010)* (pp. 303–308).

Paulheim, H., & Probst, F. (2010a). Application integration on the user interface level: an ontology-based approach. *Data & Knowledge Engineering Journal, 69*(11), 1103–1116.

Paulheim, H., & Probst, F. (2010b). Ontology-enhanced user interfaces: a survey. *International Journal on Semantic Web and Information Systems, 6*(2), 36–59.

Paulheim, H., & Probst, F. (2011). A formal ontology on user interfaces—yet another user interface description language? In *Proceedings of the second workshop on semantic models for adaptive interactive systems (SEMAIS)*.

Paulheim, H., Döweling, S., Tso-Sutter, K., Probst, F., & Ziegert, T. (2009). Improving usability of integrated emergency response systems: the SoKNOS approach. In *LNI: Vol. 154. Proceedings "39. Jahrestagung der Gesellschaft für Informatik e.V. (GI)—Informatik 2009"* (pp. 1435–1449).

Paulheim, H., Plendl, R., Probst, F., & Oberle, D. (2011). Mapping pragmatic class models to reference ontologies. In *The 2011 IEEE 27th international conference on data engineering workshops—2nd international workshop on data engineering meets the semantic web (DESWeb)* (pp. 200–205).

Rauschmayer, A. (2005). Semantic-web-backed GUI applications. In *Proceedings of the ISWC 2005 workshop on end user semantic web interaction*.

RedWhale Software (2000). The XIML specification. In *XIML Starter Kit version 1.* http://www.ximl.org/download/step1.asp.

Ruiz, F., & Hilera, J. R. (2006). Using ontologies in software engineering and technology. In *Ontologies for software engineering and software technology* (pp. 49–102). Chap. 2.

Schmidt, B., Paulheim, H., Stoitsev, T., & Mühlhäuser, M. (2011). Towards a formalization of individual work execution at computer workplaces. In *LNCS: Vol. 6828. 19th international conference on conceptual structures (ICCS 2011)* (pp. 270–283).

Simon, R., Kapsch, M. J., & Wegscheider, F. (2004). A generic UIML vocabulary for device- and modality independent user interfaces. In *WWW ALT '04: Proceedings of the 13th international world wide web conference on alternate track papers & posters* (pp. 434–435). New York: ACM.

Souchon, N., & Vanderdonckt, J. (2003). A review of XML-compliant user interface description languages. In *LNCS: Vol. 2844. Interactive systems. Design, specification, and verification* (pp. 377–391). Berlin: Springer.

Spyns, P., Meersmanand, R., & Jarrar, M. (2002). Data modelling versus ontology engineering. *SIGMOD Record, 31*(4), 12–17.

Studer, R., Grimm, S., & Abecker, A. (Eds.) (2007). *Semantic web services—concepts, technologies and applications.* Berlin: Springer.

Uschold, M., & Grüninger, M. (1996). Ontologies: principles, methods and applications. *Knowledge Engineering Review, 11*, 93–136.

Uschold, M., & King, M. (1995). Towards a methodology for building ontologies. In *Workshop on basic ontological issues in knowledge sharing*.

UsiXML Consortium (2007). *USer interface extensible markup language, v1.8, reference manual.* http://www.usixml.org/index.php?mod=download&file=usixml-doc/UsiXML_v1.8.0-Documentation.pdf.

W3C (2004a). *Composite capability/preference profiles (CC/PP): structure and vocabularies 1.0.* http://www.w3.org/TR/CCPP-struct-vocab/.

W3C (2004b). *SWRL: a semantic web rule language combining OWL and RuleML.* http://www.w3.org/Submission/SWRL/.

W3C (2009). *XForms 1.1.* http://www.w3.org/TR/xforms/1.

W3C (2010). *Delivery context ontology.* http://www.w3.org/TR/dcontology/.

W3C (2011a). *Accessible rich internet applications (WAI-ARIA) 1.0*. http://www.w3.org/TR/wai-aria/.

W3C (2011b). *HTML5—a vocabulary and associated APIs for HTML and XHTML*. http://www.w3.org/TR/html5/.

# Chapter 2
# Generating Models of Recommendation Processes out of Annotated Ontologies

**Hermann Kaindl, Dominik Ertl, Roman Popp, Ralph Hoch, Jürgen Falb, Edin Arnautovic, Ada Okoli, and Martin Schliefnig**

**Abstract** Creating content- and dialogue-based recommendation processes through manual adaptations requires a lot of time and effort. Therefore, automated generation of such processes is desirable. We present an approach for generating models of recommendation processes out of annotated ontologies. Such product ontologies have to be provided manually, but certain adaptations to them can be discovered from unstructured data (customer-generated content such as blog entries or customer feedback on products in the Web). They are given input for our approach, which applies semantic model-driven transformations to these ontologies for generating discourse-based models of recommendation processes on a high conceptual level first. These generated discourses essentially consist of questions and answers about

---

Dominik Ertl and Ralph Hoch did this work while being at the Vienna University of Technology.

H. Kaindl (✉) · D. Ertl · R. Popp · R. Hoch · J. Falb
Vienna University of Technology, Vienna, Austria
e-mail: kaindl@ict.tuwien.ac.at

D. Ertl
e-mail: ertl@ict.tuwien.ac.at

R. Popp
e-mail: popp@ict.tuwien.ac.at

R. Hoch
e-mail: hoch@ict.tuwien.ac.at

J. Falb
e-mail: falb@ict.tuwien.ac.at

E. Arnautovic
Vienna, Austria
e-mail: edin.arnautovic@gmail.com

A. Okoli · M. Schliefnig
Smart Information Systems GmbH, Viena, Austria

A. Okoli
e-mail: a.okoli@smart-infosys.at

M. Schliefnig
e-mail: ms@smart-infosys.at

T. Hussein et al. (eds.), *Semantic Models for Adaptive Interactive Systems*,
Human–Computer Interaction Series, DOI 10.1007/978-1-4471-5301-6_2,
© Springer-Verlag London 2013

those items annotated as important in the ontologies, and their possible sequences. From such a high-level model, transformation rules create a model of an operationalized recommendation process. This model also represents a so-called concrete user interface and consists of both the structure of the process and the course of events, which defines how customers may navigate through the process. From such models, an already given infrastructure can generate running processes including their final user interfaces, which have already been deployed successfully for real-world use.

## 2.1 Introduction

A content- and dialogue-based recommendation process in the Web guides its user interactively to the most suitable products, based on information it asks for and that is provided by the user. In order to reduce the costs of creating such a recommendation process for real-world use, we strived for automation. In addition or even instead of manual work on it by trained people, we investigated automating its creation for various domains through model transformations. For the overall lifecycle see Kaindl et al. (2013).

Figure 2.1 gives a schematic overview on how the transformation process is implemented. Building upon annotated product ontologies, we realize the generation of recommendation process models and a final user interface in two steps. First a model on a high conceptual level is generated as a so-called Discourse-based Communication Model (see, e.g., Popp and Raneburger 2011). This model consists of three parts, the Domain-of-Discourse Model, the Discourse Model and the Action-Notification Model. In the context of this chapter, the Action-Notification Model is not so important, because we only use predefined elements from there, whereas the other two models have to be generated. The Domain-of-Discourse Model generated in Step 1.1 contains the content of Communicative Acts (as derived from speech acts; Searle 1969), which specify the core of the Discourse Model. Properties as well as additional information from the annotated ontology provide this content. In this sense, the Discourse Model generated in Step 1.2 refers to the Domain-of-Discourse Model and defines a sequence of question and answer pairs, which are modeled as Adjacency Pairs (adopted from Conversation Analysis; Luff et al. 1990) of Communicative Acts. These questions and answers are about recommended products and, therefore created from properties from the annotated product ontology as well. Step 2 transforms such a Communication Model into a model of an operationalized recommendation process, which is presented in the Web as a final user interface of the process for customers through an already given infrastructure.

The remainder of this chapter is organized in the following manner. First, in order to make it self-contained, we present background material. Then we present our approach for generating recommendation process models as discourse-based models out of (annotated) ontologies. Based on that, we explain both our approach for generating operationalized recommendation processes and how they are presented to

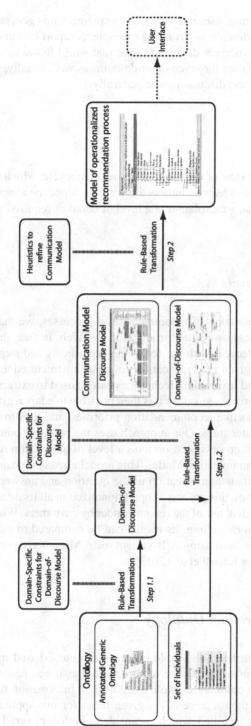

**Fig. 2.1** Transformations from annotated ontology to operationalized recommendation process

the customers in the form of user interfaces. For explaining this generation process, we use a mobile phone domain as a running example. A report on our evaluation of such recommendation processes deployed in the real world follows, for the mobile phone domain first, and then for seven other domains as well. Finally, we relate our approach to other work and discuss it more generally.

## 2.2 Background

We first provide an overview of the complete process lifecycle, which includes also the context of our approach as presented in this chapter. Since the annotated product ontology is the key input, we explain it at a level of detail as required to understand our approach.

### 2.2.1 Process Lifecycle

For semi-automatic generation of recommendation processes, we make (indirect) use of knowledge sources on related products in the Web. In fact, this involves a whole recommender lifecycle with the following ingredients and steps. First, customer feedback on the given products can be found as unstructured text reviews of products in the Web, and text mining techniques can be used to extract valuable information. With these processed values it is then possible to adapt a given ontology, including its annotations like recommendation priorities, and thus to influence the order of properties in later steps. Our approach uses the resulting ontology to generate a recommendation process, first on a high level of abstraction represented as a Discourse-based Communication Model. This model already contains the overall sequence as well as metadata information of the question and answer pairs. Using domain-specific heuristics, this process is operationalized in all its details, including a user interface for its actual use of the recommender by customers. When deploying this process in a real-world setting, its results can be compared to other processes (a manually created one first) using A/B-variant tests. More details on this process lifecycle can be found in Kaindl et al. (2013).

### 2.2.2 Annotated Product Ontology

To allow transformation from an ontology into a discourse-based model, certain specific model transformation rules are required and thus it was necessary to specify the structure of the ontology as well as additional information fields, such as annotations, and what they represent. As given input for our approach, an annotated ontology has been specified, which encapsulates both our overall structure and product individuals.[1] It is specified in a way (as a metamodel) facilitating model transformations.

This annotated ontology is designed according to GoodRelations[2] and also contains an individually defined namespace *rdf4ec*. Within this namespace all our custom properties and annotations, such as *rdf4ec:DomainSegment*, are defined and enable to configure properties. For example, Domain-Segments are used to group properties in a semantic and logical way, e.g., *WeightAndDimension*, which classifies all properties that characterize physical dimensions. Domain-Segments are defined as custom individuals in this namespace and new Domain-Segments can be introduced if necessary.

Individuals in the ontology are structured representations of kinds of real-world products, such as different mobile phone models. Note, that these are not the concrete mobile phones to be finally delivered to the customer. These kinds of products can be characterized by their multiple features they have in common, such as *weight*, *resolution*, etc., which are defined through the specified properties in our *rdf4ec* namespace. As the interpretation of these properties may vary by product domain, we use custom ontologies for different product domains.

Properties, as described above, belong to a specific domain segment and are correlated to a *rdf4ec:DomainSegment* via another annotation property that is set for all properties, *rdf4ec:belongsToDomainSegment*, allowing us to arrange properties in groups. This structure enables us in later process steps (compare Sect. 2.3) to handle properties combined that belong to the same logical segment.

For customers, particular properties may be of more interest than others and the ontology needs to support this fact. To facilitate this case, a property annotation *rdf4ec:priority* has been introduced for specifying the relative interest of properties. Properties are defined within a range of 0 to 100, where a higher value means a more important property. Comparing this to real-world products, as an example we refer to mobile phones again. Some properties, such as resolution or screen size, might be considered more important than others, weight for example, and thus would have a higher priority assigned. A higher priority means, if suitable (for a more detailed description see Sect. 2.3), a higher listing in the final recommendation process.

Figure 2.2 shows a schematic presentation of the annotated ontology as a class and an object diagram. The upper part of the figure presents the ontology concepts as a class diagram. The *Property* class defines all values that are necessary to specify a product property as well as additional annotations. Through an annotation *belongsToDomainSegment* it is related to another class *DomainSegment*. A *DomainSegment* can hold several *Properties* but one *Property* belongs only to one *DomainSegment*. The lower part of the figure shows instances of these classes in an object

---

[1] In the context of object-oriented software engineering and programming, individuals are typically called instances. Since we follow the model-transformation approach from there in addition to building on ontologies, we use these notions interchangeably in the remainder of this chapter.

[2] www.purl.org/goodrelations.

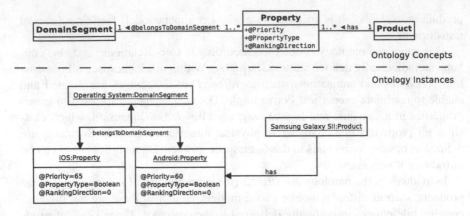

**Fig. 2.2** Excerpt of schematic structure of the annotated ontology

diagram. Each class can have multiple instances and each instance has its own custom values. More details on this annotated product ontology can be found in Kaindl
et al. (2013).

## 2.3 Generating a Recommendation Process as a Discourse-Based Model

From such a given annotated ontology, we automatically generate a recommendation process on a high conceptual level first. It is represented as a Discourse-based
Communication Model (for the background and a definition of such models see,
e.g., Falb et al. 2006; Popp and Raneburger 2011). The discourse structure (as explained in detail below) was actually predefined and given to the automated generator as a template. The overall pattern is a sequence of questions and answers
related to the recommended products, plus some background information (to be displayed optionally). This template is being filled with information about products to
be recommended as given in the product ontology. Its annotations are used by our
generator through (manually specified) heuristics to determine what to include in
the recommendation process and in which sequence.

Figure 2.3 shows an excerpt of such a Discourse Model. The pairs of related
questions and answers are modeled as so-called Adjacency Pairs and shown as dia-
monds, with opening and closing Communicative Acts (shown as lighter and darker
rounded rectangles, depending on whether they are to be executed by the system or
the customer, respectively). These Adjacency Pairs are linked with so-called Discourse Relations. In a model of such a recommendation process, only three types of
Discourse Relations are used. The first one, *Sequence*, is shown as a hexagon (since
it is more specifically a Procedural Construct), the second, *Joint*, and the third one,
*Background*, are shown as rectangles (since they are Rhetorical Relations inherited
from Rhetorical Structure Theory (RST); Mann and Thompson 1988). While such

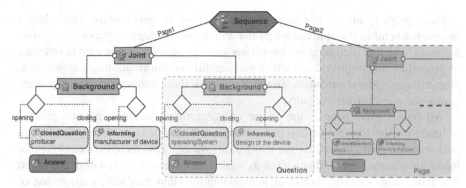

**Fig. 2.3** Excerpt of Discourse Model of recommendation process

a model can have many *Joint* relations and many Question-Answer Pairs, only one such element is shown in the figure and a second one is grayed out to indicate the existence of more elements. An earlier version of the representation of a recommendation process through a discourse-based model can be found in Ertl et al. (2011). Note, however, that both the representation and the concrete generation process of the recommender discourse have been changed meanwhile.

The automatic generation of such a model consists of two steps. In Step 1.1 of Fig. 2.1, our model-transformation approach transforms the individuals of the annotated ontology and their concrete datatypes and object property values into a model of the *content* of the communication (the Domain-of-Discourse model). In Step 1.2 of Fig. 2.1, a set of model-transformation rules matches parts of the annotated ontology (including its individuals) and transforms them automatically into corresponding parts of a Discourse Model. This step also defines the content of the Communicative Acts, so that the Discourse Model refers to the Domain-of-Discourse Model.

### 2.3.1 Domain-of-Discourse Model Generation

In more detail, Step 1.1 analyses all properties of the ontology and processes them. Each property is stored as a datatype in the Domain-of-Discourse Model. For most of the datatypes, the values used by the individuals are added to the datatype. In case of numeric properties, only the minimum and maximum values are stored as only the boundaries are important. A definable minimum percentage for individuals of properties can be set and only properties that reach this minimum percentage are selected for the recommendation process currently being generated. This means that not all properties from the ontology are taken into account in the course of generating a recommendation process. Nevertheless, all properties are stored in the Domain-of-Discourse Model and the properties that are not to be used are placed in a special container (if a different kind of heuristics will be put in place later, some of these properties might become important).

Each property also stores meta-data information as annotations. These annotations reassemble the annotations of the annotated ontology, especially *Domain-Segment*, which is used to group properties such as *priority*. These enable ordering of properties, and *propertyType*, which gives additional information on how numeric properties are to be rendered. In later process steps, these annotations are used to organize the question-answer pairs.

All further processing in the course of generating a recommendation process is based on the Domain-of-Discourse Model and thus it is necessary to allow a customizable configuration for the generation process. This includes a configurable value for minimum individual values as well as an extensible annotation container. The latter helps to easily introduce new annotations and thus allows adaptation of the generation process for other application areas.

### 2.3.2 *Discourse Model Generation*

In Step 1.2, a Discourse Model is created. For each property selected before for the currently generated recommendation process, a question-answer pair is created according to the predefined template. This template consists of a *Question* and a corresponding *Answer* Communicative Act. The *Answer* part can have different internal structure to support single-valued (numeric) as well as multi-valued (string, Boolean) answer sets. Furthermore a configuration value specifies if these answers should be mutually exclusive or not. These Communicative Acts are connected with an *Adjacency Pair*.

The description property of the transformed property is added to the defined Discourse Model part with a *Background* relation connecting the Question-Answer Adjacency Pair with an *Informing* Communicative Act, which contains the description. It is also possible that some properties of a domain segment are combined into a single question. This combination is applied, if there is more than one property of type Boolean from the same *Domain-Segment*. In our running example, the properties of the domain segment *Operating Systems* are combined. Several individual properties like *android*, *symbian*, *windowsMobile* have been combined to form a single question.

The generated Discourse Model parts are then sorted according to some heuristics. An example of such a heuristic is, that the question for the producer property is always the first question. Another heuristic is, that questions for properties with a high priority are in front of properties with a lower priority. If the priorities of some questions are the same, we apply another heuristic gained from previous tests of manually created processes. It defines that string questions are asked first, followed by numeric questions and at last combined Boolean questions.

This sorted list is then divided into logical units, which become pages in the resulting user interface. Each of these logical units has a configurable number of questions. In the Discourse Model, each of these logical units is represented with a

**Fig. 2.4** Part of an operationalized recommendation process at the CUI level (reprinted from Kaindl et al. 2013)

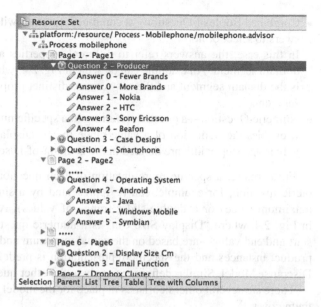

*Joint* Relation, which connects the parts created above. The generated *Joint* Relations are connected then with a *Sequence* Relation specifying the order of the logic units.

## 2.4 Generating an Operationalized Recommendation Process and Its User Interface

From such a generated high-level model, model transformations are used to create a model of an operationalized recommendation process. This model also represents a so-called concrete user interface (CUI) (Calvary et al. 2003) and consists of both the structure of the process and the course of events, which defines how customers may navigate through the process. A part of an example of such an operationalized recommendation process can be seen in Fig. 2.4.

### 2.4.1 Generation of Recommendation Process Model

To generate the operationalized recommendation process model, transformations are applied. Manually provided heuristics are used to refine the discourse-based model and to transform elements into concrete representations. To illustrate this task, we present selected specifications of the *Question* element as seen in Fig. 2.4:

- String-Question—a question that has several predefined answer sets:
  Answers refer to a specific property, e.g., the "Producer" property in Fig. 2.4, as each answer—in this case a brand—is only related to one property.

- Combined Boolean-Question—a combined question with several predefined answers to select or not:
  In this case, the answers refer to different properties and belong to a specific domain segment. An example can be seen in Fig. 2.4, where "Operating System" is the domain segment and the answers are distinct properties that belong to this segment.
- Numeric-Question—a question referring to a specific numeric property:
  It enables the definition of a value range (e.g., "Display Size Cm"). Boundary values and step-width are defined in the Domain-of-Discourse Model.

Furthermore, a specific representation of each question type is defined. A numeric question, for example, can be represented by a single-slider (minimum or maximum value) or a double-slider (range of values). An example can be seen in Fig. 2.4, where "Display Size Cm" is a numeric question. Slider-Values—like start and end value—are based on the actual minimum and maximum values of the product instances and the specific representation is predefined in the Domain-Of-Discourse Model. Similar definitions apply to the other question types as well.

There are several other heuristics in place for the model transformation. Some of them cover

- text-patterns for questions,
- definition of background information,
- restricted answers per question,
- restricted answer selection per question, etc.

The resulting model consists of the logical layers used during a recommendation process. A root element 'process' is in place as a starting point, which contains ordered pages. These pages serve as a container for question-answer pairs, where each question can have multiple related answers. Answers themselves can be restricted and special answer elements can be used to show/hide additional answers ("More/Less" switch). In addition, questions are based on product properties and have varying characteristics, which are rendered differently in the final user interface. For an example see Fig. 2.5, where two different question types and their representations are shown.

Allowing customers to easily navigate through the process and identify the parts of importance is mandatory. Thus heuristics have been put in place to support this. Let us demonstrate it with the *Producer* property. Text-patterns are used to automatically generate meaningful questions that can easily be understood by the customers. Different approaches are used for different question types. In case of a string question, the text-pattern uses the property name to create a comprehensive question. Furthermore, the number of answers is limited and only a fragment is shown, so that customers are not overwhelmed by options. A special switch can be used to show/hide additional answers ("More/Less" switch). Note, that this is a simplified description of the CUI Model as it is possible to parameterize the model transformation, and various heuristics are in place for different requirements.

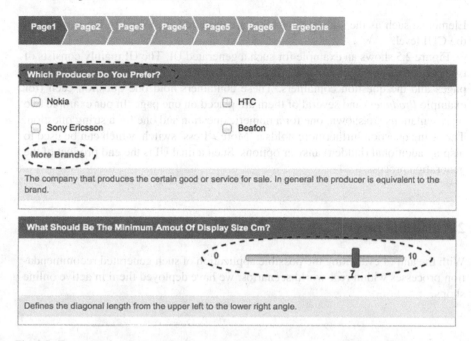

**Fig. 2.5** Example of a generated final user interface (reprinted from Kaindl et al. 2013)

Our model of the operationalized recommendation process can be seen as a 1:1 mapping for the final user interface but is still independent from a final implementation. An advantage of this method is that it supports, if necessary, manual adjustment of the process without changes at the implementation level. Adjustments can involve, for example, adding/deleting elements (pages, questions and answers) as well as changing question types. Another advantage of this approach is that it enables the use of different implementations as well as layouts for the final UI.

## 2.4.2  Final User Interface

The final user interface (UI) presented in Fig. 2.5 corresponds to the model on the CUI level in Fig. 2.4. The process together with instance data enables the recommender to give specific recommendations based on the selection of the customer. The combination of actual instance data (e.g., products of a specific Web-shop) is done during runtime by an external engine.

This specific engine provides an interesting feature in addition to what the runtime engine presented by Popp and Raneburger (2011) offers. The engine used for the recommendation process allows the user to redefine her criteria and also to go back in the process. In this case the final UI is generated as an HTML-based Web-shop where various layouts, e.g. customizable color schemes, can be applied.

Elements, such as the sliding controller, are rendered according to the settings on the CUI level.

Figure 2.5 shows an example for such a generated UI. The UI mainly consists of two parts, the top with a bar that allows the customer to navigate between different pages and the question containers. These containers hold one question each (for example *Producer*) and several of them are placed on one page. In our example two representations are shown, one for a numeric question and one for a string question. The string question furthermore holds a 'More'/'Less' switch, which can be used to display additional (hidden) answer options. Such a final UI is the end product of the generation process.

## 2.5 Evaluation

With the aim of evaluating the possible application of such generated recommendation processes within real-world scenarios, we have deployed them in active online shops.

### 2.5.1 Comparison of Recommendation Processes

In these real-world experiments, we have compared and identified differences between semi-automatically generated recommendation processes and manually created ones that have been designed by human domain experts. Both the semi-automatically generated and the manually created product recommendation processes ranked product features according to the computationally inferred relevance for customers. This is based on the underlying assumption that recommendation processes in which the selectable product features are arranged according to their relevance, would perform better than others. Prior to each test, we have set up suitable, automated monitoring services that sent out notifications whenever a decreasing performance (fewer successful recommendations) was detected. As the experiment was carried out in the real-world environment of online shops, these precautionary measures were important to anticipate and prevent any commercial losses due to potentially deficient recommendation processes.

For the comparison, we use the performance measure of the "click-out rat" to measure the success of the recommendation processes. It is a performance metric that is commonly used to measure the success of individual online strategies. In our case, it denotes the fraction of users who used a recommendation process to find a product and followed a recommendation by selecting suggested products to view them in a close-up view or by placing them into an electronic shopping cart (Performed product click-outs/Number of unique clients). This measure is opposed by the "cold exit rate", which measures the rate of customers that have used a recommendation process, but have left it without following a recommendation.

**Table 2.1** Comparison of ranking of properties in mobile phone recommendation processes

| (a) Manually created recommendation process | (b) Semi-automatically generated recommendation process |
|---|---|
| • Brand | • Brand |
| • Price | • Price |
| • Multimedia | • **Display** |
| – Camera | – Touch display |
| – Video | – Color display |
| – MP3 | – Display size |
| • Connectivity | • **Operating system** |
| – WLAN | – Android |
| – GPS | – Symbian |
| – Bluetooth | • Camera |
| • Operating system | • Connectivity |
| – Android | – WLAN |
| – Symbian | – GPS |
| | – Bluetooth |

## 2.5.2 Empirical Results

Based on this way of comparing recommendation processes, let us present empirical results from deploying semi-automatically generated processes. First, we look at the data of one specific comparison in-depth. After that, we summarize results from several different real-world domains and applications.

Let us first provide an example for mobile phones (from where our running example has been distilled as well). Comparing the generated mobile phone recommendation processes (Table 2.1), we found that the semi-automatically generated recommendation process ranked features that were related to the mobile phone *display* and the *operating system* on higher positions, while they were neglected or ranked differently in the manually created version. Also, product features that were related to *Multimedia* (Camera, Video, MP3) and *Connectivity* (WLAN, GPS, Bluetooth) were listed on lower positions in the semi-automatically generated variant. This suggests that these features have lost relevance over time, unrecognized by the domain experts in time. These results reflect the relevance of properties as given in Table 2.1. Here, the product features *touchscreen*, *displaySizeInch* and *resolutionText* (*Display*) and *android* (*Operating system*) received higher priorities than *videoFunction* and *mp3Player* (*Multimedia*) or *WLAN, GPS and bluetooth* (*Connectivity*) from the given product ontology.

In a real-world experiment, we investigated measurable performance of the pursued approach. As recommendation processes play an increasingly important role in e-commerce, we conducted the experiment within the environment of a large German online retailer. Here, recommendation processes are deployed to support online customers at finding suitable products from vast assortments. The experi-

**Table 2.2** Results of A/B-variant test with (a) manually and (b) semi-automatically generated mobile phone recommendation process instances

| Process variant | Unique clients | Click-outs | Click-out rate | Cold-exit rate |
|---|---|---|---|---|
| (a) Mobile phone rec. process (manual) | 1,068 | 421 | 0.394 | 0.781 |
| (b) Mobile phone rec. process (generated) | 1,100 | 496 | 0.451 | 0.746 |

ment ran for 14 consecutive days and involved 2,168 uninformed online customers, who accessed the recommendation processes to find suitable mobile phones.

An A/B-variant test, in which the participants were equally distributed to either process variant, was set up to compare the performance of the semi-automatically generated mobile phone recommendation process variant with the manually created variant. Table 2.2 depicts the results of the A/B-variant tests, in which the semi-automatically generated mobile phone recommendation variant (b) was tested against a manually created variant (a). It shows that the semi-automatically generated version (b) led to an increase of the click-out rate by 14 % and a decrease of the cold exit rate by 4 %. The result of this experiment indicates that our new approach may lead to a higher click-out rate and, therefore, may evoke performance increases.

Now let us provide a general evaluation of the performance values for all 8 processes that have been deployed and tested yet at the time of this writing within this experiment series. The 8 recommendation process sets within the categories bluray-player, camcorder, printer, receiver, videoprojector, DVD player, TFT screen, and mobile phone, each comprising a manually created and a semi-automatically generated variant, were tested within the experiment series.

The results are given in Table 2.3. We observe that 5 out of 8 generated product recommendation processes suggest improved data as compared with their manually created counterparts. A statistical analysis of the data is given by Kaindl et al. (2013).

The 3 product recommendation processes that led to decreasing click-out rate data (see Table 2.3c, f, g) had more complex process setups and involved higher interdependencies between the selectable product features. This may be an indicator that our current approach is better applicable for more basic process types.

Overall, the results of our real-world usage experiments provide some empirical evidence that the generation of process recommendation processes can be done semi-automatically with competitive results.

Measuring and comparing the effort of manual creation of recommendation processes with using the semi-automatic lifecycle showed that applying the latter led to a reduction of the manual work by roughly up to 60 %.

## 2.6 Related Work

Ontologies have been used in many areas of software engineering (Coral et al. 2006) and information systems (Guarino 1998). Paulheim and Probst (2010) present an

**Table 2.3** Results and comparison of A/B-variant tests of recommendation process instances in 8 product categories—manually vs. semi-automatically generated process instance

| Domain | Unique clients | Click-out rate A (manual) | Click-out rate B (semi-automatic) | Click-out increase/ decrease of B | Cold-exit rate increase/ decrease of B |
|---|---|---|---|---|---|
| (a) blurayplayer | 1,631 | 0.458 | 0.509 | +11.14 % | −2.40 % |
| (b) camcorder | 438 | 0.444 | 0.485 | +9.23 % | −2.12 % |
| (c) printer | 746 | 0.683 | 0.547 | −19.91 % | +9.61 % |
| (d) receiver | 1,363 | 0.316 | 0.319 | +0.95 % | −2.73 % |
| (e) videoprojector | 329 | 0.429 | 0.462 | +7.69 % | −0.14 % |
| (f) DVD player | 456 | 0.415 | 0.213 | −48.67 % | +12.19 % |
| (g) TFT screen | 1,019 | 0.455 | 0.348 | −23.52 % | +3.91 % |
| (h) mobile phone | 2,168 | 0.394 | 0.451 | +14.47 % | −4.4 % |

extended survey on the usage of ontologies for the development and execution of user interfaces. In particular, they focus on user interfaces "whose visualization capabilities, interaction possibilities, or development process are enabled or (at least) improved by the employment of one or more ontologies". They also propose a classification of this usage. For example, concerning the usage *domain*, ontologies can be used to represent the concepts from the real world (as, e.g., products in our case), IT system and their components, or users and their roles. Ontologies can also be classified according to their role in the lifecycle, whether being used for design or execution (or even both).

For recommendation processes, ontologies can be employed for user profiling as shown by Middleton et al. (2004), where the authors use machine-learning techniques to discover useful patterns in the users' behavior and to improve the recommendation process. In our current approach, we do not perform any user profiling, but it could be integrated.

Klan and König-Ries (2011) present an interactive approach for service selection. This approach can be compared to our approach, if we assume, that such a service can be seen as a product. This approach also includes some heuristics in the selection process. One heuristic is, that the questions are ranked according to the maximum effect in the presented list. If the answer of one question reduces the list of possible services more than another question, it is ranked higher.

The relationship between domain models and interaction models has been studied in the past. Rosson (1999) presented the integration of task models (which represent the user interactions and are related to our Discourse Models) and object models (related to our Domain-of Discourse Models). Another example of integrating processes with high-level conceptual models is the field of Semantic Web Services (Sheth et al. 2006). Adding semantics to "classical" Web Services could be done with WSDL-S (Web Service Description Language-Semantics). In WSDL-S, Web Services descriptions are annotated with domain-specific (e.g., of one particular industry) and domain-independent ontologies (e.g., for general contracts or agreements).

## 2.7 Discussion

While our approach works and even results in recommendation processes applicable in practice, a few related questions should be discussed. In particular, is it necessary or, at least useful to generate a high-level model of such a process first? Although it seems possible to generate an operationalized process in one shot, we argue that a two-step approach is useful by analogy to compiler construction. Typically, intermediate languages are used on the way from a high-level programming language to machine code. These provide useful levels of abstraction for the compiler developers, and so does our high-level model of recommendation processes.

Still, the question remains, whether other kinds of languages or models could serve the same purpose, and possibly even better. This question cannot be answered with certainty as it stands, since our approach seems to be the very first along these lines.

As our discourse-based models are primarily used for specifying models on a high abstraction level for automated generation of user interfaces, how about the most often used approach for this purpose? Instead of our discourse-based models, task-based ConcurTaskTrees from Paternò et al. (1997) may be used for bridging the semantic gap between ontologies and user interfaces. ConcurTaskTrees facilitate modeling *tasks* and their causal and temporal relations. Such models are also being transformed into a user interface semi-automatically. However, we are not aware of any approach for generating ConcurTaskTrees out of ontologies. UsiXML (Faure and Vanderdonckt 2010) is an XML-based specification language for user interface design. It allows specifying a user interface at different levels of abstraction, from high-level task models (like ConcurTaskTrees) to the concrete code of a user interface. Also for UsiXML, we are not aware of any approach for generating UsiXML models out of ontologies. Since a recommendation process of the kind generated here primarily consists of pairs of questions and related answers, Communicative Acts as used in our discourse-based approach are an excellent fit for modeling them. In contrast, tasks would have to model questions and answers in the sense of corresponding interactions with a specific kind of user interface. So, while this would certainly be feasible, it appears to be less appealing than our approach.

Since this is about modeling processes, also languages for business process modeling may be used. Such languages like Business Process Model and Notation (BPMN) focus on the dynamics of such processes. However, BPMN appears to lack means for specifying the structure of domains sufficient for the content of recommendation processes.

From Discourse-based Communication Models, it is possible to generate general-purpose graphical user interfaces according to Falb et al. (2009) and even optimized ones for devices with small screens according to Raneburger et al. (2011). Contrasting them with the user interfaces generated for recommendation processes as explained above, it is clear that the latter are preferable in terms of usability. As a matter of fact, they have been successfully used for real-world application of these recommendation processes. They are special-purpose, however, and their overall appearance was predefined, while only the content has been generated automatically for the given structure and with many given heuristics.

## 2.8 Conclusion

We show that it is possible, from a given annotated product ontology, to generate dialogue-driven recommendation processes semi-automatically. The key reason is, that such a process primarily consists of questions and answers about exactly the products from such an ontology. Therefore, a template devised by us can be filled based on products in the ontology. In addition, the annotations in this ontology are key to select products for a related recommendation process based on their priority.

The semi-automatic generation requires much less effort than the manual creation. In addition, data from real-world deployment of this new and automated approach provide empirical evidence of its usefulness. For instance, in the real-world application at a large e-commerce shop platform with about 1,500 different customers, this approach increased the rate of customers who followed recommendations by 14 %. So, the generated processes seem to be competitive with processes manually created by human experts (according to the same overall strategy).

**Acknowledgements** This research has been carried out in the SOFAR project (No. 825061), partially funded by the Austrian FIT-IT Program of the FFG.

## References

Calvary, G., Coutaz, J., Thevenin, D., Limbourg, Q., Bouillon, L., & Vanderdonckt, J. (2003). A unifying reference framework for multi-target user interfaces. *Interacting With Computers*, *15*(3), 289–308.

Coral, C., Francisco, R., & Mario, P. (2006). *Ontologies for software engineering and software technology*. Berlin: Springer.

Ertl, D., Kaindl, H., Arnautovic, E., Falb, J., & Popp, R. (2011). Discourse-based interaction models for recommendation processes. In *ACHI '11: proceedings of the 4th international conference on advances in computer-human interactions*.

Falb, J., Kaindl, H., Horacek, H., Bogdan, C., Popp, R., & Arnautovic, E. (2006). A discourse model for interaction design based on theories of human communication. In *CHI '06: extended abstracts on human factors in computing systems* (pp. 754–759). New York: ACM.

Falb, J., Kavaldjian, S., Popp, R., Raneburger, D., Arnautovic, E., & Kaindl, H. (2009). Fully automatic user interface generation from discourse models. In *IUI '09: Proceedings of the 13th international conference on intelligent user interfaces* (pp. 475–476). New York: ACM.

Faure, D., & Vanderdonckt, J. (2010). User interface extensible markup language. In *EICS '10: proceedings of the 2nd ACM SIGCHI symposium on engineering interactive computing systems* (pp. 361–362). New York: ACM.

Guarino, N. (1998). In *Proceedings of the 1st international conference on formal ontology in information systems*. Amsterdam: IOS Press.

Kaindl, H., Wach, E. P., Okoli, A., Popp, R., Hoch, R., Gaulke, W., & Hussein, T. (2013). Semi-automatic generation of recommendation processes and their GUIs. In *IUI '13: proceedings of the 2013 ACM international conference on intelligent user interfaces*.

Klan, F., & König-Ries, B. (2011). A conversational approach to semantic web service selection. In C. Huemer & T. Setzer (Eds.), *Lecture notes in business information processing: Vol. 85. E-commerce and web technologies* (pp. 1–12). Berlin: Springer.

Luff, P., Frohlich, D., & Gilbert, N. (1990). *Computers and conversation*. London: Academic Press.

Mann, W. C., & Thompson, S. A. (1988). Rhetorical structure theory: toward a functional theory of text organization. *Text*, *8*(3), 243–281.

Middleton, S. E., Shadbolt, N. R., & De Roure, D. C. (2004). Ontological user profiling in recommender systems. *ACM Transactions on Information Systems*, *22*(1), 54–88.

Paternò, F., Mancini, C., & Meniconi, S. (1997). ConcurTaskTrees: a diagrammatic notation for specifying task models. In *Proceedings of the IFIP TC13 6th international conference on human-computer interaction* (pp. 362–369).

Paulheim, H., & Probst, F. (2010). Ontology-enhanced user interfaces: a survey. *International Journal on Semantic Web and Information Systems*, *6*(2), 36–59.

Popp, R., & Raneburger, D. (2011). A high-level agent interaction protocol based on a communication ontology. In C. Huemer, T. Setzer, W. Aalst, J. Mylopoulos, N. M. Sadeh, M. J. Shaw & C. Szyperski (Eds.), *Lecture notes in business information processing: Vol. 85. E-commerce and web technologies* (pp. 233–245). Berlin: Springer.

Raneburger, D., Popp, R., Kavaldjian, S., Kaindl, H., & Falb, J. (2011). Optimized GUI generation for small screens. In H. Hussmann, G. Meixner & D. Zuehlke (Eds.), *Studies in computational intelligence: Vol. 340. Model-driven development of advanced user interfaces* (pp. 107–122). Berlin: Springer.

Rosson, M. B. (1999). Integrating development of task and object models. *Communications of the ACM*, *42*(1), 49–56.

Searle, J. R. (1969). *Speech acts: an essay in the philosophy of language*. Cambridge: Cambridge University Press.

Sheth, A., Verma, K., & Gomadam, K. (2006). Semantics to energize the full services spectrum. *Communications of the ACM*, *49*(7), 55–61.

# Chapter 3
# Cognitive Semantic Categories as a Basis for a Prototype Adaptive Information System

**Evangelos Kapros and Simon McGinnes**

**Abstract** A software application is demonstrated which exhibits conceptual data independence. The application provides domain-specific functionality, yet its structure is domain-independent. Separation between conceptual model and structure is achieved by encoding models as data and interpreting them at run-time. The overall goal is to reduce cost and delay when conceptual models change, and to provide application functionality in new domains without constructing new applications. Several conceptual models are used, to illustrate domain-specific behavior in multiple domains. Results suggest that domain-independent application design can reduce the need for application development and maintenance effort, since each domain-independent application can function in multiple domains and adapts smoothly to changing conceptual models. This is especially meaningful for end users who usually have no development skills and rely on spreadsheet and database driven applications.

## 3.1 Introduction

Current best practice in software design produces applications that are domain-specific in both behavior *and* structure. For example, accounting software might be constructed from classes representing accounts and account entries, and might store data in *Account* and *Entry* database tables. The application's architecture is described as domain-specific because its class and table structures mirror the concepts (entity types and their relationships) in the application domain's conceptual model.

The use of domain-specific architecture is a familiar and relatively simple way of constructing software. But it leads to high cost and delay when software must be altered to match new or modified conceptual models. This remains a barrier to

E. Kapros (✉) · S. McGinnes
The University of Dublin, Dublin, Ireland
e-mail: ekapros@tcd.ie

S. McGinnes
e-mail: Simon.McGinnes@tcd.ie

T. Hussein et al. (eds.), *Semantic Models for Adaptive Interactive Systems*,
Human–Computer Interaction Series, DOI 10.1007/978-1-4471-5301-6_3,
© Springer-Verlag London 2013

system evolution despite long attention from researchers (Hick and Hainaut 2006; Hartung et al. 2011). It also makes it necessary to do development work when new domain-specific functionality is required.

In conventional software design, software architectures are based on the assumption that the end user's mental concepts are relatively static. *Conceptual data dependence* is the practice of embedding these mental concepts in software architectures. Our goal is to construct applications which exhibit *conceptual data independence*, such that minimal work is required in respect of new or changed conceptual models. The motivation is to reduce the cost and delay that organizations incur when they develop and maintain software applications to match new or altered conceptual models. Development work causes cost and delay which mainly affects small and medium enterprises and organizations, which employ staff with typically little or no programming skills. Thus, they face the dilemma to buy applications that match their requirements or fund the development of custom-made applications. However, this dilemma is usually avoided and organizations rely on simple tools such as spreadsheets (Chan and Storey 1996; Raden 2005).

We propose to reduce cost and delay by building an information system that is adaptive to model changes (Adaptive Information System, or AIS). We implemented this idea to show its feasibility, and present a software application which is simultaneously the authoring environment and the user interface of applications which exhibit conceptual data independence. That is, the end users can manage the model and the data through the same user interface. Moreover, the concepts of the model and the data are represented in user-friendly forms. Thus, expert help concerning change is minimized. In addition, conceptual data independence has implications for the visual design of user interfaces.

## 3.2 Related Work

### 3.2.1 Relational Databases and Object-Oriented Design

The relational model proposed by Codd (1970) provides a standard way of translating concepts into data structures. A table represents a concept, while columns represent the concept's attributes. The concepts that describe the structure of the database form its *schema*. Research in Schema Evolution focuses on the problem of adapting a database schema to changes. This research field shows that changes in schemas represent a significant cost to organizations. In Curino et al. (2008) changes in the database schema are reported to affect up to 70 % of queries, which have to be manually reconfigured. Some theoretical models to address this problem have been constructed, but real systems incorporating schema evolution functionality are hard to find (Roddick et al. 2000).

Other types of software design are subject to the same kinds of problem. Object-oriented design in programming and in databases is one example. In object-oriented design, concepts are represented as classes. Classes serve as blueprints for objects, which are specific instances of the concept. Changes to the underlying conceptual structure implemented in a class structure make it necessary to alter the classes and their relationships. This, in turn, makes it necessary to modify code which refers to the altered classes. Hence there can be a high overhead cost arising from changes to the underlying conceptual model of an application constructed using conventional object-oriented design.

## 3.2.2 Ontologies and the Semantic Web

An ontology provides a semantic network of predefined concepts intended to describe the universe of knowledge for a particular domain. Domain-specific applications may define new end-user concepts as sub-concepts of the existing concepts in the ontology.

It has been proposed (Berners-Lee et al. 2006; Alani et al. 2005, 2008) that web applications should use ontologies as well. The so-called Semantic Web applications would, then, be able to share data freely using as mediators these predefined concepts, without any need for prior programming. For this to work in the general case, ontologies would have to be capable of being integrated with a common ontology. Various semi-automatic tools have been developed for this task (McGuinness et al. 2000; Noy and Musen 2000).

However, this is a non-trivial challenge. A lack of standardization in end-user concepts leads to the Tower of Babel (Fonseca and Martin 2004) problem: the creation, in various ontologies, of incompatible definitions for the same entity. Moreover, since the existing ontologies are domain-specific, no large-scale cross-domain implementations exist. For this reason, it is still unclear how web meta-data would follow the conceptual vocabulary of the ontologies (Shirky 2003).

The idea of handling arbitrary schemas in software applications has not been previously directly addressed. However, work on ontologies has given useful results on change in semantics while using automatically generated interfaces (Ertl et al. 2011; Wach 2011). Similarly, work on dynamic data management has given useful results (Fein et al. 2011; Kennedy et al. 2011; Sun et al. 2011) but has not, in general, addressed user-interface or usability issues. While there have been design efforts in web browsers such as LENA (LENA—a Fresnel LEns based RDF/Linked Data NAvigator with SPARQL selector support n.d.) and Tabulator (Berners-Lee et al. 2007) that offer views that depend on semantics, they are targeted to software developers and not end users (SPARQL knowledge is essential). Moreover, they differentiate the authoring environment of the applications from the applications themselves, which serves well software developers but might be confusing to end users. However, these are useful paradigms and offer valuable ideas for exploration.

## 3.2.3 Spreadsheets

Research has shown that most organizations still rely on spreadsheets for their data management (Chan and Storey 1996; Raden 2005). There is a number of reasons why that happens, including failure to deliver end-user systems with usable schema evolution. End users have been reported to "shun enterprise solutions" (Raden 2005) and 70 % of them use spreadsheets on a frequent or occasional basis most commonly for "sorting and database facilities" (Chan and Storey 1996). Spreadsheets are error-prone and miss critical database functionality. There exists work on some database functionality in spreadsheets such as managing plural relationships (Bakke et al. 2011), but not on conceptual modelling. Similarly, work on semantic spreadsheets has improved modeling in spreadsheets, but still separates authoring and application (Zhao et al. 2010; Kohlhase and Kohlhase 2011). Moreover, the problem of schema evolution remains, since the practice of conceptual data dependence is still followed.

## 3.3 Conceptual Data Independence

### 3.3.1 Soft Schemas

We approach this problem by turning conceptual models into data. Current application design practice embeds conceptual models into software structures (classes, windows, tables, etc.) When building an AIS this practice is avoided. Instead, the AIS is constructed from generic, domain-independent structures. The model-as-data is termed a *soft schema*; in our prototype it is stored as XML, although any logically-equivalent way of storing data would suffice. The soft schema is read and interpreted by the AIS at run-time. The soft schema is a properly normalized relational data model, with some additions, but it is stored as data rather than being hardcoded in application structure.

To provide domain-specific functionality, yet also exhibit conceptual data independence, the AIS must meet several conditions. First, it must react at run-time to a soft schema, providing a user interface which looks and behaves similarly to those of conventional domain-specific applications. This requires the AIS to mimic the design choices of a human designer, in real time. Our approach is to implement automated user interface design heuristics which are applied based on the contents of the soft schema. We provide specialized behavior for different types of data by responding to known semantic categories embedded in the soft schema (see Sect. 3.3.2).

An AIS must also be able to store and retrieve data corresponding to multiple soft schemas with guaranteed data integrity. The AIS has no advance knowledge of the data and schemas it will be used with, and how they may change. An AIS would be of little use if altering a schema rendered previously-stored data unusable, or if it compromised data integrity. So the data corresponding to each soft schema must be able to co-exist and be used with data stored for other soft schemas, regardless of their structures. Our solution to this problem is to store data in a broadly domain-independent way, but to retain intact the conceptual structure for each instance of data. Our prototype meets that requirement by storing the data using XML and using XML tags to denote structure. XML was chosen in this instance because of its simplicity and flexibility which are desirable properties for building a proof-of-concept prototype. But, again, any logically-equivalent storage mechanism (such as RDF or others) would suffice.

The intention in using soft schemas is to separate conceptual structure from application structure, so that change to the former does not necessitate change to the latter. But another, perhaps more far-reaching implication of this way of designing software is that an AIS could conceivably operate in many application domains, if supplied with appropriate soft schemas. Fewer applications would be required, because a single AIS could fulfill the function of many distinct (domain-specific) applications that must today be constructed separately, by hand using conventional software design practices.

### 3.3.2 Archetypal Categories and Differential Design

The AIS provides domain-specific behavior by responding to the currently-active soft schema. Each concept (entity type) in the soft schema represents something that data can be stored about. The AIS provides CRUD (create, read, update, delete) functionality in respect of every concept in the schema. Design heuristics are applied automatically to produce a "reasonably usable" interface directly from the conceptual model. This principle has been applied and tested in a number of web and client-server application environments (McGinnes 2005). Dialog design takes into account general rules of interaction and layout, as well as responding specifically to the data types used for attributes in the soft schema, the relationships between concepts, and so on.

However, for an AIS to offer true domain-specific functionality, it is insufficient to respond only to the conceptual model, because this provides a one-size-fits-all user interface style for every concept in the model. The AIS must instead offer a suitable interface style *for each* concept. Being able to do this depends on knowledge which is not normally present in conceptual models. For example, an application that stores data about geographical locations such as cities might offer an interface based on maps. Data about activities such as appointments might be represented using a calendar or timeline. Other interface styles are appropriate for other types of data. Normally, a software designer can choose appropriate interface styles using their own background knowledge about the concepts included in the conceptual model. The user interface designer recognizes what each concept signifies, and selects a suitable way of representing the concept and interacting with it (Liebenau and Backhouse 1990).

We therefore sought to embed this kind of general knowledge into soft schemas, so that it could be used automatically by an AIS to render more domain-specific interfaces and behavior. It is achieved by linking each concept in the soft schema with a particular *archetypal category* (major cognitive semantic category; Moore and Price 1999; Markman and Wisniewski 1997; Caramazza et al. 2003). The prototype AIS uses nine archetypal categories: people, organizations, places, documents, activities, physical objects, conceptual objects, systems and categories (McGinnes

**Fig. 3.1** Standard user profile design: the *upper images* represent domain-specific implementations. The generic wireframe below can load dynamically any domain-specific information at runtime. Changing its layout could result in any of the upper profile UI components

2005). Using archetypal categories allows the AIS to offer a category-specific interface style in respect of each concept in the soft schema. We refer to this process as *differential design*; it is intended to mirror the use of general knowledge by software designers (some related work exists in McGinnes 2005). An example is given in Fig. 3.1: any concept that belongs to the category people could use a standard design defined by a "user profile" visual component. This component could apply general knowledge, such as the fact that people are often identified by a name and an image, or that people usually reside at a location. This information can be required by the data structure, but everything else can be loaded dynamically in the interface and changes to the concept's definition will not break the interface.

Incidentally, the use of archetypal categories also presents advantages during modeling; for example, it allows aspects of models to be predicted, helping to speed up modeling and reduce error (McGinnes 2000).

### 3.3.3 Neurology and Cognitive Semantics

How much can we take these archetypal categories for granted? For many years a belief was prevalent that specific brain areas facilitate domain specific knowledge; this belief is referred to as *localizationism*. This idea has been challenged since 1891 (Freud 1953 (1891)). However, instances of damage to specific brain areas have been shown to affect unique knowledge domain. For example, some subjects have deficits in specific brain regions that prevented them from recognizing people (*prosopagnosia*) (Caramazza et al. 2003). Similar results have been proposed after

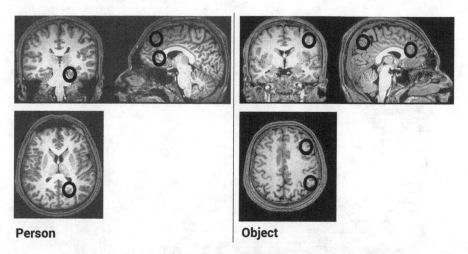

**Person** | **Object**

**Fig. 3.2** fMRI showing approximate indicative positions of activation during Person and Object trials. Composed according to data found in Mason et al. (2004), Mitchell et al. (2002), Tyler and Moss (2001)

fMRI studies, where people, objects, and activities usually trigger signals in separate brain areas (Caramazza et al. 2003; Mason et al. 2004; Mitchell et al. 2002). Evolutionary theory has suggested that pressure from the environment resulted in dedicated neural mechanisms for each domain of knowledge, effectively creating categories that are in some sense "hard-wired" and therefore *archetypal* (Caramazza et al. 2003).

Localizationism has been challenged recently, drawing from cases where subjects have recovered from deficits of the aforementioned types. A known example of regenerated brain functionality (neuroplasticity) is the ability of blind people to substitute their visual cortex functionality with haptic input: brain areas that were formerly dedicated to one function switch to another, so that blind people can "see" what they touch (Pascual-Leone et al. 1999). However, research shows that archetypal categories still emerge, but this time in a distributed neural system rather than in brain areas, and that differences in the content of concepts drive the evolutionary categorization of cognitive semantics (Tyler and Moss 2001). There is no conflict between the fMRI results of Tyler and Moss (2001) and Mason et al. (2004), Mitchell et al. (2002) (also see Fig. 3.2).

Moreover, research has shown that cognitive semantics are formed in a *middle-out* way, in contrast with a bottom-up or a top-down one. That is, humans categorize entities using *basic level* categories first, and then generalize into more abstract entities or specialize into more concrete ones (Markman and Wisniewski 1997; Klibanoff and Waxman 2003). In simple terms, one would first recognize *a person* and then specialize it to, e.g., the particular individual Joanne Wall, or generalize it to, e.g., an abstract concept such as "animate entity".

In conclusion, given the slow pace of human evolution, we can assume it is safe to use basic level cognitive semantic categories in the construction of soft schemas.

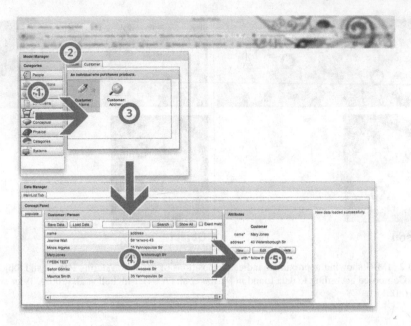

**Fig. 3.3** An interaction map of the prototype AIS. See Table 3.1 for explanation of the layout and interaction

## 3.4 How the Prototype AIS Works

In this section we describe the visual and interaction design of the prototype AIS and present a technical explanation of how it deals with soft schemas and data. The present prototype implements soft schemas and archetypal categories with real-time user interface generation. Differential design (Sect. 3.3.2) and end-user modeling have yet to be implemented.

### 3.4.1 Visual and Interaction Design

The prototype's layout, navigation, and interaction have been designed with end users in mind, particularly given that the user interface evolves over time (O'Murchú 2009). There are two main panels, aligned vertically: the Model Manager and the Data Manager (see Fig. 3.3). The Model Manager consists of a vertical button bar and a tab bar. The buttons represent the nine archetypal categories. The tab bar allows access to panels showing the soft schema and its contents.

The first panel (shown by default) offers a top-level view of the active schema. It contains tiled icons, each denoting a particular concept in the schema. Labels help to disambiguate the meaning of icons (Evamy 2003; Whitehouse 1999) (for brevity, the term "icon" is used from this point to mean a labelled icon). The remaining

**Table 3.1** Functionality of the various AIS layout elements

| Element | Functionality |
| --- | --- |
| 1. Categories button bar | Each button represents one of the archetypal categories. Clicking the button differentiates the concepts shown in the concept panel in that only concepts of the relevant category are highlighted. |
| 2. Model tab bar | Allows the user to navigate through tabs containing the soft schema and its individual concepts. |
| 3. Concept panel | Displays icons which represent concepts and attributes. Clicking an icon displays the tab panel and populates the datagrid for that concept. |
| 4. Data management panel | Allows the user to load and save data, perform search/filter operations and manipulate data displayed in a dynamic grid. Clicking each row makes relevant information appear in the attributes panel. |
| 5. Attributes panel | Offers basic data manipulation functionality; allows the user to enter, view and edit attribute values for particular concept instances and to delete concept instances. When one of the buttons is clicked a modal dialog appears, allowing the user to perform the selected function. |

sub-panels represent individual concepts in the soft schema, each with tiled icons representing attributes or related concepts. For clarity, attributes have two labels: the first (in boldface) is the parent concept and the second is the name of the attribute. This way of presenting conceptual models, using icons and windows rather than boxes and lines, has been shown to substantially improve model understandability, particularly for non-experts (McGinnes and Amos 2001).

The Data Manager contains a data management panel and an attributes panel. The data management panel includes three sets of elements. Two buttons allow loading and saving of data, a set of elements facilitate searching and filtering, and a grid displays data stored by the AIS. The grid dynamically loads columns for the currently-selected concept's attributes and rows for its instances.

A text field notifies the user on the success of their actions including loading and saving data and data manipulation functions. To assist end users, action invitations are also used throughout. Hover invitations are activated for the data management panel, tabs, load/save buttons and concept icons. A cursor invitation is activated in the search input field, and a tool-tip invitation displays information about each archetypal category.

### 3.4.2 Handling Schemas and Data

The prototype AIS reads two types of XML file: schema files and data files. Each schema file contains a soft schema. Each data file stores data consisting of a number of concept instances. Each concept instance contains data values with structure that reflects the soft schema that the instance was created with.

*Example 3.1* Schema file section describing the concept *Customer*:

```
<concept>
    <conceptName>Customer</conceptName>
    <category>People</category>
    <attributes>
        <attribute id="1">name</attribute>
        <attribute id="2">id</attribute>
        <attribute id="3">address</attribute>
    </attributes>
</concept>
```

Once a schema file has been loaded, the AIS will enforce it for any new data instances that are entered. Data instances already stored may be retrieved and viewed, but will retain their original structure. Should the schema be altered (by loading a new schema or editing the active schema), the AIS will enforce the altered schema for any data that are subsequently entered but already-stored instances will not be affected.

*Example 3.2* Data file section containing data for two customers previously entered using different soft schemas:

```
<customer>
    <name>Joanne Wall</name>
    <id>2012</id>
    <address>43 Tows Str</address>
</customer>
<customer>
    <firstname>Maurice</firstname>
    <lastname>Smith</lastname>
    <id>2002</id>
    <address>3 Yannou Street</address>
    <phone>2273034397</phone>
</customer>
```

The current schema file is not used for data retrieval and display, since any retrieved data may conform to a variety of soft schemas. Instead, the AIS interprets the data structure of each data instance, and then does its best to display the data instances together coherently, regardless of which soft schema each instance conforms to. For example, where different customers have different sets of attributes, as in the example above, the superset of the attributes is used to make up the list of columns in the data grid. Assuming that initially a concept $\Sigma$ has attributes $A = \{a, b, c\}$ and later is modified to have attributes $B = \{x, y, z\}$, then the end user will be able to read instances of $\Sigma$ with attributes $A \cup B$, add a new instance of $\Sigma$ with attributes $B$, or delete an instance of $\Sigma$ regardless of what attributes it has, subject

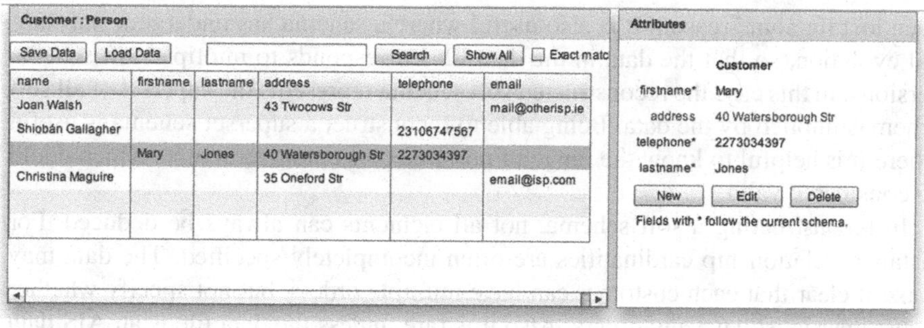

**Fig. 3.4** The data grid and the attributes panel after loading new data. Both automatically generated the columns and the text fields, thus adapting to the new data

to referential integrity constraints. Figure 3.4 illustrates the effect when a schema is changed and new data added. The columns for newly-entered instances differ from those for existing instances, yet all are displayed.

### 3.4.3 Applications in Reverse Engineering of Existing Data Structures

We note that it is a conceptually-simple operation to reconstruct the conceptual model underlying any database structure or XML data. Most of the semantics necessary to recreate the conceptual model implemented by a software application are implicit in, and capable of being determined by examination of, its data storage structures. This makes it possible, in theory, to use an AIS with any arbitrary dataset, regardless of whether its corresponding soft schema exists. The required soft schema can simply be reconstructed by examining the data, and this process can be automated.

The ability to reconstruct soft schemas automatically has been demonstrated in two AIS implementations to date. In the first, the AIS was capable of reading a database structure and thereby producing a corresponding soft schema. The resulting soft schema could be used to store and manipulate data with equivalent structure to that stored in the source database. But, unlike the source database, the AIS would permit the schema subsequently to be modified at will. This proved useful as a first stage in the reengineering of legacy database applications. The data structure from an existing application could be turned into a soft schema, which could then evolve relatively easily through a prototyping process to arrive at an improved structure matching client user requirements.

The second implementation is capable of reading an XML data file and reconstructing its corresponding soft schema. If the XML data file is an AIS data file, then the resulting soft schema can immediately be used to add to, and modify, the data in the file. This is useful, for example, if the soft schema for a particular data file has been lost for some reason. It is also useful where a schema has undergone substantial evolution, so that the data in the data file corresponds to multiple soft schema versions. In this case the reconstructed soft schema represents the superset of all soft schemas implied by the data. Being able to reconstruct a superset schema is useful where it is helpful to know the range of possible conceptual structures which could be considered valid.

In reconstructing a soft schema, not all elements can always be deduced. For instance, relationship cardinalities are often incompletely specified. The data may make it clear that each customer can have multiple orders, but not specify whether a customer *must* have any orders. Also it is rare, unless the data file is an AIS data file, for the data to be tagged with archetypal categories, icons, or other semantic information. Suitable categories and images can to some extent be automatically suggested by recognizing common terms. For example, for an item of data with XML tag `<customer>` it would be appropriate to suggest categories *person* or *organization*. Similarly for tag `<order>` it would be relevant to suggest category *activity*. Default images can be used according to the categories suggested. However, this process of deducing categories and images is inherently hit-and-miss, and so any suggested categories and images require review and possible modification by the user.

## 3.5  Discussion and Future Work

At present the prototype successfully reads schema and data files and generates suitable user interfaces, allowing basic CRUD (create, read, update, delete) functions to be performed on the data. This implementation demonstrates the feasibility of separating conceptual models from application structures, and of automatically generating user interfaces in real time from soft schemas. The next stage of our project will experimentally assess the usability of the prototype; however, related research has shown that relatively sophisticated and usable interfaces can be created this way for a variety of implementation platforms (McGinnes 2005).

Changing the schema presents no problem to the application, which continues to work effectively. Since previously-entered data can still be viewed, the user can upgrade the data to match the current schema at his or her leisure, or choose not to. We envisage that tools can be provided to assist the user in this process, identifying data which could be upgraded and automatically performing the upgrade where this is feasible. We anticipate benefits to the end user from being able to continue to use previously-entered data despite schema changes. For example, it will allow applications to grow and evolve as end user understanding improves through use. However, it also opens the possibility that data will become chaotic and unusable, particularly if many schema changes are made but data instances corresponding to earlier schema versions are not upgraded to match the new schema structure. Usability testing will reveal whether this ability to change the schema without affecting existing data is helpful for end users, or merely results in chaotic datasets which are difficult to understand and use.

At present the AIS supports only simple soft schemas, as support for relationships between concepts has yet to be implemented. We intend to add support for relationships; this will require implementation of more sophisticated user interface heuristics. Again, prior work has demonstrated that automated design can produce usable interfaces for schemas with complex relationships between concepts (McGinnes 2005). The challenge in this instance is to make the automated design occur purely at runtime rather than a mixture of design time and runtime.

In addition, functions will be added to allow the end user to visually manage soft schemas. End-user modeling using a similar schema representation has been tested in previous research (McGinnes 2000) but usability testing will help assess how easy it is for end users to do their own modeling in the context of the prototype AIS. We hypothesize that the ability to enter and retrieve data immediately upon schema change, without the need for data transformation and reloading, will facilitate understanding and learning. We also plan to implement better support for data types, with differential design, that is the dynamic selection of user interface style depending on archetypal category. For example, map views could be provided for places and calendar views for activities. It is hoped that this will improve the usability of the AIS, making it look and feel more like a hand-coded application. Again, usability testing will help evaluate and refine this feature.

Finally, the semantic categories are intended to serve as an examination ground for a potential semantic standard. This would make software more interoperable and consistent. Despite using XML at the moment, moving to OWL/RDF is an option. In this way standardization would be enforced; in any case, this option needs to be examined after adding support for relationships.

## 3.6 Conclusion

This chapter has presented a prototype user interface for an adaptive information system. The system handles various conceptual structures at runtime, treating these structures as data (*soft schemas*). It allows the user to handle (create, read, delete) data, as well as update soft schemas or data.

The intention is to evaluate the usability of a system with separate data and conceptual structures. Our hope is that software designed in this way could be more flexible for end users; one piece of software could have more uses than the domain-specific applications built according to current practices.

## References

Alani, H., Kalfoglou, Y., O'Hara, K., & Shadbolt, N. (2005). Towards a killer app for the semantic web. In *The semantic Web–ISWC 2005* (pp. 829–843).
Alani, H., Hall, W., O'Hara, K., Shadbolt, N., Szomszor, M., & Chandler, P. (2008). Building a pragmatic semantic web. *IEEE Intelligent Systems, 23*(3), 61–68.

Bakke, E., Karger, D., & Miller, R. (2011). A spreadsheet-based user interface for managing plural relationships in structured data. In *Proceedings of the SIGCHI conference on human factors in computing systems*, CHI '11 (pp. 2541–2550). New York: ACM.

Berners-Lee, T., Hall, W., Hendler, J., O'Hara, K., Shadbolt, N., Weitzner, D. J., et al. (2006). A framework for web science. *Foundations and Trends in Web Science*, *1*(1), 1–130.

Berners-Lee, T., Hollenbach, J., Lu, K., Presbrey, J., Pru d'ommeaux, E., et al. (2007). *Tabulator redux: writing into the semantic web*.

Caramazza, A., Mahon, B. Z., et al. (2003). The organization of conceptual knowledge: the evidence from category-specific semantic deficits. *Trends in Cognitive Sciences*, *7*(8), 354–361.

Chan, Y. E., & Storey, V. C. (1996). The use of spreadsheets in organizations: determinants and consequences. *Information & Management*, *31*(3), 119–134.

Codd, E. F. (1970). A relational model of data for large shared data banks. *Communications of the ACM*, *13*(6), 377–387.

Curino, C. A., Tanca, L., Moon, H. J., & Zaniolo, C. (2008). Schema evolution in Wikipedia: toward a web information system benchmark. In *International conference on enterprise information systems (ICEIS)*. Citeseer.

Ertl, D., Kaindl, H., Arnautovic, E., Falb, J., & Popp, R. (2011). Generating high-level interaction models out of ontologies. In *IUI SEMAIS* (Vol. 11, pp. 7–11).

Evamy, M. (2003). *World without words*. New York: Laurence King.

Fein, E., Razinkov, N., Shachor, S., Mazzoleni, P., Goh, S., Goodwin, R., et al. (2011). Using MATCON to generate case tools that guide deployment of pre-packaged applications. In *2011 33rd international conference on software engineering (ICSE)* (pp. 1016–1018). New York: IEEE Press.

Fonseca, F. T., & Martin, J. E. (2004). Toward an alternative notion of information systems ontologies: information engineering as a hermeneutic enterprise. *Journal of the American Society for Information Science and Technology*, *56*(1), 46–57.

Freud, S. (1953 (1891)). *On aphasia; a critical study*. Madison: International Universities Press.

Hartung, M., Terwilliger, J. F., & Rahm, E. (2011). Recent advances in schema and ontology evolution. In *Schema matching and mapping* (pp. 149–190).

Hick, J.-M., & Hainaut, J.-L. (2006). Database application evolution: a transformational approach. *Data & Knowledge Engineering*, *59*(3), 534–558.

Kennedy, O., Ahmad, Y., & Koch, C. (2011). DBToaster: agile views for a dynamic data management system. In *Proc. of the fifth biennial conference on innovative data systems research (CIDR 2011)* (pp. 284–295).

Klibanoff, R. S., & Waxman, S. R. (2003). Basic level object categories support the acquisition of novel adjectives: evidence from preschool-aged children. *Child Development*, *71*(3), 649–659.

Kohlhase, A., & Kohlhase, M. K. (2011). Spreadsheets with a semantic layer. *Electronic Communications of the EASST*, *10*, 1–18.

LENA—a Fresnel LEns based RDF/Linked Data NAvigator with SPARQL selector support (n.d.).

Liebenau, J., & Backhouse, J. (1990). *Understanding information: an introduction*. Basingstoke: Palgrave Macmillan.

Markman, A. B., & Wisniewski, E. J. (1997). Similar and different: the differentiation of basic-level categories. *Journal of Experimental Psychology. Learning, Memory, and Cognition*, *23*(1), 54.

Mason, M. F., Banfield, J. F., & Macrae, C. N. (2004). Thinking about actions: the neural substrates of person knowledge. *Cerebral Cortex*, *14*(2), 209–214.

McGinnes, S. (2000). *Conceptual modelling: a psychological perspective*. Doctoral dissertation, London School of Economics and Political Science (University of London).

McGinnes, S. (2005). *Systems and methods for software based on business concepts*.

McGinnes, S., & Amos, J. (2001). Accelerated business concept modeling: combining user interface design with object modeling. In *Object modeling and user interface design* (pp. 3–36). Reading: Addison-Wesley.

McGuinness, D. L., Fikes, R., Rice, J., & Wilder, S. (2000). An environment for merging and testing large ontologies. In *Principles of knowledge representation and reasoning-international conference* (pp. 483–493). San Mateo: Morgan Kaufmann.

Mitchell, J. P., Heatherton, T. F., & Macrae, C. N. (2002). Distinct neural systems subserve person and object knowledge. *Proceedings of the National Academy of Sciences, 99*(23), 15238–15243.

Moore, C. J., & Price, C. J. (1999). A functional neuroimaging study of the variables that generate category-specific object processing differences. *Brain, 122*(5), 943–962.

Noy, N. F., & Musen, M. A. (2000). Algorithm and tool for automated ontology merging and alignment. In *Proceedings of the 17th national conference on artificial intelligence (AAAI-00)*. Available as SMI technical report SMI-2000-0831.

O'Murchú, N. (2009). Understanding adaptive design and user experience. In *Irish human computer interaction (I-HCI) conference 2009*.

Pascual-Leone, A., Hamilton, R., Tormos, J., Keenan, J., & Catala, M. (1999). Neuroplasticity in the adjustment to blindness. In *Neural plasticity: building a bridge from the laboratory to the clinic* (pp. 94–108). Berlin: Springer.

Raden, N. (2005). Shedding light on shadow it: is Excel running your business? *DSSResources.com, 26*.

Roddick, J. F., Al-Jadir, L., Bertossi, L., Dumas, M., Gregersen, H., Hornsby, K., et al. (2000). Evolution and change in data management—issues and directions. *ACM SIGMOD Record, 29*(1), 21–25.

Shirky, C. (2003). The semantic web, syllogism and worldview. In *Networks, economics, and culture*.

Sun, Y., Gray, J., & White, J. (2011). Mt-scribe: an end-user approach to automate software model evolution. In *2011 33rd international conference on software engineering (ICSE)* (pp. 980–982). New York: IEEE Press.

Tyler, L. K., & Moss, H. E. (2001). Towards a distributed account of conceptual knowledge. *Trends in Cognitive Sciences, 5*(6), 244–252.

Wach, E. P. (2011). Automated ontology evolution as a basis for adaptive interactive systems. In *IUI SEMAIS 11* (pp. 467–468).

Whitehouse, R. (1999). The uniqueness of individual perception. In R. Jacobson (Ed.), *Information design* (pp. 103–129). Cambridge: MIT Press.

Zhao, C.-c., Zhao, L.-y., & Wang, H.-l. (2010). A spreadsheet system based on data semantic object. In *2010 the 2nd IEEE international conference on information management and engineering (ICIME)* (pp. 407–411).

# Chapter 4
# A Semantic Model for Adaptive Collaboration Support Systems

Stefan W. Knoll, Jordan Janeiro, Stephan G. Lukosch,
and Gwendolyn L. Kolfschoten

**Abstract** Dynamic environments characterize today's world. In complex design and engineering processes, dynamic environments influence the requirements of an ongoing collaboration process. They lead to process goal changes or reduce the time available to achieve a collaborative goal. In such a case, collaboration support and processes need to be adapted. Various collaboration support systems assist groups by providing technological support to structure activities, generate and share data, and to improve group communication. However, current support systems often prescribe or assume a fixed process and a known group composition. As result, collaboration support is needed that considers the changing environment and provides groups with the support they need. Such support can range from a fixed process and tool configuration to an open collaboration environment that enables groups to interact in a self-organized way. This chapter introduces an elastic collaboration approach that comprises a continuum of collaboration support, ranging from prescribed collaboration to new emerging forms of collaboration. The chapter discusses how the concept of elastic collaboration can be implemented in an adaptive collaboration support system using a semantic model to capture, manage and analyze a collaboration environment. Based on this model, a sample application of the semantic model is presented along with a collaborative problem-solving model.

S.W. Knoll (✉) · J. Janeiro · S.G. Lukosch · G.L. Kolfschoten
Delft University of Technology, Delft, The Netherlands
e-mail: s.w.knoll@tudelft.nl

J. Janeiro
e-mail: j.janeiro@tudelft.nl

S.G. Lukosch
e-mail: s.g.lukosch@tudelft.nl

G.L. Kolfschoten
e-mail: g.l.kolfschoten@tudelft.nl

T. Hussein et al. (eds.), *Semantic Models for Adaptive Interactive Systems*,
Human–Computer Interaction Series, DOI 10.1007/978-1-4471-5301-6_4,
© Springer-Verlag London 2013

## 4.1 Introduction

Nowadays, virtual teams comprise an important structural component of many organizations (Nunamaker et al. 2009). In order to lower travel and facility costs, organizations use technological support to facilitate collaborative design and engineering processes across virtual teams. In the context of engineering, "collaboration occurs when a group of autonomous stakeholders of a problem domain engage in an interactive process, using shared rules, norms, and structures, to act or decide on issues related to that domain" (Wood and Gray 1991). According to this definition, collaboration in engineering is challenging, not just because of the nature of a complex product, but also because collaboration is a dynamic process that is based on human behavior. In complex design and engineering processes, a change in the collaboration environment like a changing process goal or the reduction of time available to achieve a collaborative goal can lead to a need for a process adaptation during runtime. Furthermore, the expertise of a group constellation for the collaboration process or an adapted process stage can vary depending on the expertise of the engineers who join or leave the group during the process. To deal with these types of dynamics, teams need technological support that provide a range of flexible features to adapt a collaboration process to a new collaboration situation.

Collaboration support has been studied in various research domains such as groupware, group (decision) support systems, concurrent design and group facilitation (Nunamaker et al. 1996; Kolfschoten et al. 2007). As a result, different types of collaboration support systems exist, which offer a variety of local and web-based applications to support collaborative design and engineering processes. These systems assist groups in collaboration by providing technological support to structure activities, generate and share data, and improve group communication (DeSanctis and Gallupe 1987; Nunamaker et al. 1991).

Current collaboration support systems can be used to implement a collaboration process in different ways. On the one hand, a prescribed collaboration process can be implemented to support groups with less expertise in collaboration. Here, the system guides a group through a predefined sequence of process stages. For each stage, the system provides and configures a set of predefined tools that can be used by the group to achieve an intended outcome of a stage. On the other hand, an emergent collaboration process can be implemented to support an experienced group, who prefers to coordinate themselves rather than being coordinated by the system. Here, the system leaves the process coordination to the group and provides a set of different tools that can be freely combined and used in a collaboration process.

In a dynamic collaboration environment, such as in complex design and engineering processes, where the requirements of collaboration are not fixed, a collaboration support system needs to support different forms of collaboration in a flexible way, similar to the elastic collaboration approach (Janeiro et al. 2012a). Elastic collaboration comprises a continuum of collaboration forms, ranging from prescribed collaboration to support inexperienced groups, to new emergent forms of collaboration that enables experienced groups to interact in a self-organized way. However, a collaboration support system that implements an elastic collaboration approach needs adaptation strategies to offer collaboration support, ranging from a fixed process and tool configuration to an open collaboration environment. Furthermore, to improve the adaptation strategies over time, the system needs a component to learn from executed elastic collaboration processes. Through this component, documented collaboration processes can be analyzed by experts in collaboration or by machine learning algorithms to refine existing adaptation strategies or to define new collaboration support.

To develop such an adaptive collaboration support system, it is essential to formally describe collaboration processes, to monitor the progress of a collaboration process and to log all activities in a collaboration process. This can only be achieved by using a semantic model for collaboration processes. As a first step, this chapter analyzes the use of a process definition languages to define adaptation strategies for prescribed as well as emergent collaboration process. Different process definition languages were analyzed with respect to their feasibility to describe, capture and analyze elastic collaboration processes. The analysis shows that given languages only provide limited process information to define adaption strategies as well as to assess the quality of a collaborative process. As a result, the chapter introduces a first approach of a semantic model that makes use of an ontology-based approach to describe and capture more knowledge about the collaboration process than given process definition languages. The chapter closes with a presentation of a sample application of the semantic model to define adaptation strategies for elastic collaboration and how the semantic model can be used to assess the quality of a collaboration process.

## 4.2  Background

Based on a series of workshops and conference calls with experts from the construction industry, collaboration in complex design and engineering processes was analyzed (Janeiro et al. 2012b). Here, a product lifecycle process was used as a possible scenario for a dynamic environment that involves collaboration between groups with different needs. The experts analyzed different phases of the product lifecycle against existing collaboration processes. During the workshop new challenges for collaboration in a dynamic situation were identified, which are not traditionally considered in collaboration process design. These challenges originate in the dynamics and short problem-solving cycles in the process, causing uncertainty about the time available, the goals, requirements and participants for the collaboration process.

As an example for such collaboration processes, consider a diagnosis process of a manufacturer that wants to increase the availability of its machines. These machines, e.g. wheel loaders, are connected through a remote infrastructure that monitors their performance data. If the machine emits degrading signals, the manufacturer has to investigate a certain issue, according to a well-defined deadline to avoid a machine breakdown. This situation forces engineers that have different backgrounds (e.g.

mechanical engineering, stress engineering and fluid engineering) to team up and collaborate, formulating a diagnosis and preparing action plans.

## 4.2.1 A Collaborative Problem-Solving Model

Based on the workshop results, a process model was developed to describe the different collaborative processes that were identified during the workshop. The experts indicated that most of these processes represent problem-solving and decision-making processes. As both processes combine similar phases of convergent and divergent thinking, a collaborative problem-solving model was developed to identify and discuss challenges of collaboration in dynamic environments of product lifecycle.

This section introduces a model for collaborative problem solving. The model is based on different stepwise models for problem solving (Wallas 1926; Osborn 1963; Simon 1977; Warr and O'Neill 2005), which in common define problem solving in three stages: Intelligence, Design and Choice. According to Simon (1977), the stage Intelligence involves the identification and analysis of a problem. The resulting knowledge about a problem is then used in the stage Design to develop or identify alternative solutions to the problem. In the final stage Choice, these solutions are evaluated and a solution is selected for implementation.

During the industry workshops, experts indicated that depending on the problem complexity, a problem-solving process in a product lifecycle can be implemented as an individual or collaborative process. As a result, the three-stage model was adapted with respect to methods and components that can be used to support individual as well as collaborative processes in a product lifecycle. The resulting collaborative problem-solving model considers the following stages (see Fig. 4.1):

- *Problem Definition:* This stage begins when an event in the product lifecycle initiates a problem-solving process. Similar to the stage Intelligence (Simon 1977), the problem is analyzed by collecting relevant information, which will be used to generate and select a problem definition. During the workshop, experts indicate that the process can be supported by structuring the analysis of data related to the event. In a collaborative mode, a group may need further support to create shared understanding about possible problem definitions as well as to create consensus during the selection of a working definition for the next stage. If the problem cannot be defined, the stage can be repeated with further data or a new group constellation.
- *Solution Search:* This stage represents a part of the original stage Design (Simon 1977). The subdivision in Solution Search and Solution Generation was made in regard to the workshop results, where the experts indicate that a solution generation is only needed if there are no known existing solutions to a problem. As a result, the stage is used to search for "off-the-shelve" solutions that can be used as a whole or in a modified form to solve the problem. Support can be needed during the gathering and analyzing process of data related to the problem definition.

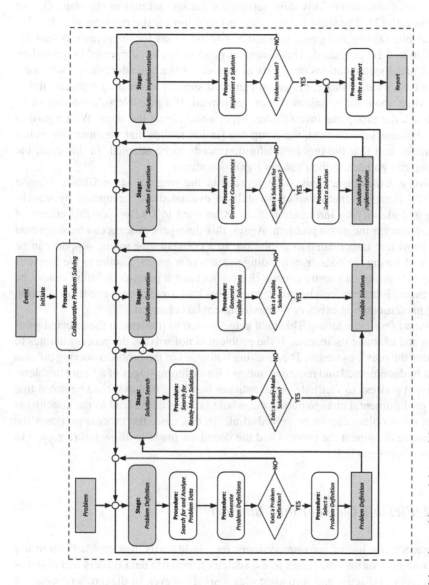

**Fig. 4.1** A collaborative problem-solving model

Here, participants can be guided in exploring previous cases, lessons learned and other documentations of organizational knowledge to find an existing solution. Furthermore, during the collaborative phase, collaboration support can be needed to create a shared understanding among the group members.

- *Solution Generation:* This stage represents the second part of the stage Design (Simon 1977). The stage begins when no solution for the problem as defined is available. During this stage, new alternative solutions for the given problem situation will be generated. This divergent process can be supported by providing data like documentations or reports as stimuli for the brainstorming of solutions. In a collaborative mode, the group can need support in creating a shared understanding about the solutions that are generated. If a possible solution cannot be defined, the group can invite further experts and repeat the stage. With regard to the dynamic environment, the group can further realize that the environment has changed and that the problem definition needs to be adapted. In this case, the group can go back to the\\*Problem Definition* stage.
- *Solution Evaluation:* This stage represents the original stage Choice (Simon 1977). Here, alternative solutions will be evaluated and compared by searching and identifying information that can be used to foresee possible effects of a solution on the given problem. Again, this divergent process can be supported by providing data related to a solution. In a collaborative mode, support can be needed during the consensus building process of a group. Similar to the previous stages, a group can invite experts if the effects of a possible solution cannot be foreseen. Furthermore, the group can go back to a previous stage if no solution for implementation exists or the environment has changed.
- *Solution Implementation:* This final stage is used to implement the selected solution and evaluate its success. If the problem is not solved, the process iterates to one of the previous stages. The resulting outcomes of the problem-solving process can be documented and reused as support for different stages of a future problem-solving process to facilitate organizational learning. It also should be noted that an environmental change during the whole process could lead to the conclusion that the problem cannot be solved at all. In this case, the process proposes the group to document the process and the decisions made to allow future groups to reuse their knowledge.

### 4.2.2 Flexible Collaboration Support

Engineers make use of software systems, e.g. dashboards, that enable them to use and configure various diagnosis tools, such as telemetric data readers and collaboration tools to discuss and formulate diagnosis. However, in diagnosis processes a change in the machine performance may require process adaptations. For example, assume the situation in which experts have a deadline to fix an underperforming cooling sub-system of a machine. Based on the available time, they plan to discuss and investigate the problem before taking actions. However, a faster overheating in the machine's engine forces the team to abandon the original plan and to quickly brainstorm to prevent a machine breakdown. In this situation, the team needs guidance from the software system to collaborative solve the problem in a short amount of time. Need for support is also given if experts join or leave the team during the diagnosis process. For example, it might be that an expert is required to analyze the cooling sub-system. If an expert is not available, the team needs guidance to analyze the cooling sub-system on their own.

The above collaborative problem-solving model covers such different collaboration processes. Suitable support for the engineers, however, needs to be flexible and adaptable to cover the different collaboration processes. Elastic collaboration offers such support, as it comprises a continuum of collaboration support, ranging from prescribed collaboration to emergent forms of collaboration (Janeiro et al. 2012a). On the one extreme, prescribed collaboration supports less experienced groups by predefining collaboration procedures and tools for every step of the collaborative process. Here, a technological support system can be used to monitor the collaboration environment and to provide support based on predefined rules. On the other extreme, emergent collaboration supports expert groups that do not need guidance and coordination during collaboration. Here, the group monitors the collaboration environment and coordinates the use of collaboration methods and tools based on their needs. During collaboration, the group or system can shift from one type of collaboration to the other as in a continuum of collaboration.

Such elastic collaboration either needs context-aware or process-aware collaboration support. Process information can be used to define adaption strategies for dynamic environments as well as to assess the quality of a collaborative process during runtime. Context information about, e.g., the provided system components can be used to define rules for their adaptation in relation to a possible change in the collaboration environment. The following sections discuss such support.

## Context-Awareness

The main goal of context-aware systems is to achieve automatic self-configuration according to the context in which they are inserted, preventing users to deal with such cumbersome task. This type of systems often employs adaptation mechanisms based on rule systems. Once an event is detected and a condition satisfied, the system executes actions, which represent foreseen adaptations.

As systems aim at performing automatic context-aware adaptations in different application domains, it becomes difficult to establish a generic context model. Rather, context models were categorized to tackle specific domains (Schilit et al. 1994): hardware context, user context, physical context and time context. Based on this initial set, various context-aware systems emerged but the majority of the systems mainly focused on three context entities (Dey et al. 2001): places (rooms and buildings), people (individuals and groups) and things (physical objects and computer components).

Besides the popularity of these entities, other types of context-aware systems focusing on the adaptation of collaborative work environments evolved. Haake et al. (2010) propose a framework for modeling context information and description of adaptations in a shared workspace. In one of the scenarios the framework is used to quickly switch tools for users, according to the projects in which they are assigned to. Gross and Prinz (2004) propose a model for processing awareness context information enabling the presentation of notifications in the appropriate user situation about: shared artifacts, presence of group members and user activities. Prinz and Zaman (2005) propose a context model based on individual and group activities combined with a content analysis of documents in shared workspaces. The context model is used in a system to assist users in finding the right place for storing their contributions.

Although using context models to execute adaptations, there is still a lack of efforts in exploiting and defining models that provide contextualized guidance in collaboration systems.

**Process-Aware Systems**

Process-Aware Systems have a process description that aims at coordinating users to accomplish a goal. In this type of system the process logic is separated from the application code to keep system flexibility if the process changes.

This type of systems is used for distribution and coordination of activities between users (Ellis et al. 2005) or to guide a group of users to accomplish expected tasks (Knoll et al. 2009) through a set of collaboration techniques named thinkLets (Briggs et al. 2003). However, these systems do not define support for the execution of dynamic context-aware adaptations. In line with dynamic adaptations, Reichert et al. (2003) propose the ADEPT-flex, a graph-based model that enables structural adaptation of workflows. However, there is no context model that supports adaptation. Instead, the adaptation is only interpreted as a user choice.

Rather than supporting just a process for collaboration, Bernstein (2000) proposes to bridge the existing gap between process-aware systems and non-process-aware systems (ad-hoc systems), which are open workspaces like dashboards. This type of system allows users to have different types of system support, along a spectrum called the Specificity Frontier. Differently from the other process-aware systems of this section, the system implementing the Specificity Frontier (referred in this chapter as the Specificity Frontier System) supports the transition between the prescribed and ad-hoc execution types. However, the system does not define a context model to support process adaptation or collaboration-based adaptations.

## 4.2.3 Summary

This section introduced a collaborative problem-solving model for complex and dynamic collaboration situations in design and engineering. The proposed model covers a range of different collaboration processes that require flexible collaboration support. Many context-aware collaboration systems evolved since the popularization of the term. Often, these systems execute automatic adaptations to customize shared workspaces. However, there is a lack of context-aware systems that can provide process guidance to a group. Such support is indirectly offered by process-aware systems by specifying a process that leads users to achieve expected outcomes. However, there is not a process-aware system that executes context-aware adaptations based on a specific collaboration context model. Prerequisites for an elastic collaboration support are the possibilities to formally describe collaboration processes, monitor the progress of a collaboration process and log all activities in a collaboration process. The following section analyzes different process definition languages with respect to their feasibility to support the elastic collaboration approach by expressing prescribed as well as emergent collaboration processes.

## 4.3 Analysis of Process Definition Languages

Common process definition languages are designed to define the underlying process logic of a collaboration process. Collaboration support systems make use of this information to guide collaboration and provide technological support in relation to a prescribed collaboration situation. These process definition languages are:

- *XML Process Definition Language (XPDL):* A graph-structured language to interchange business process definitions between different workflow products (Workflow Management Coalition 2008). XDPL provides an approach to support prescribed collaboration by expressing executable processes that can be executed collaboratively using groupware support. A process workflow is described by flow objects like the entity activity, which represents Gateways, Events and Tasks of a business process. However, process and workflow languages typically describe what needs to be done, not how it needs to be done (Deokar et al. 2008). The language therefore provides less information about the end-user or the application that will be used to execute a process task. These entities are represented by attributes of a flow object. This characteristic reduces the feasibility of XPDL to represent emergent collaboration processes in detail. However, detailed information about the entities component, participant and activity could be used to assess the quality of a collaboration process in more detail, which could help to define adaptation strategies for dynamic environments. Especially, to detect group behaviors that require a process adaptation, further knowledge about the participants and their activities can be needed.
- *WS-Business Process Execution Language Extension for People (BPEL4People):* A block-structured programming language for specifying human interactions within business processes with web services (Alves et al. 2012; Kloppmann et al. 2005). In contrast to BPEL, BPEL4People provides an approach to express executable processes that model human interactions as services implemented by people. These human activities represent standalone tasks that could offer a callable web service interface. Similar to XPDL, BPEL4People provides less information about the process environment.

- *IMS Learning Design (IMS LD):* A meta-language to represent learning design and units of learning (IMS Global Learning Consortium 2012). The language uses the metaphor of a theatrical play to subdivide a learning process called Method into one or more concurrent sub processes called Play. A Play contains different sequential processes called Act, which are related to the entities participant and activity via a role concept. With regard to the objective to express a learning process, participants are defined as learner or staff who can execute learning or support activities. IMS LD can support prescribed collaboration by adapting the given entities to a collaborative context. An interesting approach is the use of the entity Objective to specify the outcome of a process for the participants. Furthermore, the use of a metaphor to structure the learning process into sub processes can also be used to structure a collaboration process. However, similar to XPDL and BPEL4People, the concepts of the IMS LD provide fewer details to express the environment of an emergent collaboration process.
- *Collaborative Task Modeling Language (CTML):* A formal task based specification language to model actors, roles, collaborative tasks and their dependency and impact on the domain (Wurdel et al. 2008). The language is based on the assumptions that in limited and well-defined domains the behavior of an actor can be approximated through a role. This behavior can be associated to a collaborative task, which execution depends on the current state of the environment. The language uses a task tree notation to express a collaboration process. CTML represent an interesting approach to support prescribed collaboration by its expression of a collaborative task and its dependency and impact on the environment. However, the task tree notation seems not to be feasible to express an emergent collaboration process.
- *Collaboration Engineering Pattern Language:* A pattern language for collaboration using design patterns for best practices of facilitation (Briggs et al. 2003). The approach classifies the collaboration process into patterns of collaboration. Design patterns called thinkLets are used to prescribe reusable collaborative work practices for groups. Here, a thinkLet provides information on how a group can create a pattern of collaboration by using a set of capabilities (e.g. collaboration support tools) in a specific configuration. A prescribed collaboration process can be expressed by a sequence of thinkLets. However, the resulting process is documented as a paper-based script that provides guidelines for a facilitator or practitioner on how to support the collaboration process. This characteristic reduces the feasibility of this language approach to be used as a machine-readable process definition language for a collaboration support system.

To summarize, the analyzed process definition languages are feasible to express prescribed collaboration, but shows limitation in the expression of emergent collaboration. Most languages provide only abstract concepts to express information about the participant or the application that will be used during collaboration. However, detailed information about process, participants and environment is needed to assess the quality of a collaboration process during runtime and to define adaptation strategies that support collaboration in dynamic environments. As a result, this chapter proposes the need for a new formal model to express elastic collaboration processes in a dynamic environment. In this context, the chapter defines the following requirements:

R1: To guide collaboration, a formal model needs to express the underlying process logic of a prescribed collaboration process. This captured data has to allow an adaptive collaboration support system to provide technological support in relation to a prescribed collaboration situation.

R2: To detect the need for collaboration support, a formal model needs to capture data about prescribed as well as emergent collaboration processes and their context at runtime. This data has to allow an adaptive collaboration support system to assess the quality of a collaborative process and if needed to adapt the collaboration process.

R3: To improve collaboration support, a formal model needs to log all activities of a prescribed and emergent collaboration process. This data can be used to evaluate existing collaboration processes as well as adaptation strategies.

Instead of adapting a process definition language, the chapter proposes a semantic model to express elastic collaboration processes in dynamic environments. Haake et al. (2010) shows that a model approach can be used to describe context information in a collaboration environment, which can be used to configure a collaboration support system. As a result, the chapter extends given context model approaches by common entities of given process definition languages. Thereby, the chapter makes use of an ontological approach.

By definition, an ontology is a formal specification of a conceptualization of a domain of interest (Gruber 1993) that specifies a set of constraints that provide a data dictionary for a class of systems. Ontologies are used to identify what is or can be in the world. It is the intention to build a complete world model for describing the semantics of information exchange. An adaptive collaboration support system, implementing elastic collaboration, may benefit from ontologies to monitor and log activities represented by ontology concepts.

## 4.4 A Semantic Model for Elastic Collaboration

Ontology engineering aims at building a formal representation of domain knowledge (concepts in a domain) and creating a common understanding of the structure of information in the domain (relations between the concepts) among people or software agents (Studer et al. 1998; Gruber 1995). Today, several methods and methodologies for developing ontologies exist (Corcho et al. 2003). This chapter adopts these methodologies for ontology building (Grueninger and Fox 1995; Pinto and Martins 2004) and used the following steps:

- *Purpose and scope:* To conduct a literature research on collaboration as well as to use the introduced collaborative problem-solving model to define possible scenarios for elastic collaboration in the context of a product lifecycle management. Here, a set of questions is defined that a semantic model should be able to answer, called competency questions.

- *Capture and formalization:* To explore and structure all potentially relevant terms and phrases in a collaboration session and use the resulting elements to capture key concepts and relationships. Common process definition languages and given ontology-based approaches are analyzed to use previously established conceptualizations. A graphical representation is used to build a conceptual model for collaboration that is transformed into a semantic model.
- *Evaluation:* To evaluate the semantic model in relation to the purpose and the defined requirements. Here, the competency questions are used to verify the model regarding its consistency and completeness.
- *Documentation:* To document the concepts and relationships in a data dictionary, where each concept is describes by its name, description, cardinality, etc.

### 4.4.1 Purpose and Scope of the Semantic Model

The objective in developing a semantic model for elastic collaboration is to describe, capture and analyze knowledge about collaboration in dynamic environments. The chapter assumes that resulting information can be used to define adaptation strategies for elastic collaboration as well as to assess the quality of a collaboration process.

In this chapter collaboration is defined as an interactive process of a group in which the group members work together to achieve a shared goal. To describe this process, different entities from given process definition languages can be used to define the workflow of a process (Thiagarajan et al. 2002; zur Muehlen and Indulska 2010). To integrate human interaction into this definition, the entity *Participant* needs to be included. The following resulting entities are required to define a collaboration process:

- *Process:* Describes a logically ordered set of activities and relevant data to produce a result.
- *Activity:* Describes a step within a process with a name, a type, pre- and post-conditions and scheduling constraints.
- *Component:* Describes tools or artifacts that are used by an activity.
- *Data:* Describes the type and the value of the data elements that will be used or developed by an activity.
- *Flow connector:* Describes the order in which activities are executed and data is used between activities.
- *Participant:* Describes a human that act as the performer of the various activities.

These entities were used as a starting point to classify and define a set of competency questions that a semantic model for collaboration should be able to answer. For example, for the entity Process, questions were asked like "What is the objective of a process?", "Who uses the process?", "What are the activities of a process?", "What is the logical order of activities in a process?" or "When is a process effective?".

## 4.4.2 Defining and Formalizing a Semantic Model

Defining a semantic model demands to identify abstract entities (key concepts), naming important properties and defining relationships between the entities. To make use of previously established conceptualizations, the chapter analyzes common process definition languages, given ontology-based (Rajsiri et al. 2008; Oliveira et al. 2007; Pattberg and Fluegge 2007) as well as domain model approaches (Haake et al. 2010) to capture knowledge about collaboration.

### Existing Approaches to Capture Knowledge about Collaboration

An ontology-based approach to conceptualize and formalize a common vocabulary for a collaboration domain is given by Oliveira et al. (2007). Here, collaboration ontology is used to support the integration among different collaboration software applications within an organization. A collaboration session is defined by the concepts participants, objectives, artifacts, coordination and communication. Participants are the agents that can contribute in a meaningful way to achieve the objectives of the session. The ontology defines these actions of the participants by the concept participation, which denotes an atomic event that uses the concept protocol to coordinate actions between the participants. During a collaboration session different collaboration artifacts can be consumed or generated. The exchange of information between the participants is defined by the send and receive participations. Here, information is represented by the concept message that is expressed through a language. In conclusion, the presented collaboration ontology divides the key concepts for a collaboration domain into the sub-ontologies cooperation, communication and coordination. However, the ontology provides no concepts to define the software components that can be used in a collaboration process. Furthermore, the ontology provides no information about the logical order of activities in a process, which are needed to define and log collaboration processes.

Pattberg and Fluegge (2007) use a design pattern approach to capture knowledge about collaboration by creating an ontological approach that uses a structure of various levels of abstraction. These levels clarify the relation of a collaboration pattern (proven solution for a collaboration problem) to collaboration services (reusable implementation services) to the underlying communication technology of a collaboration process. This approach seems to be feasible to combine different concepts of collaboration patterns and pattern language. However, the given approach leaves the question open how detailed the information on the given layers need to be described.

Rajsiri et al. (2008) define an ontology-based approach to automate the specification of collaborative processes for virtual organization networks. Their approach of a collaboration network ontology consists of a collaboration ontology, a collaborative process ontology, and deduction rules to automate the specification of a collaborative process into a BPMN relevant model. Here, the collaboration ontology regards the characterization of collaborative network, details and abstract services of participants. The collaborative process ontology defines the task of the participants at

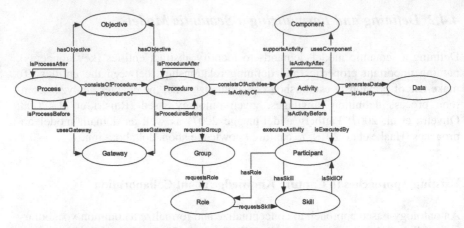

**Fig. 4.2** A semantic model for elastic collaboration

a functional level, which has input and output resources. The authors provides a supporting tool that applied the ontology, but indicates that the resulting BPMN models miss elements such as gateways and events, which are also not defined by the ontologies.

A collaboration domain model for describing collaboration environments and collaborative situation is presented by Haake et al. (2010). Here, a global collaboration space is defined by the interaction between the actors who uses the services of different applications to work and share artifacts between different workspaces. The concept of a role is used to define possible actions that an actor can execute within an application. Each actor is assigned to a workspace that defines a set of available applications. These applications implement the model-view-controller paradigm to operate on shared artifacts. In conclusion, the proposed collaboration domain model seems to be feasible to express collaboration situations as well as to define meaningful adaptations of a user workspace for specific situations. However, the model provides no concepts to define a collaboration process by a logical order of activities that an actor needs to execute to achieve a shared goal.

To sum up, the analyzed ontology-based approaches and domain model capture knowledge about collaboration in different ways. However, none of the approaches provide all concepts to model a collaboration process in relation to a changing environment or human behaviors. As a result, the chapter introduces a first approach of a semantic model for collaboration that reuses and combines some of the provided concept. Here, the competency questions were used to verify the resulting model and the defined relationships between the entities.

**A First Approach of a Semantic Model**

A first approach of a semantic model for elastic collaboration is illustrated in Fig. 4.2 by the key concepts and their relations. Here, the concept *Participant* describes a human being taking part in a process. This entity has certain *Skills* that can be a prerequisite of a *Role* in a process. Similar to Haake et al. (2010), the concept *Role* is used to denote abstractly a set of behaviors, rights and obligation of a *Participant*. A *Participant* can be assigned to a *Group* in a specific *Role*. Besides the concept *Role*, the concept *Skill* is used to distinguish different participants and thus to be able to define requirements for the participants of a process. These concepts can be used by an adaptive collaboration support system to define adaptation rules that suggests experts for a team extension.

The entity *Process* describes a process in which a *Group* makes effort toward a goal. Similar to Oliveira et al. (2007), a *Process* has an *Objective*, defining its main purpose or goal. The chapter intents that a collaboration process can be character-ized by observable group behaviors and the state of the concepts with which the group works. How a group moves through this process to create an intended state in the process can be prescribed by work tactics of a group, similar to the concept of a collaboration pattern (Pattberg and Fluegge 2007). The semantic model represents these work tactics by the concept *Procedure* that is related to a *Group*. During a *Procedure* a *Group* of *Participants* moves through a sequence of activities. Similar to given concepts like *"Participation"* (Oliveira et al. 2007) or Action (Haake et al. 2010), the concept *Activity* represents an atomic activity that will be executed by a *Participant* using a software artifact represented by the concept *Component*. To con-trol the collaboration process and allow the representation of parallel procedures, the concept *Gateway* is used to implement given workflow patterns like parallel split, exclusive choice or simple merge (van der Aalst et al. 2003).

## 4.5 Evaluation and Application

This section describes a first evaluation of the semantic model with regard to the identified requirements (R1–R3) and presents an application scenario in which the semantic model is used to support elastic collaboration.

### 4.5.1 To Guide a Collaboration Process (R1)

The semantic model can be used to define different collaborative problem-solving processes with different task and group constellations as defined in the collaborative problem-solving model (see Fig. 4.1). Here, competency questions are used to ver-ify the consistence and completeness of the models. First analyses show that the se-mantic model can be used to predefine the underlying process logic of a prescribed collaboration process. For example, a stage of the problem solving model can be prescribed by the concept *Process*. Here, the concept *Process* is related to different *Procedures* that represent different work tactics of a stage (for example, the stage *So-lution_Evaluation* can be divided into the procedures *Generate_Consequences* and

*Select_a_Solution*). Each *Procedure* is related to a specified *Group*, which requires *Participants* with a specific *Role*. The *Procedure* itself defines a sequence of *Activities* that are related to predefined *Components* (for example, the activity to generate consequences for a possible solution can be implemented by a brainstorming tool).

### 4.5.2 To Detect the Need for Collaboration Support (R2)

The semantic model can be used to detect the need for collaboration support. The language describes the concept Component by its fundamental and optional activities. For example, a component that implements a brainstorming process in a number of ways can be defined by the fundamental activities: *Create_Idea* and *View_Generated_Ideas*, which are used to generate and share ideas in a global list. By using optional activities like *Select_Idea*, *Create_Comment* and *View_Comment*, the component can further provide the functionality to comment on generated ideas. By knowing possible activities that can be executed by a component, a model can be used to express a more specific relation between the concepts of a *Participant*, its *Skills*, the executed *Activities* and the used *Components* to generate or use *Data*. This data can be used to assess the quality of a collaboration process during runtime. For example, the quality of an ideation process can be assessed by monitoring the number of a data element: *Idea* that a participant: *Participant_A* generates using the activity: *Create_Idea* and the component: *Brainstorming* during the procedure: *Idea_Generation*. However, a well-defined approach to measure the quality of a collaborative problem solving still has to be defined. Especially, the identification of group behaviors via a process log represents a challenge for future research. As a result, the given semantic model is a first approach to assess the quality of elastic collaboration.

### 4.5.3 To Improve Collaboration Support (R3)

Data from the semantic model can be used in a rule concept to describe the relation between an intervention and a specific collaborative situation. In this context, the concept of event-condition-action (ECA) rules seems to be feasible to define this relation (Goh et al. 2001). Currently, different approaches offer libraries to handle ECA-based rules, such as: the rule markup language (Boley et al. 2001) and Java Expression Language (JEXL 2013). The semantics of an ECA rule (ON event IF condition DO actions) can be defined as follows:

- *Event:* Specifies the situation in which a rule is used to coordinate the use of interventions that are related to this situation. For example, the activation of a predefined *Procedure* can be seen as an event were different rules are used to monitor the process and provide support if needed.

- *Condition:* Defines a logical test that, if satisfied or evaluated to be true, causes the action to be carried out. The expression of a condition can make use of given logical operations and can refer to the concepts of the semantic model. For example, a condition could check if a specific *Procedure* has been activated by a *Participant* with a specific *Role*.
- *Action:* Defines a change or update in a collaboration process by means of an intervention. These interventions can support collaboration by adapting the collaboration process, the involved participants or the resources used. For example, the action component can specify the use of a specific *Data* element as a stimulus for an *Activity* of the active *Procedure*.

Related to Niederman et al. (2008), adaptation rules can define interventions at different levels:

- *Design Level:* Interventions guide participants in choosing appropriate tools, techniques, and participants to structure a collaboration process that is effective in achieving the group goal.
- *Execution Level:* Interventions guide a group step-by-step through the process or workflow of a collaboration process and to adapt this workflow if needed.
- *Activity Level:* Interventions analyze the structure of activities of a collaboration process and provide support to adapt these activities to stimulate effective, efficient and rigorous problem solving.
- *Behavior Level:* Interventions analyze interaction and behavior of participants to stimulate and reward collaborative behavior.

Adaptation rules can be defined concerning the identified stages of the introduced collaborative problem-solving model. Each of these rules describes a possible intervention with a specific level and a condition that causes its activation. Related to a specific stage of a collaboration process, different adaptation rules at different levels can be combined in rule-sets. For example, a rule-set for solution generation stage can combine different adaptation rules at design and activity level to monitor the ideation process and provide support, for instance to invite experts or to provide additional data about a problem to improve the effectiveness of the collaboration. Experts in collaboration can use the concept of a rule-set to define reusable adaptation strategies for specific collaboration situation that can be used by an adaptable collaboration support system in different processes.

### 4.5.4 Application Scenario

This section discusses the application of the semantic model to define adaptation strategies for elastic collaboration. Consider a diagnosis process of a manufacturer that wants to increase the availability of its machines.

According to the collaborative problem-solving process (see Fig. 4.1), an adaptive collaboration support system initiates a diagnosis process by contacting a group of available engineers. To contact the engineers that best fit to the diagnosis process, the system makes use of interventions at design level. Here, adaptation rules use the semantic model for collaboration to define and evaluate conditions for the selection of an engineer, i.e. by focusing on the skills a participant may have to join a group in a specific role.

```
ON   Activation.Process.ProcessType == "'diagnosis"'
IF   Group.RequiresRole("'manager"')
     && Group.RequiresSkill("'hydraulics"')
DO   InviteParticipant("'manager"',"'hydraulic"')
```

As the invited engineers are novices in using the tools of the adaptive collaboration support system, the system uses a prescribed collaboration process to guide the group along the diagnosis process. Related to the semantic model, such a process is predefined by different procedures that represent different work tactics for the identified stages. Each procedure itself represents a sequence of activities that are related to predefined component. Again adaptation rules make use of the captured knowledge to select a procedure that is suitable to the invited group and to provide components that allow the group to execute the intended activities. For example, during the problem definition stage, the system provides the composition of tools enabling the group to analyze real-time machine telemetric data and define hypothesis for a machine problem.

```
ON   Activation.Process.Procedure.ProcedureType
     == "'Generate_Problem_Definition"'
IF   Process.Procedure.Group.RequestSupport == true
DO   ActivateComponent ("'Data_Analyzer"')
ProvideActivity ("'Analyze_Data"',"'Create_Problem_Definition"')
```

After defining a problem definition, the group continues the process with the solution search stage. Here, the system provides a documentation exploration tool to search for similar solutions that were previously documented. However, the engineers could not find a possible solution. As a result, the solution generation stage is used to identify and describe a possible solution for the previous formulated problem. During the solution generation stage, the system makes use of the semantic model to log the process. The log establishes a relation between the participants, skills, the executed activities and the used components to generate or use data. This captured knowledge is used by different adaptation rules to assess the quality of the process and to provide interventions at execution level. For example, if the system detects that the group still analyzes data instead of generating possible solutions, an intervention is to draw the attention of the group on the generation of possible solutions.

```
ON   Process.Procedure.CurrentActivityTime
     < Process.Procedure.ActivityTimeLimit
IF   Active.Process.Procedure.Component.ComponentType
     == "'Data_Analyzer"'
DO   ActivateWarning ("'You reached the deadline for analysis."')
CloseComponent ("'Data_Analyzer"')
ActivateComponent ("'Brainstorming"')
```

During the process, interventions at an activity level are supported by enabling the group to detect the need for adaptation and to initiate an intervention. Here, the adaptive collaboration support system provides tools and methods to monitor the diagnosis process. For example, during the solution generation phase, the group members realize that they need to analyze historic machine telemetric data, and not just current real-time data. However, the prescribed collaboration process does not provide this functionality. This situation motivates the group to switch from a prescribed to a more flexible form of collaboration. The group initiates an emergent collaboration process and requests the system to provide different tools that can be freely combined and used by the group to analyze historic machine telematics data.

```
ON  Process.Procedure.collaborationForm == "'changed"'
IF  Process.Procedure.collaborationForm == "'flexible"' &&
    Active.Process.Procedure == "'Generate_Possible_Solutions"'
DO  ActivateComponent ("'Data_Analyzer_A"', "'Data_Analyzer_B"',
    "'Data_Analyzer_C"')
```

Still in the solution generation stage, the group generates a set of possible solutions and continues the process with the solution evaluation stage. Here, the group uses a rating tool to establish a priority among the proposed solutions. The group is aware that during the evaluation of solutions consensus is important to create a behavioral state where participants commit to a solution for implementation. However, the group detects a conflict between some of the engineers and asks the system for support. As a result, the system requests the group to describe the problem and compare their description to a set of possible behavioral state. By selecting a similar state the system can provide a set of possible interventions to support the group, for example by providing a template that support rational evaluation during the solution evaluation. This intervention helps the group to overcome the conflict and the most rated proposed solution is then implemented in the solution implementation stage. The success of the implementation will be documented for future diagnosis processes.

## 4.6 Discussion and Conclusion

Collaboration has become a critical success factor for many organizations, as products and services are becoming increasingly complex and cannot be designed individually. However, in complex design and engineering processes, a dynamic environment can lead to process goal changes or reduce the time available to achieve a collaborative goal. In such a case, a collaboration process needs to be adapted to the dynamic environment. Available collaboration support systems often prescribe or assume a fixed process and a known group composition. As result, such support systems provide technological support for a predefined environment.

Based on a collaborative problem-solving model the chapter identified the need for adaptive collaboration support systems that provide flexible collaboration support in dynamic environments. This collaborative problem-solving model can be used to describe different collaborative problem-solving processes which use different forms of collaboration support. The chapter proposed that an adaptive collaboration support system can implement this flexible support by detecting the need for collaboration support in dynamic environments by adapting collaboration in relation to dynamic environments and by learning from collaboration in dynamic environments.

An analysis of existing collaboration support shows that current support systems either implement prescribed or emergent collaboration but do not provide a continuum of collaboration support between process guidance and emergent collaboration. Current systems lack feasible functionalities to detect adaptation needs, trigger adaptation mechanisms and learn from user activities. A prerequisite to offer such support is a formal model for collaboration processes. Existing process definition languages are feasible to express prescribed collaboration, but do not provide detailed process information to detect the need for adaptation. As a result, the chapter proposed an ontology approach to develop a semantic model for elastic collaboration that allows us to describe and capture knowledge about collaboration in dynamic environments.

The chapter presented a first version of a semantic model that can be used to capture, share and reuse knowledge about collaboration. This semantic model combines characteristics of process languages such as XPDL, BPEL4People or IMS LD as well as domain model approaches to define collaboration processes and at the same time provide more detailed information about the participants and used components. First analyses showed that the semantic model can be used to prescribe, adapt and log collaborative problem-solving processes.

The chapter discussed the application of the semantic model to define intelligent adaptation strategies for elastic collaboration. Here, a new rule concept for a collaboration support system is introduced, which describes the relation between an intervention and a specific collaborative situation. These rules can be combined in rule-sets and related to a specific part of a collaboration process. The chapter presented first examples of possible adaptations for collaborative diagnosis process in a dynamic environment. These adaptations go beyond existing technological support for collaboration by providing support at different levels. These levels provide interventions to improve the selection of tools, techniques, and participants; to guide a group through the process; to adapt process activities to stimulate effective, efficient and rigorous problem solving; and to stimulate and reward collaborative behavior.

In the current form, the semantic model provides entities to describe the collaboration environment. New concepts are needed to capture and analyze the behavior of participants in detail. Finally, more research is needed to define a formal assessment method to measure the quality of a prescribed as well as an emergent collaboration process.

**Acknowledgements** This work has been partially supported by the FP7 EU Large-scale Integrating Project SMART VORTEX (Scalable Semantic Product Data Stream Management for Collaboration and Decision Making in Engineering) co-financed by the European Union. For more details, visit http://www.smartvortex.eu.

# References

Alves, A., Arkin, A., Askary, S., Barreto, C., Bloch, B., Curbera, F., et al. (2012). *WSBPEL: web services business process execution language version 2.0.*

Bernstein, A. (2000). How can cooperative work tools support dynamic group process? Bridging the specificity frontier. In *Proceedings of the 2000 ACM conference on computer supported cooperative work*, CSCW 00 (pp. 279–288). New York: ACM.

Boley, H., Tabet, S., & Wagner, G. (2001). Design rationale of RuleML: a markup language for semantic web rules. In *Proceedings of the international semantic web working symposium* (pp. 381–402).

Briggs, R. O., de Vreede, G.-J., & Nunamaker Jr., J. F. (2003). Collaboration engineering with ThinkLets to pursue sustained success with group support systems. *Journal of Management Information Systems, 19*(4), 31–64.

Corcho, O., Fernández-López, M., & Gómez-Pérez, A. (2003). Methodologies, tools and languages for building ontologies. Where is their meeting point? *Data & Knowledge Engineering, 46*(1), 41–64.

Deokar, A. V., Kolfschoten, G. L., & de Vreede, G.-J. (2008). Prescriptive workflow design for collaboration-intensive processes using the collaboration engineering approach. *Global Journal of Flexible Systems Management, 9*(4), 13–24.

DeSanctis, G., & Gallupe, R. B. (1987). A foundation for the study of group decision support systems. *Management Science, 33*(5), 589–609.

Dey, A. K., Abowd, G. D., & Salber, D. (2001). A conceptual framework and a toolkit for supporting the rapid prototyping of context-aware applications. *Human-Computer Interaction, 16*(2), 97–166.

Ellis, C. A., Barthelmess, P., Chen, J., & Wainer, J. (2005). Person-to-person processes: computer-supported collaborative work. In M. Dumas, W. M. van der Aalst, & Arthur H. ter Hofstede (Eds.), *Process-aware information systems* (pp. 37–60). New Jersey: Wiley.

Goh, A., Koh, Y. K., & Domazet, D. S. (2001). ECA rule-based support for workflows. *Artificial Intelligence in Engineering, 15*(1), 37–46.

Gross, T., & Prinz, W. (2004). Modelling shared contexts in cooperative environments: concept, implementation, and evaluation. *Computer Supported Cooperative Work, 13*(3–4), 283–303.

Gruber, T. R. (1993). A translation approach to portable ontology specifications. *Knowledge Acquisition, 5*(2), 199–220.

Gruber, T. R. (1995). Toward principles of the design of ontologies used for knowledge sharing. *International Journal of Human-Computer Studies, 43*(5–6), 907–928.

Grueninger, M., & Fox, M. S. (1995). Methodology for the design and evaluation of ontologies. In *Proceedings of the international joint conference on artificial intelligence, workshop on basic ontological issues in knowledge sharing*, IJCAI'95.

Haake, J. M., Hussein, T., Joop, B., Lukosch, S. G., Veiel, D., & Ziegler, J. (2010). Modeling and exploiting context for adaptive collaboration. *International Journal of Cooperative Information Systems, 19*(1–2), 71–120.

IMS Global Learning Consortium (2012). *IMS learning design best practice and implementation guide.* http://imsglobal.org/learningdesign/ldv1p0/imsld_bestv1p0.html.

Janeiro, J., Lukosch, S. G., & Brazier, F. M. T. (2012a). Elastic collaboration support: from workflow-based to emergent collaboration. In *Proceedings of the 17th ACM international conference on supporting group work* (pp. 317–320). New York: ACM.

Janeiro, J., Knoll, S. W., Lukosch, S. G., Kolfschoten, G. L., & Brazier, F. M. T. (2012b). Designing collaboration support for dynamic environments. In A. T. de Almeida, D. C. Morais & S. de Franca Dantas Daher (Eds.), *Proceedings of the group decision and negotiation 2012.* Recife: Universitaria da UFPE.

JEXL (2013). *Website of the Java expression language.* http://commons.apache.org/jexl/.

Kloppmann, M., Koenig, D., Leymann, F., Pfau, G., Rickayzen, A., von Riegen, C., Schmidt, P., & Trickovic, I. (2005). *WS-BPEL extension for people (BPEL4People).*

Knoll, S. W., Hörning, M., & Horton, G. (2009). Applying a ThinkLet- and ThinXel-based group process modeling language: a prototype of a universal group support system. In R. H. Sprague Jr. (Ed.), *Proceedings of the 42nd Hawaii international conference on system sciences*, HICSS'42 (pp. 1–10). Los Alamitos: IEEE Comput. Soc.

Kolfschoten, G. L., den Hengst-Bruggeling, M., & de Vreede, G.-J. (2007). Issues in the design of facilitated collaboration processes. *Group Decision and Negotiation, 16*(4), 347–361.

Niederman, F., Briggs, R. O., de Vreede, G.-J., & Kolfschoten, G. L. (2008). Extending the contextual and organizational elements of adaptive structuration theory in GSS research. *Journal of the Association for Information Systems, 9*(10), 633–652.

Nunamaker Jr., J. F., Dennis, A. R., Valacich, J. S., Vogel, D. R., & George, J. F. (1991). Electronic meeting systems to support group work. *Communications of the ACM, 34*(7), 40–61.

Nunamaker Jr., J. F., Briggs, R. O., Mittlemann, D. D., Vogel, D. R., & Balthazard, P. A. (1996). Lessons from a dozen years of group support systems research: a discussion of lab and field findings. *Journal of Management Information Systems, 13*(3), 163–207.

Nunamaker Jr., J. F., Reinig, B. A., & Briggs, R. O. (2009). Principles for effective virtual teamwork. *Communications of the ACM, 52*(4), 113–117.

Oliveira, F. F., Antunes, J. C. P., & Guizzardi, R. S. S. (2007). Towards a collaboration ontology. In *Proceedings of the 2nd workshop on ontologies and metamodeling in software and data engineering*, WOMSDE'07 (pp. 97–108).

Osborn, A. F. (1963). *Applied imagination: principles and procedures of creative problem-solving.* New York: Scribner's.

Pattberg, J., & Fluegge, M. (2007). Towards an ontology of collaboration patterns. In *Proceedings of the international workshop on challenges in collaborative engineering*, CCE.

Pinto, H. S., & Martins, J. P. (2004). Ontologies: how can they be built? *Knowledge and Information Systems, 6*, 441–464.

Prinz, W., & Zaman, B. (2005). Proactive support for the organization of shared workspaces using activity patterns and content analysis. In *Proceedings of the 2005 international ACM SIGGROUP conference on supporting group work*, GROUP'05. New York: ACM.

Rajsiri, V., Lorre, J.-P., Benaben, F., & Pingaud, H. (2008). Collaborative process definition using an ontology-based approach. In L. Camarinha-Matos & W. Picard (Eds.), *IFIP—the international federation for information processing: Vol. 283. Pervasive collaborative networks* (pp. 205–212). New York: Springer.

Reichert, M., Rinderle, S., & Dadam, P. (2003). ADEPT workflow management system: flexible support for enterprise-wide business processes. In W. Aalst & M. Weske (Eds.), *Lecture notes in computer science: Vol. 2678. Business process management* (pp. 370–379). Berlin: Springer.

Schilit, B., Adams, N., & Want, R. (1994). Context-aware computing applications. In *Proceedings of the first workshop on mobile computing systems and applications*.

Simon, H. A. (1977). *The new science of management decision.* New York: Prentice Hall.

Studer, R., Benjamins, V. R., & Fensel, D. (1998). Knowledge engineering: principles and methods. *Data & Knowledge Engineering, 25*(1–2), 161–197.

Thiagarajan, R. K., Srivastava, A. K., Pujari, A. K., & Bulusu, V. K. (2002). BPML: a process modeling language for dynamic business models. *Proceedings of the fourth IEEE international workshop on advanced issues of e-commerce and web-based information systems*, WECWIS '02. Washington: IEEE Comput. Soc.

van der Aalst, W. M. P., ter Hofstede, A. H. M., Kiepuszewski, B., & Barros, A. P. (2003). Workflow patterns. *Distributed and Parallel Databases, 14*(1), 5–51.

Wallas, G. (1926). *The art of thought.* New York: Harcourt, Brace & World.

Warr, A., & O'Neill, E. (2005). Understanding design as a social creative process. In *Proceedings of the 5th conference on creativity & cognition*.

Wood, D. J., & Gray, B. (1991). Toward a comprehensive theory of collaboration. *The Journal of Applied Behavioral Science, 27*(2), 139–162.

Workflow Management Coalition (2008). *Workflow process definition interface—XML process definition language (XPDL) version 2.1a* (Technical Report No. WFMC-TC-1025).

Wurdel, M., Sinnig, D., & Forbrig, P. (2008). CTML: domain and task modeling for collaborative environments. *Journal of Universal Computer Science*, *14*(19), 3188–3201.

zur Muehlen, M., & Indulska, M. (2010). Modeling languages for business processes and business rules: a representational analysis. *Information Systems*, *35*(4), 379–390.

References

# Chapter 5
# A Semantics-Based, End-User-Centered Information Visualization Process for Semantic Web Data

Martin Voigt, Stefan Pietschmann, and Klaus Meißner

**Abstract** Understanding and interpreting Semantic Web data is almost impossible for novices as skills in Semantic Web technologies are required. Thus, Information Visualization (InfoVis) of this data has become a key enabler to address this problem. However, convenient solutions are missing as existing tools either do not support Semantic Web data or require users to have programming and visualization skills. In this chapter, we propose a novel approach towards a generic InfoVis workbench called VizBoard, which enables users to visualize arbitrary Semantic Web data without expert skills in Semantic Web technologies, programming, and visualization. More precisely, we define a semantics-based, user-centered InfoVis workflow and present a corresponding workbench architecture based on the mashup paradigm, which actively supports novices in gaining insights from Semantic Web data, thus proving the practicability and validity of our approach.

## 5.1 Introduction

With the advent of the Semantic Web technologies like RDF, RDFS, and OWL, more and more organizations publish their information as so-called *Linked Open Data* in the form of open semantic knowledge bases.[1] Consequently, there is an increasing need for tools to manage and process this rapidly-growing amount of data. One important aspect in this regard is how to enable end-users, i.e., knowledge workers, to analyze and gain insights from these data sets. Unfortunately, this task is mainly reserved to tech-savvy users (Dadzie and Rowe 2011). Here is why:

---

[1] As of February 2013, the *Data Hub* (http://thedatahub.org/) hosts about 5100 data sets from various domains.

M. Voigt (✉) · S. Pietschmann · K. Meißner
TU Dresden, Dresden, Germany
e-mail: martin.voigt@tu-dresden.de

S. Pietschmann
e-mail: stefan.pietschmann@tu-dresden.de

K. Meißner
e-mail: klaus.meissner@tu-dresden.de

T. Hussein et al. (eds.), *Semantic Models for Adaptive Interactive Systems*,
Human–Computer Interaction Series, DOI 10.1007/978-1-4471-5301-6_5,
© Springer-Verlag London 2013

Primarily, end-users lack an understanding of Semantic Web data, its syntax and structure. They may know spreadsheets and have an idea what the rows and columns mean. However, they do not (and need not) know about concepts like triples, multiple inheritance, or that properties are not hardly tied to classes. Hence, tools need to present Semantic Web data in a reasonable, understandable way.

Various RDF browsers (Dadzie and Rowe 2011) and ontology visualization methods have been proposed (Katifori et al. 2007). However, they are usually limited to graph- or list-based data representations and thus do not exploit capabilities of prevalent visual analytic systems, e.g., support for generic charts, multiple coordinated views, iterative mapping refinement, or the recommendation of visualizations. Even more important, they are tailored (and limited) to specific domains and data sets.

Unfortunately, well-established, generic InfoVis tools like Tableau[2] do not support Semantic Web data, and there is no sign this is going to change soon. While slowly, more promising concepts for generic RDF InfoVis are emerging like the SPARQL result set visualization from the *Data-Gov* project (Ding et al. 2010), they require users to employ expert knowledge in Semantic Web, programming and visualization.

Finally, even with proper Semantic Web InfoVis tools at hand, interpreting and finding the right visualization for a certain data set and goal is a challenging task for novices, because they lack the necessary visualization knowledge (Grammel et al. 2010). Knowledge-assisted visualization (Chen et al. 2009) tries to fill this gap by using formalized expert knowledge and reasoning. Despite innovation in this direction, existing solutions, such as (Kadlec et al. 2010; Wang et al. 2009), are domain-specific, self-contained, and not applicable for Semantic Web data. Furthermore, they do not recognize and incorporate context information of the used device, e.g., screen estate, and the user, e.g., explicit or implicit preferences, to present the data in a suitable manner.

In this chapter, we propose a novel concept for a generic, user-centered InfoVis workflow geared towards novices, which allows for the context-aware mapping of arbitrary data to appropriate visualization components. Further, we present the key challenges as well as our solutions for its application on Semantic Web data. Finally, we give an architectural overview of our InfoVis workbench VizBoard which implements our novel approach based on the mashup platform CRUISe (Pietschmann 2009) and, thus, allows for presenting any Semantic Web data in a dashboard-like, composite, and interactive visualization.

Our chapter is structured as follows: After giving a brief overview of related work in the next section, we introduce the foundations of our concept in Sect. 5.3: a context-aware application composition framework and a visualization knowledge-base. In Sect. 5.4 we define a novel, user-centered InfoVis workflow which employs shared semantics to assist the visualization process. Further, we highlight the challenges and solutions found while realizing this workflow for Semantic Web data.

---

[2]http://www.tableausoftware.com/.

Then, Sect. 5.5 presents a corresponding software architecture which realizes the process based on the mashup platform CRUISe to illustrate and evaluate its applicability. Finally, we discuss our findings and point out future work in Sect. 5.6.

## 5.2  Related Work

Both the Semantic Web and InfoVis have received lots of attention by the research community in the recent years. Thus, we need to analyze existing concepts with respect to the goals and challenges lined out in the previous section. First, we give an overview of how knowledge models can assist the visualization process in general. Thereafter, we analyze existing generic approaches for the visualization of Semantic Web data.

### 5.2.1  Understanding and Supporting the Visualization Process

As mentioned before, the vision of a semantics-based InfoVis for novices requires both a formal knowledge model and a structured process which defines how to bridge the gap from raw data to an appropriate graphical representation. To this end, various visualization-specific process models and InfoVis concepts addressing novices have been proposed.

The pipeline model is commonly used to describe visualization as a process. In its elementary version it defines a sequence in which raw data is filtered and enriched, mapped to an abstract visualization specification, and finally rendered to a displayable image (Haber and McNabb 1990). This model has been successively enhanced, e.g., to include the user and his tasks (Card et al. 1999) or to allow for the coordination of independent views (Boukhelifa et al. 2003). In contrast to our work, the pipeline model focuses firstly on system-side functionalities and not on the (lay-)user in his struggle to gain insights from his data. Further, it does not employ formalized knowledge to represent which graphic representation is the best within a specific context.

Within the area of knowledge-assisted visualization, several authors have proposed ways to support the visualization process using knowledge models. Wang et al. (2009) describe how knowledge "moves" through the visualization process in a number of conversion steps, e.g., to externalize tacit user knowledge to explicit system knowledge. Yet, information on how to employ these steps in generic InfoVis systems to assist users in visualizing (Semantic Web) data, is missing. Chen et al. (2009) sketch a high-level knowledge-based infrastructure in parallel to the visualization system, which extracts information from data and uses it together with predefined expert knowledge to adapt the visualization process. Despite the similar goals, users' interaction steps and the integration of the formal knowledge in every stage of the InfoVis process is missing.

Both the pipeline model and knowledge-assisted visualization are primarily focusing on how a system can create appropriate visualizations. An additional, orthogonal aspect we consider important in our work is active user support. The first notable guidelines in this direction were given by Heer et al. (2008). They include easy data input, user assistance in selecting graphical representations, and the use of default mappings from data to visual variables. These principles have been underpinned by a recent user study (Grammel et al. 2010), wherein the authors suggest some additional guidelines and requirements, such as (semantics-based) search facilities to narrow the data set, adaptation to the iterative nature of the visualization process, and support for partial and uncertain input specifications of novices. Finally, Shneiderman's mantra (Shneiderman 1996) defines the most fundamental design guideline for all interactive systems addressing information search: "Overview first, zoom and filter, then details-on-demand". This is especially true for novices, who need a lightweight overview of the Semantic Web data before they dive into details in an iterative way afterwards.

In summary, previous work shares our goal of actively supporting novices during the InfoVis process by providing valuable advices. However, only Grammel et al. emphasize the power of semantics to support novices.

### 5.2.2 Information Visualization of Semantic Web Data

With the growing amount of Semantic Web data sets, more and more methods (Katifori et al. 2007) and tools (Dadzie and Rowe 2011) for their visualization have been proposed. Mostly, they focus on text- or graph-based visualization and are tailored towards special purposes and data sets. In the following, we focus on the few very generic InfoVis approaches.

An increasing number of US governmental data is made accessible in RDF (Ding et al. 2010) by the Open Government Directive. Tutorials on their visualization using popular APIs and widget libraries are published[3] which imply, that every user has the freedom to build his or her InfoVis of choice. Unfortunately, these tutorials—including a proxy for data transformation—are little help for novices, as Semantic Web, programming, and visualization skills are needed for their use.

Alternatively, the UISPIN framework provides means to describe user interfaces for rendering Semantic Web data. This includes a chart library[4] with various widgets to visualize Semantic Web data. The library can be embedded in Semantic Web tools, as it is the case for the TopBraid Composer.[5] Thereby, users can include charts without programming skills, but still need to define SPARQL queries for the data to be visualized. As further assistance, e.g., recommendation of suitable widgets, is

---

[3]http://data-gov.tw.rpi.edu/wiki/How_to_use_Google_Visualization_API.

[4]http://uispin.org/charts.html.

[5]http://www.topbraidcomposer.com.

missing, users must know, which visualization to choose and how to define queries in SPARQL.

A solution to one of these problems is given by Leida et al. (2010), who annotate SPARQL queries with a shared vocabulary of visualization-specific concepts to (semi-)automatically map RDF data to graphic representations. Since this promising approach focuses on the mapping only, a concrete semantic model for defining visualization-specific knowledge is missing as well as its integration in an overall, (lay-)user-centered InfoVis workflow.

Finally, Mazumdar et al. (2012) propose the .view. framework which employs the dashboard metaphor to visualize Semantic Web data with well-know charts in multiple views. We are also developing an interactive system to provide composite visualization of any RDF data but our approach is more sophisticated as we employ semantic models to allow for a context-aware, automatic mapping of data to the widgets without the need to manually define any configuration files for the data set. Furthermore, we provide a user-centred workflow comprising a data filtering and widget selection geared towards novices.

All in all, current solutions from this field solely focus on the visualization of SPARQL query results. Their common limitation on SELECT statements implies, that graph-based visualizations are mostly excluded, even though these are better suited and commonly used for Semantic Web data. With these concepts we share the idea of combining arbitrary data sources with existing, web-based widgets from different libraries, following the mashup paradigm. However, and most importantly, prevalent solutions do not support novices adequately.

Before we present our concepts of a user-centered visualization process, the next section provides details about the conceptual and practical basis we are building on.

## 5.3 Conceptual Foundation

As can be seen from the discussion so far, realizing a context-aware InfoVis workflow is far from trivial, since a broad number of challenges has to be addressed. To this end, our solutions and the corresponding tooling are built on top of existing concepts and practical results from other research projects.

Most importantly, we use the concept of *universal* application composition which allows us to freely combine two types of building blocks: (semantic) data sets and generic visualization components. This composition is supported by visualization knowledge formalized as an ontology. In the following, we present some insights on these foundations.

### 5.3.1 Universal Context-Aware Mashup Composition

In our work, we build on the results from the CRUISe project (Pietschmann 2009), which provides a conceptual foundation as well as an ecosystem for the dynamic,

**Fig. 5.1** Architectural overview of the CRUISe ecosystem

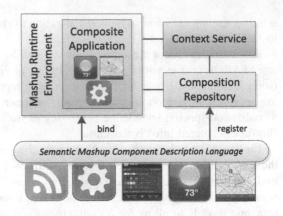

context-aware composition of web applications from distributed building blocks. The following paragraphs provide a brief overview of the corresponding concepts and infrastructure parts illustrated in Fig. 5.1.

The idea of universal composition implies a uniform component model, to which all parts of an application adhere. Such components are black-box pieces of independent software that provide a dedicated functionality. It is important to note, that this explicitly includes user interface, i.e., visualization components to be reused in different contexts.

In our conceptual space, components are characterized by three abstractions, namely *Property*, *Event*, and *Operation*. The set of properties resembles the component state and allows for its configuration. Whenever the internal state changes, events are issued to inform the runtime system and other components. Finally, state changes, calculations and other arbitrary functionality of a component can be triggered by invoking its operations with the help of events. Events and operations may themselves contain semantically typed *parameters*, thereby realizing the data flow between components.

Using the *Semantic Mashup Component Description Language* (SMCDL), components are described in a platform-independent, declarative way—comparable to WSDL for the description of web services. SMCDL is used to specify the above-mentioned interface parts as well as non-functional properties and information on how concrete implementations are bound to the abstract interface at runtime.

End-user-oriented authoring tools are employed to create interactive applications from these components, e.g., including search and recommendation features. Those applications can be expressed formally as instances of the Mashup Composition Model (MCM) (Pietschmann et al. 2010)—a description of the components, the data and control flow, the visual layout and the adaptive behavior of a composition on a platform-independent level.

For the visualization of Semantic Web data, our goal is to create a step-by-step InfoVis workflow which semi-automatically binds generic visualization components to given data providers, e.g., by finding and recommending suitable components with respect to a given context, resulting in a composite application.

For the interpretation and execution of universal compositions, CRUISe has come up with a reference architecture of a *Mashup Runtime Environment* (MRE) and the corresponding infrastructure. During the model interpretation, a MRE requests components from a given Component Repository (CoRe). The latter always returns those component instances, which fit the application requirements and context best. In this discovery process, both implicit and explicit rules are used, e.g., to consider the technological compatibility (implicit) or user preferences (explicit). There are more services involved in the composition, but those are the main ones involved in our approach.

This integration process and composition infrastructure form the basis for our InfoVis workflow, as it allows to include visualization knowledge in the dynamic, context-aware composition of applications. To realize this vision, a formalized representation of this knowledge is required, though. Therefore, the next section introduces a modular visualization ontology, which does just that.

## 5.3.2 Formalizing Visualization Knowledge

The fundamental problem of InfoVis, regardless if done manually or automatically, is to find an appropriate mapping between data and visual attributes. Therefore, visualization knowledge is required. Tools like Tableau already provide limited support for novices, who lack this kind of knowledge. However, they do not cover the complete parameter space, e.g., including the used device or users' preferences. As mentioned in Sect. 5.2, few approaches facilitate semantic technologies to assist the visualization process, yet a generic, formal, and freely distributed knowledge model is still missing.

For this reason, we developed the modular visualization ontology (VISO, cf. Fig. 5.2-1) (Voigt and Polowinski 2011). It provides a well-documented vocabulary of concepts and relations to formally describe data, graphics, human activity, as well as the user and system context. Since we focused on the first two modules, we re-used existing and well-established ontologies whenever possible, such as the DEMISA task ontology (Tietz et al. 2011). Based on the defined entities, we also modeled factual expert knowledge (cf. Fig. 5.2-2), e.g., that using *position* instead of *color coding* is more suitable to visualize *quantitative* data, which is used to rank different mapping alternatives. Equally, users' input data (cf. Fig. 5.2-3) can be annotated with visualization semantics, e.g., an RDF property *price* may have a *quantitative* scale of measurement and an assigned domain *UnitPriceSpecification* of the GoodRelations ontology.[6]

With the help of VISO, user interface components of the CRUISe ecosystem can be described (cf. Fig. 5.2-4) with regard to visualization specific aspects. Therefore, the domain-independent SMCDL is extended to link to VISO concepts and properties. We annotate the data structures of the component interface—in Operations,

---

[6]GoodRelations ontology: http://purl.org/goodrelations/v1.

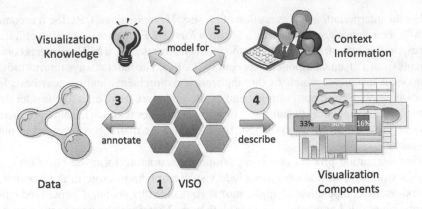

**Fig. 5.2** Generic visualization ontology (VISO) as conceptual foundation of our visualization workflow (reprinted from Voigt et al. 2012d)

Events, and Properties—the kind of graphic representation used (map, scatter plot), the visual complexity (high, low), or the interaction potential (zoom, filter). Finally, the user and system contexts (cf. Fig. 5.2-5) are represented based on CRUISe's context service (cf. Fig. 5.1), e.g., in terms of *preferences* and user *skills*, the *display size* or the available *software* infrastructure.

All in all, by using VISO as a common vocabulary, all stakeholders of an Info-Vis process, including contextual information, are combined in one knowledge base, thereby facilitating the context-aware recommendation of visualization components. In the following section, we present the steps of this semantics-driven InfoVis workflow in detail.

## 5.4 Context-Aware Information Visualization Workflow for Semantic Web Data

To address the problems lined out in Sect. 5.1, we propose a novel interactive, user-driven InfoVis workflow (cf. Fig. 5.3) which builds on the common semantic vocabulary provided by VISO and some insights retrieved from related work discussed in Sect. 5.2. The workflow can be applied to arbitrary data models, however, the following discussion specifically focuses on the visualization of RDF data and the corresponding challenges.

The workflow design is inspired by the way (lay-)users naturally interact when analyzing data. It consists of five stages users needs to pass: choosing or uploading a data set (cf. Fig. 5.3-1), getting an overview of the data and choosing a subset (cf. Fig. 5.3-3), selecting relevant data variables and suitable visualization components (cf. Fig. 5.3-5), configuring them (cf. Fig. 5.3-7) and, finally, interacting with the rendered data to gain the desired insights (cf. Fig. 5.3-9). Due to the interactive nature of the visualization process, users can sequentially pass through, but may

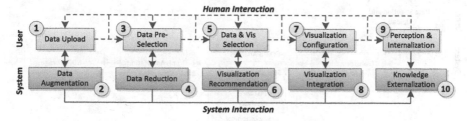

**Fig. 5.3** Overview of the semantics-based visualization workflow (reprinted from Voigt et al. 2012d)

also move backwards. For instance, the configuration step can be skipped by using default mappings. Furthermore, users may choose to search and integrate multiple, alternative visualizations to benefit from multiple coordinated views of their data after completing the workflow.

This user-driven process is supported by five system-side functionalities which make use of the VISO (the lower rectangles in Fig. 5.3). Elementary functionalities like storing, querying, and supplying the data, graphic representations or knowledge are omitted from the figure for the purpose of simplification. In the following, we discuss each step of the workflow, point to major requirements and obstacles to realize them, and—as far as we already solved them—present our solutions.

### 5.4.1 Data Upload and Augmentation

The starting point of every visualization process is the provision of the data set, i.e., *raw data* (Card et al. 1999) (cf. Fig. 5.3-1). This data first needs to be transformed into a suitable format for the remaining process steps. After this, it must to be augmented (cf. Fig. 5.3-2) with visualization-specific knowledge, e.g., the kind of *scale of measurement* (nominal, ordinal, or quantitative), using the VISO vocabulary. This (semi-)automatic augmentation is the foundation for nearly all of the following system-side tasks, like the recommendation of appropriate visualization components or their coordination support.

The **Data Upload** is the most trivial part of the complete workflow. It requires the user to select an RDF or OWL file, a URI of a data dump or a Web service API and to submit it to the visualization system. It is also possible to support other data formats, like tabular (spreadsheets, etc.) or relational data sets (MySQL database) through a transformation step, as indicated in Fig. 5.4-2. In these cases, the data needs to be transformed into RDF triples using corresponding APIs. Especially for the mapping from relational databases to RDF a broad range of tools is already available (Sahoo et al. 2009).

**Data Augmentation** is split in two parts: First, evident visualization knowledge about the data is reasoned using information-retrieval techniques (cf. Fig. 5.4-3). Second, the data is augmented with this semantics using the VISO vocabulary

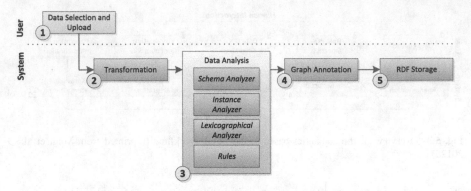

**Fig. 5.4** Data upload and augmentation in more detail

(cf. Fig. 5.4-4). Here, the benefits of the Semantic Web come in handy, as the data can be easily linked to other concepts.

In this augmentation step, four distinct analyzers can be employed: (1) a *schema analyzer* which extracts information about simple data types if they are not explicitly provided; (2) an *instance analyzer* which calculates metrics like the number of distinct instances; (3) a *lexicographical analyzer* to identify more generic concepts as well as categories from DBPedia[7] with help of the WordNet[8] knowledge base to provide additional information to support the data to visualization mapping step; (4) a *rule engine* can be used to add custom relationships in a flexible manner. A common problem is the automatic identification of the *Scale of Measurement* of a property according to its basic data type, instances, and already identified domain concepts. A typical example would be to identify that a property called "school grade" has an ordinal scale instead of a nominal.

In the end, the annotated RDF graph needs to be stored within a homogeneous data layer—an RDF triple store—to allow for system-wide uniform data access in the following workflow steps (cf. Fig. 5.4-5). As a side note, we suggest to include a manual step in order to let an expert check and edit the automatically generated annotations and the declarative rules.

### 5.4.2 Data Pre-Selection and Reduction

One of the key problems of a generic approach to visualize Semantic Web data is the size of the data sets. In contrast to the findings of Sicilia et al. (2012) that most OWL ontologies are small and flat, there exist quite a number of huge OWL ontologies, especially in the public and medical sectors, e.g., the NCI thesaurus.[9] Moreover,

---

[7]DBPedia: http://dbpedia.org/About.

[8]WordNet: http://wordnet.princeton.edu/.

[9]http://ncicb.nci.nih.gov/download/evsportal.jsp.

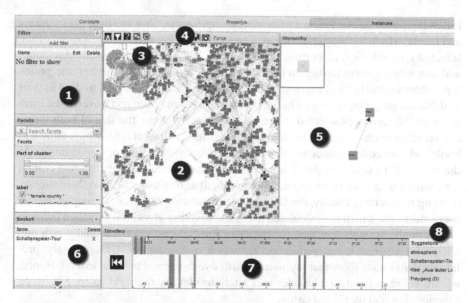

**Fig. 5.5**  Screenshot of our first prototype of the pre-selection

OWL has not yet "arrived" in the Linked Open Data (LOD) cloud (Glimm et al. 2012), which heavily relies on RDF and RDFS sets. Currently, it comprises 295 sets with approximately 32 billion triples, which implies an average 107 million triples per data set.[10]

In order to handle this amount of data, two challenges have to be addressed: First, the data sets must be visualized in an understandable, interactive manner with the goal to select classes, properties, or instances for more in-depth informations visualizations (cf. Fig. 5.3-3). Second, techniques are required to reduce the data sets to the relevant entities and point to interesting areas for the user respectively (cf. Fig. 5.3-4). In the following, we present our solutions to these challenges.

Based on Shneiderman's mantra, the purpose of the **Data Pre-Selection** (cf. Fig. 5.3-3) is to give users a high-level view of a data structure. Through interactions like zooming, panning, searching, or filtering he is able to find interesting subsets of the data which are selected for an in-depth Information Visualization through suitable components afterwards. For our InfoVis workflow this means to provide novices with intelligent visualizations and convenient metaphors to interact with data sets of more than a million entities.

A first prototype of a corresponding user interface is shown in Fig. 5.5. Its development is based on best practices from related tools, e.g., the TopBraid Composer[11] as well informal user studies with software prototypes. The frontend comprises the

[10]Information based on the State of the LOD Cloud report from October 2011, http://www4. wiwiss.fu-berlin.de/lodcloud/state/.

[11]TopBraid Composer: http://www.topquadrant.com/products/TB_Composer.html.

following parts: At the left, we offer various options to filter the data (1) by terms and facets, which are discussed below. The main view (2) shows all resources of the selected type (classes, properties, or instances). Within this view, users may zoom and pan while always having an overview of the dataset in (3). Further, the proto-type offers methods for clustering, key concepts extraction, and path finding as well as different graph layouts (4). On the right (5), users may see and traverse the hier-archy of the resources selected in the main view. Of course, the size of both views can be adapted on-demand. Our solution also offers a "basket" (6), which allows to bookmark and collect resources of interest for later investigation or visualization. At the bottom (7) a time line shows breakpoints of user interactions in different colors, e.g., setting up a filter or zooming. Clicking them allows users to undo their interac-tions up to this task. Finally, the UI suggests interesting resources (8) depending on user selections, which are calculated using the pivoting algorithm sketched below.

All in all, the user interface for the Data Pre-Selection is functionally rich and allows for a versatile navigation and reduction of the dataset. Unfortunately, pre-liminary user tests show that lay-user are still overburdened to some extend. Hence, we are going to conduct a broader user study to identify the right balance between functionality and user satisfaction.

To assist the Data Pre-Selection in the frontend, a **Data Reduction** (cf. Fig. 5.3-4) must take place. Therefore, we suggest to use different data mining strategies as proposed in Fayyad et al. (1996): classification, clustering, summarization, or link analysis. Unfortunately, many of those techniques are commonly geared towards tabular data or relational databases. Thus, an adaptation is required which necessi-tates a distinction of the different ingredients of an ontology, namely classes, (object and data) properties, and instances. Currently, our conceptual workflow includes the following techniques in combination to allow for differentiated data reduction.

*Faceted-Based Filtering* Based on different kinds of metrics, facets and facet values can be created to allow for a target-oriented data filtering. The metrics calculation depends on the resource type. For classes we suggest to use topological character-istics like the number of subclasses, the number of instances, and the betweenness (Brandes 2001). Properties can be filtered using their domain, range, and hierarchy. Finally, instances may be distinguished by their class membership.

*Clustering* A number of different clustering algorithms like the wide-spread k-Means algorithm allow to find and summarize similar entities. The metrics men-tioned above can also be applied as distance functions for them to cluster classes, properties, and instances.

*Path Finding* Another concept we employ for reducing the data set is path finding. Here, the idea is to calculate the shortest path(s) between two or more classes or instances of interest, and to filter out all resource outside these paths.

*Key Concept Extraction* Furthermore, we include the *key concept extraction* (Per-oni et al. 2008) approach to identify and highlight the most relevant resources within a data set. Therefore, it makes use of insights from cognitive science, net-work algorithms, and lexicographical statistics. However, this solution is only ap-plicable for classes.

*Pivoting*   Another way to provide only a small subset of the data and to extend it on-
demand is called pivoting (Popov et al. 2011). To calculate potentially interesting
items we apply different metrics, e.g., the topological similarity for classes and
properties or the semantic similarity for instance data.

*Association Rule Mining*   Finally, the tracking of navigation trails within the data set
in the Data Pre-Selection are analyzed using association rule mining techniques.
Its results allows to highlight interesting resources or reduce the cumbersome information overload.

### 5.4.3   Interactive Data and Visualization Selection

After a user has narrowed down his data set to a region of interest, the following
**Selection** step (cf. Fig. 5.3-5) covers the exploration and selection of interesting
data variables and suitable visualization components to represent them. This is especially challenging for end-users, as their lack of InfoVis knowledge often leads
to unsatisfying visualizations results (Grammel et al. 2010). In order to assist them,
the workflow must include support mechanisms, e.g., suggesting appropriate graphical representations based on the selected data attributes and visualization characteristics. While the latter recommendation algorithm is explained in Sect. 5.4, the
following paragraphs focus on the user interface and interaction.

For the design of a suitable search interface in this context it is fundamental to
decide between querying and browsing. For the user it is less mental work to scan
and choose from a list of entities than to think about appropriate query terms to
describe his information need (Hearst 2009). Thus, with respect to our target group
of novices, we suggest to use a browsing approach—in particular the interactive
*faceted browsing* paradigm. Thereby, empty result sets can be avoided and users
gain immediate feedback and can refine their queries iteratively. However, in our
research we also faced some problems with using faceted browsing for data and
visualization selection. Most importantly, users need to assign priorities to facets
within a search query. Thus, we extended the paradigm to *weighted faceted browsing*
introduced in Voigt et al. (2012b). In the following, be briefly describe these novel
concepts, which address the definition of search criteria, the result ranking, and the
corresponding, intuitive user interface.

First of all, we distinguish between mandatory and optional search criteria. To
narrow the results, a facet value needs to be added to the mandatory set where all
criteria are linked conjunctively—the standard behavior of a faceted browser. In
contrast, optional facets are combined disjunctively within a dedicated set and thus
do not constrain but rank the results. That way, the more optional criteria an item
satisfies the higher it is ranked. If multiple items meet the same number of optional
criteria, their ranking is the same. However, every criterion may be given an explicit
weight (between 1 and 100), which directly influences its ranking. Zero value is
neglected, as this means that facet can be omitted.

The input for calculating the overall result set is a query set of mandatory and
optional criteria. While the mandatory part simply constraints the set by removing

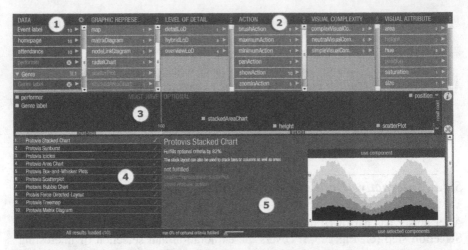

**Fig. 5.6** Screenshot of our weighted faceted browsing prototype (reprinted from Voigt et al. 2012b)

all items not supporting a chosen facet value, the relevance ranking using multiple optional facets is more complicated. To solve the multi-criteria optimization, we combine the *weighted sum model* with *lexicographic ordering* in an iterative way to interpret the criteria. If some elements still have the same weight we order them alphabetically.

Of course, these theoretical concepts of weighted faceted browsing need not be visible to the lay-user. Instead, we have designed an intuitive user interface which consequently builds on the principles of existing facet browsers. The running prototype is shown in Fig. 5.6. As can be seen, the view is split into three main areas: facet widgets at the top (1), (2), the query visualization—called *querycloud*—in the middle (3), and the results view at the bottom (4), (5). To search for a visualization component, the user simply needs to drag a desired facet value—a RDF resource to visualize (1) or a visualization characteristic (2)—and drop it at a desired spot in the querycloud which is split into a mandatory and (weighted) optional area. The result set visualization (4) updates subsequently. By selecting an item from the result list, detailed information are displayed in (5).

We conducted a preliminary user study to test our hypotheses and the practicability of weighted faceted browsing for visualization selection. After an introduction, users had to handle five basic and five advanced search tasks to find appropriate visualization for given data sets. To our delight, the subjects answered all questions correctly. They generally enjoyed the intuitive approach, in particular of the querycloud. Whereas the basic tasks were solved without any help, we needed to give some assistance at solving the advanced issues. This was mostly caused by the missing understanding of the data set and the metadata of the visualization components within the facet widgets. An exemplary questions was: "What does *neutral visual complexity* mean?". Thus, providing additional information on facet values should prove beneficial.

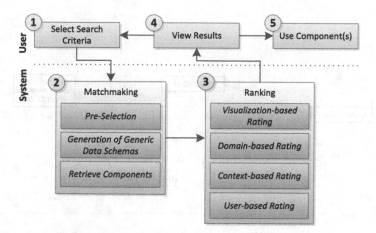

**Fig. 5.7**  Overview of our visualization recommendation process

## 5.4.4  Context-Aware Recommendation of Visualization Components

With respect to the knowledge and experience of novices, the exploration and selection of data variables and visualization facets as described in the previous section should be actively supported with **Visualization Recommendation** techniques (cf. Fig. 5.3-6). Of course, this functionality constitutes the heart of every visualization process and it comes with a number of challenges: First, an algorithm needs to discover appropriate visualization components based on the selected Semantic Web data using the aforementioned semantic annotations (cf. Sect. 5.3). Second, the algorithm needs to rank every identified component due to its applicability within the current context. In the following, we summarize the main concepts of our recommendation algorithm which is described in more detail in Voigt et al. (2012a).

Figure 5.7 gives an overview of our recommendation process. It starts with the selection of search criteria (1) which is realized by the weighted faceted browser. Based on the selection, the matchmaking process (2) starts with a pre-selection step. Thereby, the amount of components is reduced by matching the visualization-specific criteria, e.g., the kind of representation, the level of detail, or the interaction potential needed. Afterwards, a generic data schema is generated by mapping the data structure selected by the user to a generic one based on VISO. This schema then forms the basis for the retrieval of appropriate visualization components.

Subsequently, the list of suitable components is ranked (3) making use of the semantic annotations and VISO rules introduced earlier. The ranking step includes four criteria: First, the appropriateness is calculated with respect to visualization-specific knowledge, e.g., the visual encodings for quantitative data (Cleveland and McGill 1984). Second, the assigned domain concepts or categories of the data variables and the visualization component are employed. For each combination of those, the semantic similarity is calculated. Third, contextual knowledge is included. Thus,

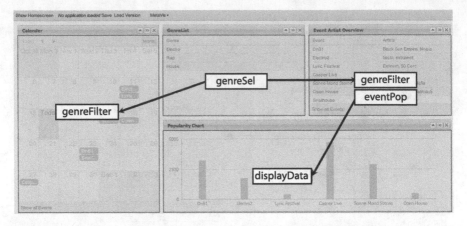

**Fig. 5.8** Screenshot of the meta-visualization which allows to show and edit the coordination between the integrated components

the context model is queried for user or device characteristics, such as the screen real estate, in order to identify the best fitting visualization. Last but not least, we consider user-based ratings of existing components. The collection of this information is further described in Sect. 5.4.

Finally, combined rating for each component allows to establish a ranking order. This sorted list is presented to the user, who may either adjust his search criteria (1) or select one or more components to visualize the selected data with (5).

### 5.4.5 Visualization Integration and Configuration

Having selected one or more components to visualize his Semantic Web data, the work of the user is done. For the underlying system it means, that all those components need to be loaded and instantiated, "bound" to the selected data, configured with respect to the users' needs (cf. Fig. 5.3-7), and integrated with each other resulting in a homogeneous user interface (cf. Fig. 5.3-8).

For the integration, we heavily build on the concepts and infrastructure of CRUISe (cf. Sect. 5.3). It already provides means to load the selected, possibly distributed components and to manage their life cycle including instantiation and configuration. In a next step, we establish the "binding" to the selected Semantic Web data. The corresponding data and mapping information directly result from the previous workflow steps. By choosing several visualization recommendations iteratively in the previous steps, users are (implicitly) building *multiple coordinated views* of their data, which are finally presented interactively using CRUISe's runtime platform MRE.

Figure 5.8 shows such a user interface, overlayed with a meta-visualization. As can be seen, the data set—in this case concert data—is shown with respect to four different aspects (time, genre, artist, popularity) and corresponding visualizations (calendar, lists, and a bar chart).

The meta-visualization in Fig. 5.8 is one way to let novices establish (or edit existing) coordination links. The latter allow for the integration of visualization components on the data level by connecting their data variables for synchronization or filtering. This way, selected data in one view, e.g., the genre in this example, can be highlighted or act as a filter in another one. By establishing such links, users intuitively create *coordinated multiple views* on their data sets from which they may gain a better understanding of the displayed information.

Further mechanisms for user-driven adaptation may be provided, such as component configuration, which highly depends on their implementation. Typical configuration parameters include color schemes and filters. If multiple mappings between the underlying data and the component interface are possible, the user may as well adapt them, e.g., to switch the data mapping between the axes of a scatter plot. More sophisticated adaptation is possible as well, such as component exchange or layout changes. These mechanisms are provided by the underlying platform—in our case CRUISe—yet, their impact on user satisfaction are yet to be evaluated.

### 5.4.6 Perception and Knowledge Conversion

Once the coordinated view has been set up, novices can study and interact with the visualized data with the goal of increasing their knowledge or solving specific tasks. This phase is referred to as internalization Wang et al. (2009) (cf. Fig. 5.3-9). As stated in van Wijk (2005), the amount of knowledge gained depends on the kinds of visual representations used, the users' prior knowledge and their perceptional capabilities. Thus, we took care to address three requirements in our workflow to enhance the internalization process.

To foster **Perception and Internalization** (cf. Fig. 5.3-9), we follow two approaches. First, as for every interactive application, the user interface and interaction design of the visualization platform must be geared towards novices. As an example, this includes self-descriptive and intuitive mechanisms to configure the coordination as discussed above (cf. Sect. 5.4). Based on our prototypes and a number of small user studies, we are continuously working on these issues towards an elaborated user study. Second, beside the platform itself, the visual representations, i.e., the resulting composite application plays the key role for successful internalization. Thus, we consider the users' contexts in the recommendation algorithm of visualization components (cf. Sect. 5.4) to offer him the most suitable and understandable graphical representations. Contextual triggers for this are basic user properties (age, mother tongue, disabilities), preferences, usage (mobile vs. stationary) and device characteristics (e.g., the available screen real estate).

**Knowledge Tracking and Externalization** (cf. Fig. 5.3-10) is a background task that actively supports several phases of the Information Visualization workflow. As Fig. 5.3 shows, its purpose is to extract implicit visualization knowledge in every

**Fig. 5.9** Visualization component with rating bar at the bottom

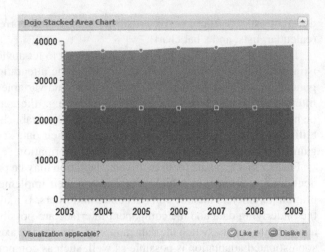

workflow step to support the upcoming phases. In the following, we briefly present possibilities we see and use in this regard.

*Augmentation* It is worth considering an expert review step for the data augmentation (cf. Sect. 5.4). By checking and updating automatically generated annotations, their knowledge is externalized, which can be the input for further formalization. Here, the proposed the usage of declarative annotation rules proves its value as they (1) are independent of a special dataset and (2) can be revised by Semantic Web experts without programming.

*Reduction* As mentioned in Sect. 5.4, we apply association rule mining based on the navigation trails of users in their data sets during the data pre-selection phase. This way, users' understanding of entities and relations of the data is externalized.

*Data and Visualization Selection* Association rule mining can be employed here, as well. Selected facet values, their assignment as mandatory or optional search criteria, and the previewed visualization components can provide insights into the users' understandings and goals, and they can used to enhance the selection step, e.g., by ordering or highlighting suitable facet values.

*Configuration* Tracking and externalization in the configuration stage includes the analysis of chosen data mappings to a component, and of user-established coordination patterns between components.

*Perception* Finally, we use a mechanism to rate single combinations of data and visualization components. Therefore, we distinguish between implicit and explicit ratings. The former are deduced automatically based on the usage of a component in different usage contexts, e.g., a *repeated use* leads to a higher implicit rating while having only a *glimpse* on the component after the integration lowers the rating. The explicit rating is given manually by users clicking "Like" or "Dislike" buttons added beneath every component (cf. Fig. 5.9). Using a collaborative filtering algorithm we then exploit this knowledge to improve recommendations (cf. Sect. 5.4).

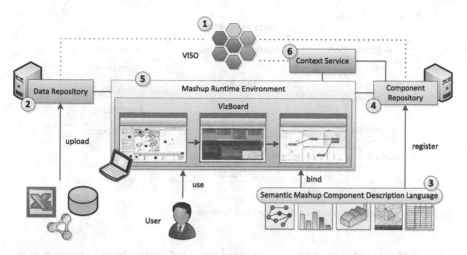

**Fig. 5.10** Overview of the architecture of VizBoard

Having presented all the steps of our semantics-driven, context-aware visualization workflow for Semantic Web data, the following section covers our approach of a corresponding software architecture to cover the whole process.

## 5.5  Component-Based Software Architecture

We specified a component-based software architecture for our visualization system—called VizBoard—according the requirements which come along with our user-centered, semantics-driven InfoVis workflow. As already mentioned in Sect. 5.3, we are building on the CRUISe ecosystem which allows for the dynamic composition of web applications from distributed building blocks. Figure 5.10 gives an overview of the architecture of VizBoard. It comprises six primary parts. In comparison to the architectural overview of CRUISe (cf. Fig. 5.1) we added the visualization-specific vocabulary (1) defined by the **VISO**, which is the glue between the data and visualization components, and the **Data Repository** (DaRe) (2) which provides a common data layer. In the following, we describe the DaRe and the extension made within the CRUISe ecosystem (3)–(6) in more detail. Then, in Sect. 5.5 we give a brief overview of some implementation details.

### 5.5.1  Data Repository

CRUISe allows for the composition of any data source, i.e., web service, with any user interface widget as long as they are compatible according their semantic de-

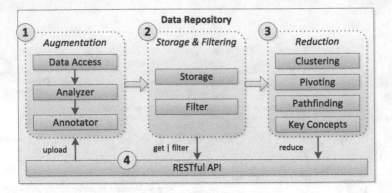

**Fig. 5.11** Separation of concerns within the Data Repository

scription of the API. Since its also a desired behavior for the InfoVis domain, it is not applicable in the same way due to the following reasons.

*Common Data Access* The data to visualize arises from different sources, e.g., web service, files, or databases, and may vary in their formats. Therefore, components are required which allow for a common data access and hide data format specifics like the connection or the query format.

*Augmentation and Reduction* The aforementioned workflow comprises essential functionality to augment and reduce the data. Our prototypical test demonstrates clearly that most of these functionalities are time consuming and not applicable during the runtime so that a preprocessing is required. Further, the data needs to be available for the asynchronous management of the annotations by an expert.

*Performance and Scalability* Another problem is the varying performance of the data sources. An own storage layer provides a stable performance and allows to scale on demand.

*Security* Also if its out of scope, a common data layer enables the management of access rights but also to use security mechanism, e.g., to prevent SQL injections.

For this reasons, a common data layer for all visualizations components, the **Data Repository**, is integrated. Its main components are presented in Fig. 5.11. They could be distinguished into four blocks according their functionality needed within the workflow. Hence, the data access, the analyzers, and the annotator are forming a building block (1) to augment and thus to prepare the data for the following process steps. Subsequently, the homogeneous data is stored within a triple store which allows to request but also to filter the data (2). These functions are required for instance during the integration of the visualization components (cf. Sect. 5.4). To facilitate the data reduction (cf. Sect. 5.4) the components in block (3) query and process the data from (2) on-demand. In the end, the DaRe offers a RESTful web service interface (4) to allow for a platform-independent data access.

## 5.5.2 CRUISe Extensions

To enable the visualization of Semantic Web data according the proposed workflow we also had to extend the CRUISe architecture. First, **Visualization Components** (cf. Fig. 5.10-3) are specialized user interface components focusing on presentation but mostly neglect other "CRUD" functions like the creation of new data. Thus, we can rely on the component model of CRUISe without any difficulties but the SMCDL is extended to describe visualization features with VISO concepts, e.g., the kind of graphic representation. As the properties as well as the parameters of operations and events are already semantically typed, we can simply point to their generic, semantics-based description of the data structure (Voigt et al. 2012a).

Also the **CoRe** (cf. Fig. 5.10-4) is extended to allow for the semantic-driven management of visualization components based on the enhanced SMCDL. Further, the recommendation for appropriate components (cf. Sect. 5.4) need to be integrated as a multi-level process comprising the discovery and ranking (Voigt et al. 2012a). And some of the knowledge externalization functionalities (cf. Sect. 5.4) are added, especially the collaborative filtering approach for the user-based rating which is employed during the recommendation.

The **MRE** (cf. Fig. 5.10-5) provides the interface between the user, DaRe, and CoRe. Therefore, the complete user-driven workflow is implemented as wizard-like composite CRUISe application comprising specialized and thus, efficient user interface components for each stage. To enable novices to create, edit, and delete communication connections between visualization components, we added a more abstract coordination layer and a helpful meta visualization to show existing communication relations (cf. Fig. 5.8). Further, the runtime is extended to handle RDF data received from the DaRe as shared data layer for all components.

Finally, we utilize the CroCo context service (cf. Fig. 5.10-6) to track the user and device context. We slightly extended its knowledge model using the VISO vocabulary to store visualization specific preferences.

## 5.5.3 Implementation

All the parts presented in the architectural overview are prototypical implemented to allow for an evaluation. Only single features, e.g., the association rule mining within the data and visualization selection to extract implicit knowledge (cf. Sect. 5.4), are missing. In the following, we highlight some of the implementation details of the DaRe and CRUISe on the whole.

The DaRe is implemented using Java and is accessible through a RESTful web service API using Java Jersey.[12] Its core is a RDF triple store which allows to store

---

[12]http://jersey.java.net/.

and filter the datasets. To identify an appropriate one, we conducted a benchmark using different real-world datasets on freely available triple stores (Voigt et al. 2012c). Although no store stands out in this test, we decided on Jena TDB[13] due to the existence of an extendable rule engine required for the analysis within the augmentation step. We implemented various data access components to use RDF datasets from uploaded files or received from web services. Further, we integrated Apache POI[14] and the D2RQ engine[15] to use Excel spreadsheets and MySQL databases as data sources. To carried out the data reduction we implemented and integrated numerous algorithms. For example, we employ the JGraphT[16] library for graph calculations, we reuse the key concept extraction API,[17] and integrated RapidMiner 5.2[18] including the RMonto plug-in (Potoniec and Ławrynowicz 2011) to cluster the Semantic Web data.

As aforementioned, we are relying on the CRUISe ecosystem to enable the user-centered, semantics-driven visualization of Semantic Web data. Therefore, we had to extend the existing implementation mainly at three points. First, we integrated the algorithm to recommendation visualization components into the Java-based CoRe. In this regard, we had to extend the semantic model, which stores the information about the registered components, according the visualization specifics from VISO. Our algorithm makes use of the already integrated Apache Jena API and its SPARQL functionality. Second, we developed CRUISe user interface components to implemented the user-centered visualization workflow (cf. Fig. 5.3), e.g., the data pre-selection, and to visualize the data. Like other components, we rely on HTML, JavaScript—using frameworks like D3.js[19] or jQuery[20]—and partly on Adobe Flash. Third, we extended the JavaScript-based MRE to enable the user to create and manage the coordination behavior between components on runtime. To visualize the connections in the meta-visualization we rely on the Raphael library.[21]

The mashup paradigm coming along with CRUISe allows to easily extend our system with new visualization components but also the DaRe is adaptable to use other data sources. All in all, our web-based visualization system VizBoard could be adapted on current needs and thus is applicable on different devices in various domains.

---

[13]http://jena.apache.org/documentation/tdb/.

[14]http://poi.apache.org/.

[15]http://d2rq.org/.

[16]http://jgrapht.org/.

[17]http://sourceforge.net/projects/kce/.

[18]http://rapid-i.com/.

[19]https://github.com/mbostock/d3.

[20]http://jquery.com/.

[21]http://raphaeljs.com/.

## 5.6  Conclusion and Future Work

Gaining insights from the growing amount of available Semantic Web data has become seemingly impossible for novices. However, this is exactly the situation that domain experts are facing, as more and more data is provided in the form of RDF, RDFS or OWL. To address this need for user-centered Information Visualization, we have proposed three ingredients: (1) a semantic model formalizing visualization knowledge, (2) a user-centered, semantics-driven visualization workflow utilizing the shared visualization model, and (3) a corresponding software architecture to realize the workflow. While the model has been covered extensively in Voigt et al. (2012a), this chapter has focused on the workflow and its application.

In contrast to existing InfoVis processes, e.g, the pipeline model, our novel visualization workflow actively guides novices from a given set of semantic input data to suitable visualization components using the shared visualization knowledge and contextual information. Even though we have presented a corresponding software system and composition architecture, all steps of the workflow are generic enough to be realized and supported by other tools and frameworks. It should also be noted, that the process itself remains independent from the underlying data models and can thus be employed for arbitrary Semantic Web data. Thus, we facilitate and welcome implementations and evaluations by the community.

As a manifestation of our concepts, we have presented an architecture which implements the workflow and utilizes VISO as the semantic model. To this end, we employ the mashup paradigm whose goal is the combination of existing web resources—in our case RDF data and InfoVis widgets—to create an added value for the user. The architecture is easily extensible with both new visualization components and new data connectors. As it is web-based and includes context knowledge in the composition process, it can be utilized on different devices, such as desktops, tablets, and smartphones, independent of location and time.

As mentioned before, this chapter provides an overview of our work on a user-centered, semantic-driven InfoVis workflow and its implementation in an extensible, open workbench. While the core concepts—the *recommendation* and *selection* of suitable visualization components—has already been validated (Voigt et al. 2012a, 2012b), a high-performance triple store for the DaRe has been identified (Voigt et al. 2012c), and large parts of the workbench have been realized based on the CRUISe platform, a few things remain to be done. In particular, we are planning to conduct three user studies to evaluate our concepts and prototypes of the data reduction (cf. Sect. 5.4.2) and knowledge externalization (cf. Sect. 5.4.6) as well as the acceptance of VizBoard in general.

## References

Boukhelifa, N., Roberts, J. C., & Rodgers, P. J. (2003). A coordination model for exploratory multiview visualization. In *Coordinated and multiple views in exploratory visualization* (pp. 76–85).

Brandes, U. (2001). A faster algorithm for betweenness centrality. *The Journal of Mathematical Sociology*, 25(2), 163–177. doi:10.1080/0022250X.2001.9990249.

Card, S. K., Mackinlay, J. D., & Shneiderman, B. (1999). *Readings in information visualization: using vision to think*. San Francisco: Morgan Kaufmann. ISBN: 1558605339.

Chen, M., Ebert, D., Hagen, H., Laramee, R. S., van Liere, R., Ma, K.-L., et al.(2009). Data, information, and knowledge in visualization. *IEEE Computer Graphics and Applications*, 29(1), 12–19. doi:10.1109/MCG.2009.6.

Cleveland, W. S., & McGill, R. (1984). Graphical perception: theory, experimentation, and application to the development of graphical methods. *Journal of the American Statistical Association*, 79(387), 531–554.

Dadzie, A.-S., & Rowe, M. (2011). Approaches to visualising linked data: a survey. *Semantic Web*, 2(1), 89–124. doi:10.3233/SW-2011-0037.

Ding, L., DiFranzo, D., Graves, A., Michaelis, J., Li, X., McGuinness, D. L., & Hendler, J. A. (2010). TWC data-gov corpus: incrementally generating linked government data from data.gov. In *WWW'10* (pp. 1383–1386). doi:10.1145/1772690.1772937.

Fayyad, U., Piatetsky-Shapiro, G., & Smyth, P. (1996). The KDD process for extracting useful knowledge from volumes of data. *Communications of the ACM*, 39(11), 27–34. doi:10.1145/240455.240464.

Glimm, B., Hogan, A., Krötzsch, M., & Polleres, A. (2012). Owl: yet to arrive on the web of data? In *Linked data on the web (LDOW2012)*.

Grammel, L., Tory, M., & Storey, M.-A. (2010). How information visualization novices construct visualizations. *IEEE Transactions on Visualization and Computer Graphics*, 16, 943–952.

Haber, R., & McNabb, D. A. (1990). Visualization idioms: a conceptual model for scientific visualization systems. In *Visualization in scientific computing* (pp. 74–93).

Hearst, M. A. (2009). *Search user interfaces*. Cambridge: Cambridge University Press.

Heer, J., van Ham, F., Carpendale, S., Weaver, C., & Isenberg, P. (2008). *Creation and collaboration: engaging new audiences for information visualization* (pp. 92–133). Berlin, Heidelberg: Springer. doi:10.1007/978-3-540-70956-5_5.

Kadlec, B. J., Tufo, H. M., & Dorn, G. A. (2010). Knowledge-assisted visualization and segmentation of geologic features. *IEEE Computer Graphics and Applications*, 30(1), 30–39. doi:10.1109/MCG.2010.13.

Katifori, A., Halatsis, C., Lepouras, G., Vassilakis, C., & Giannopoulou, E. (2007). Ontology visualization methods—a survey. *ACM Computing Surveys*, 39(4), 10. doi:10.1145/1287620.1287621.

Leida, M., Afzal, A., & Majeed, B. (2010). Outlines for dynamic visualization of semantic web data. In *LNCS: Vol. 6428. On the move to meaningful internet systems: OTM 2010 workshops* (pp. 170–179). Berlin: Springer.

Mazumdar, S., Petrelli, D., & Ciravegna, F. (2012). Exploring user and system requirements of linked data visualization through a visual dashboard approach. *Semantic Web Journal*. doi:10.3233/SW-2012-0072.

Peroni, S., Motta, E., & d'Aquin, M. (2008). Identifying key concepts in an ontology, through the integration of cognitive principles with statistical and topological measures. In *LNCS: Vol. 5367. The semantic web* (pp. 242–256). Berlin: Springer.

Pietschmann, S. (2009). A model-driven development process and runtime platform for adaptive composite web applications. *International Journal on Advances in Internet Technology*, 4(1), 277–288.

Pietschmann, S., Tietz, V., Reimann, J., Liebing, C., Pohle, M., & Meißner, K. (2010). A metamodel for context-aware component-based mashup applications. In *Proc. of the 12th int. conf. on information integration and web-based applications & services*.

Popov, I., Schraefel, M., Hall, W., & Shadbolt, N. (2011). Connecting the dots: a multi-pivot approach to data exploration. In *International semantic web conference*.

Potoniec, J., & Ławrynowicz, A. (2011). RMonto: ontological extension to RapidMiner. In *10th international semantic web conference (ISWC2011)*.

Sahoo, S. S., Halb, W., Hellmann, S., Idehen, K., Thibodeau, Jr. T., Auer, S., et al. (2009). *A survey of current approaches for mapping of relational databases to RDF*. W3C RDB2RDF Incubator Group.

Shneiderman, B. (1996). The eyes have it: a task by data type taxonomy for information visualizations. In *Proc. of IEEE symp. on visual languages* (pp. 336–343). doi:10.1109/VL.1996. 545307.

Sicilia, M. A., Rodríguez, D., García-Barriocanal, E., & Sánchez-Alonso, S. (2012). Empirical findings on ontology metrics. *Expert Systems with Applications*, *39*(8), 6706–6711. doi:10.1016/j.eswa.2011.11.094.

Tietz, V., Blichmann, G., Pietschmann, S., & Meißner, K. (2011). Task-based recommendation of mashup components. In *Proc. of the 3rd intern. workshop on lightweight integration on the web (ComposableWeb 2011)*. Berlin: Springer.

van Wijk, J. J. (2005). The value of visualization. In *Proceedings of IEEE visualization* (pp. 79–86). doi:10.1.1.75.6547.

Voigt, M., & Polowinski, J. (2011). *Towards a unifying visualization ontology* (Tech. Report No. TUD-FI11-01). Dresden, Germany, TU Dresden. ISSN: 1430-211X.

Voigt, M., Pietschmann, S., Grammel, L., & Meißner, K. (2012a). Context-aware recommendation of visualization components. In *Proc. of the 4th intern. conf. on information, process, and knowledge management (eKNOW 2012)*.

Voigt, M., Werstler, A., Polowinski, J., & Meißner, K. (2012b). Weighted faceted browsing for characteristics-based visualization selection through end users. In *Proc. of the 4th symp. on engineering interactive computing systems*, Copenhagen, Denmark (pp. 151–156). doi:10.1145/2305484.2305509.

Voigt, M., Mitschick, A., & Schulz, J. (2012c). Yet another triple store benchmark? Practical experiences with real-world data. In *Proc. of. the 2nd intern. workshop on semantic digital archives (SDA)*.

Voigt, M., Pietschmann, S., Meißner, K. (2012d). Towards a semantics-based, end-user-centered information visualization process. In *Proc. of the 3rd international workshop on semantic models for adaptive interactive systems (SEMAIS 2012)*.

Wang, X., Jeong, D. H., Dou, W., Lee, S.-W., Ribarsky, W., & Chang, R. (2009). Defining and applying knowledge conversion processes to a visual analytics system. *Computers & Graphics*, *33*(5), 616–623.

# Chapter 6
# PASTREM: Proactive Ontology Based Recommendations for Information Workers

Benedikt Schmidt, Eicke Godehardt, and Heiko Paulheim

**Abstract** Information work involves the frequent (re)use of information objects (e.g. files, web sites, emails) for different tasks. Information reuse is complicated by the scattered organization of information among different locations. Therefore, access support based on recommendations is beneficial. Still, support needs to consider the ad-hoc nature of information work and the resulting uncertainty of information requirements. We present PASTREM, an ontology-based recommender system which proactively proposes information objects for reuse while a user interacts with a computer. PASTREM reflects the ad-hoc nature of information work and allows users to switch seamlessly between recommendations for more multitasking oriented or more focused work. This chapter describes the PASTREM recommender, the used data foundation of interaction histories, data storage in an ontology and the process of recommendation elicitation. PASTREM is evaluated in comparison with other, activity related recommendation approaches for information reuse, namely last recently used, most often used, longest used and semantically related. We report on strength and weaknesses of the approaches and show the benefits of PASTREM as recommender which considers the difference between single task focused and multitasking oriented recommendations.

## 6.1 Introduction

Information is a resource for as well as a product of information work. Within the daily work process, numerous information objects (e.g. files, web sites) are created, modified or consumed using different applications. The sheer amount of accessed

B. Schmidt (✉) · E. Godehardt
SAP Research, Darmstadt, Germany
e-mail: benedikt.schmidt@sap.com

E. Godehardt
e-mail: eicke.godehardt@sap.com

H. Paulheim
University of Mannheim, Mannheim, Germany
e-mail: heiko@informatik.uni-mannheim.de

T. Hussein et al. (eds.), *Semantic Models for Adaptive Interactive Systems*,
Human–Computer Interaction Series, DOI 10.1007/978-1-4471-5301-6_6,
© Springer-Verlag London 2013

information and the difficulty or impossibility of managing the information results
in information overload (stated in a study among 124 managers) (Farhoomand and
Drury 2002), threatening the effective and efficient use of information to execute
work. As an effect, information retrieval and access present themselves as dominant
activities of the workday (Jensen et al. 2010). Interestingly enough, the same information object might be searched for several times. Information objects are reused
when an interrupted task is resumed, when they seem appropriate in the context of
another task or as a template or data provider for other information objects (Jensen
et al. 2010). Each time, the location of an information object is forgotten a duplication of earlier retrieval activities follows.

Different tasks and different state of knowledge of the worker foster different
information needs and result in an uncertainty of an information workers' information requirements throughout the work day. An uncertainty which complicates the
support of retrieval and access activities.

The reuse of already accessed information objects is supported by features like
histories, recently used file lists or manually maintained favorite lists (Bergman
et al. 2009). Histories and recently used file lists show a list of previously accessed
information object (e.g. the last 10 accessed documents). Favorite lists are manually maintained lists used to structure frequently used information objects. One
limitation of these approaches is the scope: generally they are limited to one specific application (e.g. history of a web browser, recently used files of a text processor). Additionally, the size of the lists is frequently restricted to maintain readability
(a list of more than 10 items is hard to read). Due to the limitations, other retrieval
techniques—not considering the reuse characteristic—like information search are
frequently applied for reused objects.

In this chapter, the access of previously used information objects is supported by
a recommender approach named PASTREM.[1] Recommenders are generally used
to help users to explore information collections under uncertainty. This is achieved
based on rating the suitability of items for a user by identifying preference information (Adomavicius and Tuzhilin 2005). Preference information results from observed activities (e.g. which products were watched and which were bought in an
online store). The reuse of information in information work can benefit from a similar approach. We consider user activities at the computer desktop as criteria for the
recommender system and previously accessed information objects as data source
to develop the PASTREM recommender. PASTREM uses a topic model based approach, resulting in the unsupervised recommendation of information objects based
on recent activities.

PASTREM has been developed in the context of a toolset to support information
work based on data collected from user activities (Schmidt et al. 2011a, 2012). The
existing architecture creates an ontology that contains detailed information about
the activities of the user, including accessed information objects, time spent with
the information objects, the respective content and the activities performed on the

---

[1]PASTREM refers to the supported process: the REMembering of useful information objects
which already have been used in the PAST.

information objects. PASTREM uses this data, extends it by a representation of topics, relevant for the user, created by a topic model approach. The identified topics are composed of words and are linked to information objects. While the user is working, PASTREM basically identifies active topics based on the content of the information objects in the interaction stream of the user. Within the ontology, the active topics link to information objects which are ranked and which are proactively proposed to the user.

The remainder of this chapter is structured as follows. First, information work is discussed to underpin the claim that uncertainty with respect to the information requirement exists, and to highlight the relevance of user activities to derive information requirements. Second, existing recommender approaches in the domain of information work are presented and claims for further research on recommender approaches are derived. Third, the ContAct monitor is presented which is the core component of the toolset PASTREM belongs to. The description of ContAct helps to understand the data used by PASTREM to create recommendations. Core element of ContAct is the computer work ontology (CWO) which formalizes identified user activities. Fourth, the PASTREM recommender approach is described and evaluated. PASTREM is evaluated by comparing the performance of PASTREM to other recommendation approaches, namely last recently user, most often used, longest used and semantically related. All recommenders are compared by measuring the recommendation quality on two existing interaction history data sets of 24 work days. Summary and outlook conclude the chapter.

## 6.2 Information Work

This section provides a basic understanding of information work. The relevance of information within information work is shown while specific consideration is given to the unpredictability of the information demand due to the dynamicity of work execution. This is the foundations for the later review of existing recommender systems for information work within this chapter.

### 6.2.1 Multitasking Coordinated by Interruptions

Information workers frequently have a set of different tasks they have to work on. The ad-hoc nature of the information work process results from the way information workers deal with those multiple tasks. Notably, tasks are not processed sequentially, finalizing one task after another. To address constraints (e.g. time) or to react on events, information workers switch tasks, which means that a task is set on hold before it is finalized to start or continue working on a different tasks. Thus, tasks are processed in parallel or in rapid succession (Link et al. 2005), coordinated by interruptions.

Two general types of interruptions can be distinguished (González and Mark 2004; Salvucci and Taatgen 2008): internal and external interruptions. Internal interruptions result from the information worker himself. The information worker decides to switch tasks because of internal stimuli. External interruptions result from events in the environment, external stimuli. Different studies have shown independently that interruptions are evenly distributed among internal and external interruptions (González and Mark (2004) talks about 50 %, Czerwinski et al. (2004) talks about 40 % self-initiated interruptions).

Interruptions at the computer workplace have become increasingly relevant with the computer becoming a multi-task machine (Salvucci and Taatgen 2008). One-task computers discouraged multitasking, whereas the ability to start multiple programs at the same time and access multiple information objects at a time encourages the described multitasking.

A study among Fortune 100 companies (Gallup and San Jose State University and Park, Institute for the Future in Menlo 1999) showed that eighty-four percent of the staffers are interrupted at least three times per hour by messages. In this group, 51 % are interrupted six or more times per hour. Seventy-one percent feel overwhelmed by the message traffic. Czerwinski et al. (2004) reports on an average of 50 goal shifts over a week that were relevant to realize complex goals. Most shifts were triggered by interruptions. Apart from coordinative interruptions, interruptions may as well provide necessary information that is required to realize a goal (González and Mark 2004; Morteo et al. 2004). In this sense, interruptions may even be a core characteristic of work, as Sproull identifies for managers (Sproull 1984).

### 6.2.2 Uncertainty of Information Requirements

Information is outcome as well as raw material of information work (Aral and Brynjolfsson 2007). First, information work produces information as instrument for illocutionary and perlocutionary acts in Austin's sense (Austin 1962). The individual executes an act by creating a certain piece of information (illocution)[2] or the individual disseminates information (which can also be the modification of symbols in computers) to have a following effect in the real world (perlocution). Second, the work execution itself builds on information, external information accessed and transformed within the work process as well as information which is internalized in the individual (Polyanyi 1966).

Uncertainty with respect to the actual information requirements within information work processes follows. Due to the lack of predefined work processes, the overall information requirement for a work task is unknown. Even if the information requirement can be derived, the fragment of internalized information of the information worker is unknown. Only the activities performed by the information worker at least indicates the overall work domain and possible information requirements.

---

[2] An example is a priest who contracts a marriage.

### 6.2.3 Information Reuse

Each task switch modifies the information requirement of the information worker and triggers processes of information retrieval and information access to find the relevant information for the task the information worker switched to. If a task is resumed, the search and access activities are duplications of earlier efforts. When a task was tackled earlier, the subject already identified relevant information but probably needs to identify this information again, once the task is resumed after an interruption.

Barreau and Nardi (1995) classified information reuse as (1) ephemeral information, (2) working information and (3) archived information. Ephemeral information is information which has only a short lifespan, e.g. like some emails or a todo list. Reuse of ephemeral information is unlikely. Working information is the information which is actively produced or modified by the information worker over a longer period of time. Reuse of working information is simple, as the information worker generally spends much time with it and knows where he put it. Archived information is information which is used in the work process and has relevance over a long or very long period of time (e.g. weeks and month). Studies show that the reuse of ephemeral and archived information is complex (Barreau and Nardi 1995). The short time span and the large amount of different information types complicates the access of this type of information.

Although the study by Barreau et al. is from 1995, the results seem not outdated. Techniques which support the quick and simple retrieval of earlier accessed information objects without requiring substantial manual maintenance effort are required. Next to the already mentioned software features of recently used lists and favorites additionally, different personal organization techniques may be applied. Examples of personal organization techniques are tags as categorization system, folder structures as classifying system, post-its etc. All techniques are frequently used and require substantial manual maintenance effort while an increasing complexity of the technique additionally complicates the retrieval (e.g. folder structure depth and size positively correlate with retrieval time; Bergman and Whittaker 2012).

## 6.3 Related Work

Various recommender approaches exist to support information reuse. One way to address the uncertainty of information requirements is the use of interaction histories. Interaction histories are logs of user system interactions generated by software sensors (Kaptelinin 2003). This basic representation of activities gives an understanding of the information relevant for the information worker at that specific moment and to derive potential information requirements. The main differences of the systems exist with respect to a limitation of recommended information types (e.g. only web-sites) and the data source of information to be used for support.

## 6.3.1 Overview of Approaches

The Dyonipos system (Makolm 2008; Rath and Weber 2008) uses the interaction history to recommend documents, people and locations from the users' personal and the organizational information stores. The recommendations are based on classifiers trained during design time for a set of tasks. The APOSDLE system analyzes user work and identifies documents related to the activities of the user based on a distinction of navigational goals, information goals and transactional goal (Lokaiczyk et al. 2007). Like Dyonipos, the APOSDLE system recommends based on trained classifiers. A limitation of the Dyonipos and the APOSDLE approach is the need to know about existing tasks and information requirements at design time of the system. The TaskTracer system, a personal information management system, uses an extension called TaskPredictor to train classifiers during work execution (Shen et al. 2006). Thus, the limited information about work tasks that occurs in information work is addressed.

Dyonipos, APOSDLE and TaskTracer encapsulate the recommendation logic and sometimes even the used data foundation in the trained model. The black box characteristic of trained models complicates system maintenance and extension. An open and transparent formalization of the used data source and the recommendation logic in form of an ontology is an alternative approach. Middleton et al. developed the Quickstep and the Foxtrot system (Middleton et al. 2004). The system creates interaction histories for the access of research papers and uses the IBk (Aha et al. 1991) classifier to determines a paper class, a research paper belongs to which is added to an ontology. The ontology is used to create recommendations based on the types of research papers accessed over a day and additionally considers explicit user feedback on paper types of interest.

The SPREADR system uses features of user history, location and local time to create recommendations in a spreading activation network which is built based on ontologies (Hussein et al. 2007). Activated features spread the activation among the network. SPREADR has been used to recommend events and artists in an adaptive music portal web-site.

While approaches like Dyonipos,[3] APOSDLE and TaskTracer address all types of information work at the computer workplace, a very straight forward method of training recommendation is used, which requires training effort, during design time, while later maintenance and extension is complex. The recommendations have a short lifespan and are updated frequently. The approaches that use ontologies have been used for specific domains like research papers or a music portal, considering recommendations with a long lifespan.

To address information work based on recommender system that use ontologies, respective domain ontologies are required. Two examples and important results of

---

[3]Dyonipos uses ontologies only to capture events in interaction histories. The classifiers do not extend the ontology.

this research have been developed in the context of social semantic desktops, within the Nepomuk[4] and the Calo project (Cheyer et al. 2005). Both projects provide an initial ontology which allows a basic classification of things which may have relevance in different information work scenarios, including elements like files, locations and tasks. The ontology of the Nepomuk project is a RDF-S ontology named PIMO (Personal Information Model). Similarly, IRIS provides a personal topic map based on OWL ontologies. After crawling information stores, both ontologies provide a rich presentation of data users are working with. The main use of the data is browsing of the personal information structure. We have developed a comparable ontology, named computer work ontology (CWO) (Schmidt et al. 2011b). The computer work ontologies is capable of managing very different types of information objects which may be used in information work. It has been designed to be used by tools to collect and process interaction histories.

## 6.3.2 Requirements for Information Reuse Support

Based on the reviewed recommender approaches, requirements for further research in the domain of recommender for information reuse can be identified:

1. *Characteristic*: During design time, there is a lack of knowledge which types of user tasks will be executed and which information requirements may occur when the tool is used.
   *Requirement*: Recommendation models need to derive recommendations based on data which emerges when a recommender is used, not based on design time assumptions.
2. *Characteristic*: Every required user input, e.g. the maintenance of models or the supervision of a training is a potential interruption.
   *Requirement*: The creation of recommendation models should require no, or minimal user input.
3. *Characteristic*: System requirements may change over times, requiring maintenance or extension.
   *Requirement*: Recommender approaches should structure the trained data and the used data source in a way which is open to access, to increase maintainability and extendibility.
4. *Requirement*: Information requirements change frequently during the work time due to multitasking.
   *Characteristics*: A recommender approach needs to monitor indicators of information requirements closely to align the recommendations, especially if task switches occur.

---

[4]http://nepomuk.semanticdesktop.org/nepomuk/.

## 6.4 ContAct Monitor and the Computer Work Ontology

This section presents the ContAct monitor. The ContAct monitor collects interaction histories, processes the interaction data and creates a formal representation of the information workers' work process. The PASTREM recommender approach presented later in this chapter builds on the output of the ContAct monitor.

Basically, the ContAct monitor realizes an interaction history management process, composed of the steps (1) data collection, (2) data processing and (3) data organization. A detailed overview of these steps is given in Schmidt and Godehardt (2011). In this chapter, we give a summary of the involved components with a focus on the computer work ontology, used to formalize the work process.

### 6.4.1 Data Collection

Data collection in the ContAct monitor is realized with software sensors to store an interaction histories. The existing implementation of the ContAct monitor can be used for Windows 7 and Windows 8. Each time the foreground process changes or the user interacts with the computer, an event is generated which specifies the foreground process, the information object accessed (if available) and the textual content displayed by the object (if available). This data gives a detailed overview of the sequence of the work process with detailed information about the type of information, the user interacts with.

### 6.4.2 Data Processing

The data processing step enriches the interaction history and derives additional information from the history. The output is a classification of the user activities and an aggregation of activities which were repeated during execution. For example, in an interaction history, multiple switches to a word processor with a similar open document may exist, always accompanied by multiple keyboard inputs. The data processing classifies this as authoring of the respective document and aggregates all respective events.

### 6.4.3 Data Organization

The work process data that results from the data collection and data processing is stored in the computer work ontology (CWO). The CWO offers a vocabulary of user system interactions based on the DOLCE foundation ontology (Gangemi et al. 2002). This brief presentation follows a detailed discussion of CWO in Schmidt et al. (2011b). In the following, the specific characteristics of DOLCE and CWO are provided.

## DOLCE

*DOLCE*, the "descriptive ontology for linguistic and cognitive engineering" (Gangemi et al. 2002), is a foundational ontology with its roots in cognitive science and linguistics. It provides a top level of categories in which entities can be classified. Notably, the top level category is "particular"—where a particular is something which cannot have direct instances, whereas a "universal" is something which *can* have direct instances. For example, the Eiffel Tower is a universal, since there is a direct instance of it. A building, on the other hand, is a particular, since there is nothing that would be denoted as *the building*. Universals are members of the sets defined by particulars (Masolo et al. 2001).

The top level of DOLCE is composed of four basic categories: ENDURANT, PERDURANT, QUALITY, and ABSTRACT. An endurant is something whose parts a fully present at a given point in time (like a car), while a perdurant is something whose parts are not fully present at a given point in time (like the process of driving with a car). As a consequence, the parthood relation for endurants is only fully defined when adding a time span (e.g. "Alan Wilder was a member of Depeche Mode from 1982 to 1995"), while the parthood relation for perdurants does not require such a time span (e.g. "the 1980s were part of the 20th century"), as explained by Masolo et al. (2001).

Typically, endurants *participate* in perdurants (like a car participating in the driving of that very car). Important distinctions of endurants encompass physical vs. non-physical and agentive vs. non-agentive endurants.

Qualities are entities that can be perceived or measured, like the color and the prize of a car. Every entity may have a set of qualities that exist as long as the entity exists. DOLCE distinguishes physical qualities (such as size or color), temporal qualities (like the duration of a process), and abstract qualities (such as a prize).

Abstracts are entities that neither have any qualities nor are qualities by themselves. A typical abstract is a spatial region or a time interval.

Several extensions to DOLCE exist (see Fig. 6.1). One of the most frequently used is the DOLCE DNS (Descriptions and Situations) module, which is used to formalize communication scenarios. The DNS ontology provides useful concepts for describing such interoperations, such as parameters, functional roles, and communication methods. Due to its wide usage, DOLCE and DOLCE DnS are bundled together in one ontology as DOLCE-Lite. DOLCE-Lite consists of 37 classes, 70 object properties, and 349 axioms.

Based on the DnS extension, two other extensions to DOLCE have been proposed, which are useful foundations for using ontologies in the field of software engineering. The *DDPO* (Dolce and DnS Plan Ontology) (Gangemi et al. 2004), which defines categories such as tasks and goals, as well as constructs needed to account for the temporal relations, such as preconditions and postconditions. The *information object ontology* (Gangemi et al. 2004) defines information objects (such as printed or digital documents) and their relations to actors and real world entities. Based on these foundations, Oberle et al. (2006) have defined ontologies of software and software components.

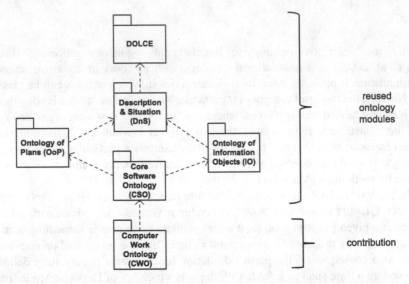

**Fig. 6.1** Overview of the ontologies. *Dotted lines* represent dependencies between ontologies. An ontology $O_1$ depends on $O_2$ if it specializes concepts of $O_2$, has associations with domains and ranges to $O_2$ or reuses its axioms

## CWO Modeling Computer Work

The CWO is modeled by considering the computer workplace as an environment that offers functionalities of generating, displaying and transforming data which can be consumed as information. The functionalities and the available information define a possibility-space for the execution of work. Functionalities are encapsulated in software tools and information is stored in files.

Aspects related to the computer like data are modeled based on the CSO ontology (Oberle et al. 2006). Files realize a connection between meaningful information and software as data in a digital encoded representation.

First, we describe the representation of information by files (see Fig. 6.2). We model a CWO:FILE[5] as a role played-by only CSO:DATA. As CSO:SOFTWARE is a subclass of CSO:DATA, we cover software as files (see Fig. 6.2). CSO:Abstract Data is another subclass of CSO:DATA, containing data that identifies something different from itself, e.g. the word *tree* that stands for a mental image of a real tree. As a file may be abstract data or software, two aspects of files are supported: (1) being a static information object, and (2) being an information object for execution to make plans accessible in a runtime representation. A file as a static information object is modeled by relating the file as CSO:DATA by DNS:ABOUT with a DNS:DESCRIPTION. A file as an executable information object relates

---

[5]From now on and throughout the paper entities that belong to CWO are given without prefix. For all other entities, the respective prefix is given.

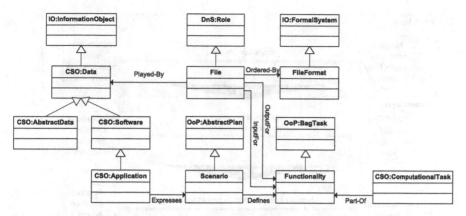

**Fig. 6.2** The classification of software with scenarios, functionalities, and files. Concepts taken from DOLCE and accompanying ontologies are labeled with the respective name space

CSO:SOFTWARE with OOP:PLAN by the DNS:EXPRESSES relation. This is given by the following definitions:

(D1) File-Format(x) → IO:Formal-System(x)

(D2) specializes(x, y) ∧ File-Format(x) → File-Format(y)

(D3) uses(x, y) ∧ File-Format(x) → File-Format(y)

(D4) File(x) =$_{def}$ DnS:Role(x) ∧ ∃y(ordered-by(x, y) ∧ File-Format(y)) ∧ ∃z (played-by(z, x) ∧ (AbstractData(z) ∨ Software(z))) ∧ ∀f(inputFor(x, f) → Functionality(f)) ∧ ∀g(outputFor(x, g → Functionality(g)))

A CWO:FILE is DNS:ORDERED-BY a CWO:FILE-FORMAT. A CWO:FILE with specific CWO:FILE-FORMATS can be input for CWO:FUNCTIONALITY. This connection organizes the file access by functionalities, which may range from opening the file to displaying content in a work processor or to the interpretation of a web page by a web browser.

To express content extracted from a file, a DNS:ABOUT relation between CSO:ABSTRACTDATA and the respective entity is created.

By modeling files in a way that they can stand for software, a file which represents a website can capture a service. CSO:SOFTWARE is IO:REALIZEDBY a CSO:COMPUTATIONALOBJECT. Services use functionalities to express scenarios. This is given with the following definitions:

(D5) CSO:Functionality(x) =$_{def}$ OoP:BagTask(x) ∧ ∃y(DOLCE: part-of(y, x) ∧ ComputationalTask(y))

(D6) Scenario(x) =$_{def}$ OoP:Abstract-Plan(x) ∧ ∀y(DnS: defines(x, y) → Functionality(y))

(D7) CSO:Application(x) =$_{def}$ CSO:Software(x) ∧ ∃y(IO: realizedBy(x, y) ∧ CSO: ComputationalObjects(y)) ∧ ∀z(IO: expresses(x, z) → Scenario(z))

The described aspects allow the use of the CWO ontology to create personal information models comparable to those given with PIMO and the IRIS ontologies.

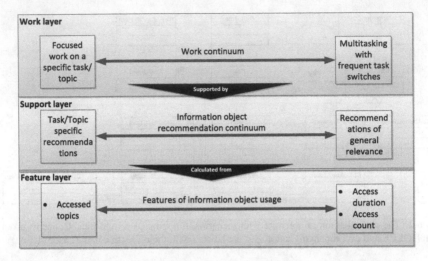

**Fig. 6.3** Work continuum, related recommendation continuum and influence of features

The output of the organization step of the ContAct monitor is a CWO representation of the user work. This data can be stored to create an archive of user system
interactions, or it can be directly forwarded to subscribed applications. In the following, both types will be used. The stored history is used to get an understanding of the
general history of the user. The direct forwarding helps to understand the short term
activities of the user which describe his situation and hint to existing information
requirements.

## 6.5 PASTREM Recommender

This section presents the PASTREM recommender approach. The PASTREM recommender builds on the CWO instance data created by the ContAct monitor and
extends it. The PASTREM recommender approach supports information reuse for
information workers for a more focused or a more multitasking oriented work. The
approach especially tackles the requirements of (1) creating models for the recommender based on and within the actual work process, (2) limiting the required user
input for the recommender system (3), structuring recommendation data in an easily accessible way to improve maintainability, and (4) respecting the dynamism of
information work.

### 6.5.1 PASTREM Recommendation Continuum

PASTREM builds recommendations for information object reuse with respect to a
work continuum which goes from an extremely focused, single task work to multitasking with frequent task switches (see Fig. 6.3). The assumption is that the actual

useful recommendations differ. A very focused work may be supported by information objects which are closely related to the task, considering even information objects which have been accessed very few times until that moment. In contrast, a multitasking oriented work requires recommendations which support the task switches by providing information objects as anchor points for upcoming tasks. An anchor point is an information object of high relevance which helps the user to quickly recall conditions and requirements of a task, like a memory cue that supports a task switch. Therefore, multitasking oriented work would probably be supported best by information objects of general importance. Thus, the work continuum triggers a continuum of recommendations, focusing more or less on focused or multitasking work respectively.

For PASTREM three activity features are used: user topics, access count and access duration. Topics capture an abstract representation of information requirements of the user generally related to the task a user works on. A latest time segment of user interaction is used to identify relevant topics which hint to related information objects in the interaction history of the user captured by the CWO. Topics can be understood as an information requirement following the assumption that a user continues to work on a focused task. Thus, topic related recommendations help users to focus on specific topics. Access count and overall access duration are global characteristics, not related to the given focus task. Therefore, access count and access duration support task switches as they result in information object recommendations of general high relevance, possibly unrelated to an active task but serving as memory cues for task switches.

In the following, information about topic modeling and the integration of topics into the CWO is provided. Then, the overall process of PASTREM is presented, including data preparation and recommendation elicitation (see steps in Fig. 6.4).

### 6.5.2  Topic Modeling for CWO

Topic modeling stands for a group of approaches which use Bayesian parameter estimation on multinomial distributions frequently used to derive the latent semantics of a text corpus. PASTREM uses the Latent Dirichlet Allocation (LDA) (Blei et al. 2003) to derive topics as latent semantics from a user interaction history as text corpus. In the following, a brief description of LDA is provided and the integration of topics, extracted from interaction histories, into the CWO is described.

The model assumption of LDA is that documents are composed of topics, while each topic is a set of words. Creating a document means choosing the required topics, their relevance for the document and sampling the words from the set of topics. LDA reverts this process and extracts a generative probabilistic model from a text corpus using Bayesian methods (for a good introduction, see Heinrich 2009). The model describes the probability that a word is part of a topic and the probability that a topic was used to generate a document.

Input for LDA is a bag of words representation of documents, i.e. the words used in the corpus are enumerated and for each document the count of each word is noted.

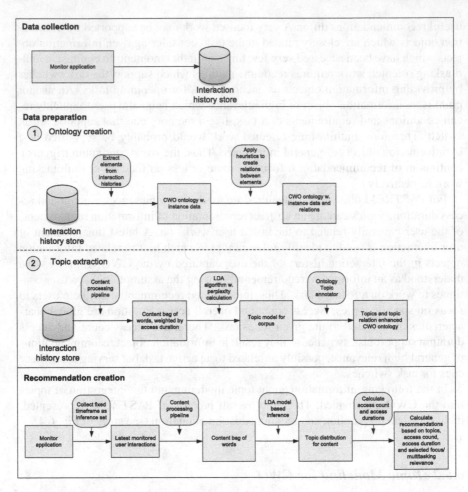

**Fig. 6.4** Processes involved in the recommendation creation

## 6.5.3 Adding Topics, Access Count and Access Duration to CWO

The extended information object design pattern (Gangemi et al. 2004) describes the modeling of an information object. An information object can be realized by any sort of entity and can be about any sort of entity. To express that a file has a content which stands for different topics the following model applies: the file plays the role of abstract data, as discussed above, and the abstract data expresses a topic which is modeled using the subject entity. As the topic extraction identifies a value which stands for the relatedness of the data to the topic we have applied reification.

An IO:SUBJECT gets connected to a CSO:MEASUREMENT unit with a property of type DNS:REFERENCES. The CSO:MEASUREMENTUNIT is again connected to an IO:INFORMATIONOBJECT. The measurement unit contains the relatedness value.

For access count and access duration, the extraction is simpler. They can be derived from the CWO based on the logged work situations which refer to information objects. The situation number for each information object needs to be counted to get the access count while the access duration is provided by the sum of the situation durations for each information object.

## 6.5.4 Data Preparation

The data preparation described in the following especially focuses on the extraction of topics from the interaction which requires most effort within the recommendation process. Data preparation creates two artifacts which are used in the recommendation process. On the one hand, an instance of the CWO ontology is created and annotated with information about topics and the relatedness values for information objects. On the other hand, a model of the user topics is created, which is later used to infer topic distributions of new documents.

Data preparation is a time consuming task which needs to be performed on a regular basis (e.g. daily):

1. *Ontology creation*: First, the CWO ontology is filled with instance data about the elements the user interacts with. Based on the classification of information objects and additional heuristics, CWO instances are extracted. The resulting CWO ontology links information about the information objects, services and applications a user interacted with. The CWO also includes information about work episodes, thus providing data about access count and access duration of the information objects. This is the output of the ContAct monitor.
2. *Topic model creation and ontology enrichment*: Second, the content of the interaction history is used to identify topics of the accessed content. This is done using LDA, which requires a bag of words representation of the content as input. The bag of words is created in a document processing pipeline, as it is frequently used in natural language processing tasks (Nadkarni et al. 2011). The pipeline contains the following elements: tokenizer, language detection based on n-grams, part of speech tagging and stopword detection. Stopwords are deleted and only nouns and verbs are processed further.

   The pipeline creates content representations as bags of words: lists of words with the number of occurrences.

   The corpus represented by sets of bag of words is input to LDA. The LDA algorithm creates two distributions: a distribution of words to topics and a distribution of topics to documents. The LDA algorithm requires the input of topics before the algorithm runs. As the amount of useful topics generally is not known, a workaround can be used. The perplexity "is monotonically decreasing in the likelihood of the test data, and is algebraically equivalent to the inverse of the geometric mean per-word likelihood" (Blei et al. 2003). The lower the perplexity score, the better the generalization performance. If LDA is executed several times for different amounts of topics, the perplexity indicates the topic amount with the best generalization performance.

The ontology created in the previous step is enriched by the new data. Each topic is added as a topic entity represented by IO:Subject to the ontology. As described in the previous section, a CSO:MEASUREMENT unit connected with DNS:REALIZES connects CSO:ABSTRACTDATA played by the file and the IO:Subject.

The output of the step is not only the ontology enriched with the topic and topic relatedness data. The second output is the model of document, word and topics created by the LDA algorithm which is used later for inference.

### 6.5.5 Recommendation Creation

Recommendations are proactively generated while the user is working. While access count and access duration are directly available, the relevant topics are derived from the latest interaction history. Therefore, the most recent segment of the users' interaction history is used as inference set to identify the relevant topics.

The textual content of the interaction history fragment is used to identify recommendations based on the CWO ontology. To create recommendations, first a bag of word representation of the content is created using the document processing pipeline mentioned. The access date has no influence on the recommendation creation. The topic distribution for the content is inferred based on the model of document, word and topics created in the previous step. As a result a numerical representation of the topic relevance for the work in the considered latest time frame is created. The information object relevance ($IOTOPIC_{Rel}$) value is composed of the accumulated relatedness of the inference set to the topics and of the topics to the information objects: $IOTOPIC_{Rel} = (\sum_{t=1}^{T}(IS_t + \sum_{i=1}^{I} IO_{it}))$ with $T$ = number of topics, $I$ = number of information objects, $IS_t$ = relatedness of Inference set to topic $t$, $IO_{it}$ as relatedness of information object $i$ to topic $t$. Thus, the relevance of a topic for the latest time segment adds to the relevance of all information objects for the topic.

For each information object, the relevance ($IO_{Rel}$) for the recommendation is calculated as a product of the topic relevance, the access count and the access duration weighted by factors to increase or decrease the relevance of focused or multitasking work respectively: $IO_{Rel} = IOTOPIC_{Rel}^{\beta} * ac^{\alpha} * ad^{\alpha}$ with $ac$ as access count, $ad$ as access duration in minutes and $\alpha$ and $beta$ to trigger the relevance of topics for focused work and of $ac$ and $ad$ for multitasking oriented work.

### 6.5.6 PASTREM Discussion

PASTREM addresses the needs identified for recommendation approaches for information reuse based on topic extraction on the long term interaction history and topic inference on the short term history. The specific demands are tackled by this approach in the following way:

1. *Requirement*: Creating models for the recommender based on and within the actual work process.
   *Addressed*: The topic model created by LDA is the model used to generate recommendations based on the interaction history of a user.
2. *Requirement*: Limiting the required user input for the recommender system.
   *Addressed*: LDA is an unsupervised algorithm which only requires the work process information provided by the ContAct monitor and captured in the CWO. Access count and access can be calculated from the interaction history.
3. *Requirement*: Structuring recommendation data in an easily accessible way to improve maintainability.
   *Addressed*: The use of the CWO to capture an abstract representation of the computer work, accessed information objects, topics and the relatedness of topics to information objects provides simple access to the data used for recommendation elicitation. Extension of CWO to other types of accessed information is simple, as long as a textual representation of the information is given.
4. *Requirement*: Respecting the dynamism of information work.
   *Addressed*: The frequent creation of recommendations based on the most recent interaction history segment helps to consider the latest topic of interest which may change the information requirement quickly within the recommendation. The ability to increase or decrease the relevance of topics on the one hand and access count/access duration on the other hand helps to increase or decrease the relevance of focused or multitasking oriented work episodes.

## 6.6 Evaluation

In the following, the PASTREM recommender is evaluated and compared to the results of other activity related recommenders: last recently used (LRU), semantic relatedness (TR), most often used (MOU) and longest used (LOU). LRU, MOU and LOU are-self explaining. The TR algorithms recommends only based on the relatedness of the topic of the considered time segment to stored topic models with related information objects. Especially, MOU and LRU are frequently used recommender types used in applications (often referred to as *recently used lists* or *histories*).

The evaluation is conducted in an ex post manner. Two interaction history data sets are used to identify the number of correct recommendations at a given position in the history by checking whether the elements actually accessed by the user would have been recommended. This results in a binary decision whether a used resource was recommended or not with a hit percentage.

The evaluation process is described in the following. Information objects are identified which have been used in a real use time segment after a randomly selected starting point (see Fig. 6.5, start point) in the interaction history and which were used earlier. The information objects of the real use time segment are compared to

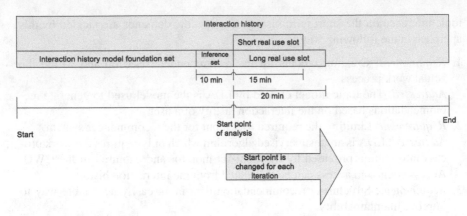

**Fig. 6.5** Timeframes relevant for recommendation analysis for a given starting point

the recommendations generated by the recommender approaches, i.e. it is checked how many of the reused information objects in the real use slot are recommended by the algorithms (see Fig. 6.5, use slots).

The events before the start position are used to create recommendations. Therefore, they are separated in two sets: (1) Model foundation set (2) Inference set. To ensure a sufficiently large number of events to build the model, it was enforced that the start position was in the middle or later of the interaction history. The recommendation inference set is a time segment of 10 minutes before the selected position. This time segment is used for the recommendation creation. All events that occurred before than the recommendation inference set are used to build the ontology and to perform topic extraction (see Fig. 6.5, model foundation and inference set).

## 6.6.1 Evaluation Configuration

The performance of PASTREM as well as the performance of LRU is scaled by the amount of elements included in the recommendation list. If both propose a list of all elements the user ever interacted with, both have the best possible recall but a low precision. This has practical relevance for the user interface of the recommender. A longer list of recommendations complicates user interactions due to limited cognitive capabilities. Therefore, the number of recommended elements is of high importance: the lower the number of recommendations required to make a valid recommendation, the better.

To address this, different recommendation set sizes have been compared: 10, 15, and 20 information objects. The ranking was performed as follows. For LRU the last $n$ elements which were used directly before the begin of the inference set have been used. MOU uses the $n$ most often used elements and LOU uses those $n$ information objects used for the longest amount of time. TR calculates the relatedness of the inference set to topics of the model and the relatedness of the topics to the information objects (actually the calculation of $IOTOPIC_{Rel}$ described in the previous section). Based on the resulting values, TR recommends the $n$ elements with the highest relatedness. In all cases, elements from the inference set were excluded from the list of potential recommendations, as they are already used.

Another influence factor is the length of the real use slot. The longer the slot, the higher the probability that a recommendation might fit. This has been addressed by considering two different real use slot lengths: 15 and 20 minutes.

A third influence factor is the temporal length of the inference set. Based on experience, we have set the length to 10 minutes. This value has not been changed in the study, although it is worth to investigate it further. The assumption is that the length of a useful inference time segment length depends on the homogeneity of work as measure for multitasking. An inhomogeneous work probably requires smaller inference time segments than homogeneous work.

Two interaction history data sets have been analyzed, using the described process. The $\alpha$ and $\beta$ value were both set to one, to balance between task-focus and multitask orientation.

## 6.6.2 Evaluation Process

The interaction history data sets were created by researchers at an IT company. Data set 1 contains 15 363 interaction events (e.g., mouse clicks, window focus, etc.) for a period of 9 work days. Data set 2 contains 18 311 interaction events for 4 work days. Information objects were only considered, if they were at least 10 seconds focused. The data sets represent the normal working day of the two people, starting emails, browsing the internet, reading emails, etc.

For data sets 1 (100 data points) and for data set 2 (80 data points) were chosen randomly with the constraint that at least one third of the overall event number was recorded before the selected event as starting point. The constraint assured that enough information objects and data for reasonable recommendations and topic model creation existed.

Data set 1 contains 620 different information object accesses in all 100 real use time segments for a 15 minutes time segment (elements not included in the inference set). Of those 620 elements, 384 elements had not been used earlier, while 272 elements were reused. For all 20 minute real use slots, overall 765 information objects were used, 436 had not used been before, while 329 were reused. The average number of reused information objects for a 15 minutes real use time segment was 2.7 and 3.2 for a 20 minutes real use time segment. Only three real use slots for 15 minutes as well as for 20 minutes reused more than 20 information objects which means that only for these three elements the largest recommendation set would be insufficient to recommend all items.

Data set 2 contained 287 different information objects accessed in all 80 real use time segments of 15 minutes length. The 287 elements contained 237 elements not used before and 50 reused elements. Within the 20 minute time segments 336 elements were accessed, 267 were unknown before and 69 were reused. An average number of 0.6 elements were reused within 15 minutes, 0.86 were reused within 20 minutes. No slot for 15 or 20 minutes contained more than 20 information objects, thus the recommendations could have been sufficient to recommend all actually used information objects.

The numbers already hint to different work styles captured by the data sets. In the following evaluation, we will see that data set 1 is more multitasking oriented while data set 2 stands for work with less multitasking which has effects on the different assessed recommender algorithms.

### 6.6.3 Evaluation Results

The accuracy of recommended information objects for PASTREM, LRU, MOU, LOU and TR for data set 1 is given in Table 6.1 and for data set 2 in 6.2. PASTREM shows a good performance on both data sets, as up to 67.2 % and 71.0 % (15 min) of accuracy is reached for a list of 20 recommendation elements and a 15 minutes time segment. For 10 elements 58.1 % (data set 1), 54.7 % (data set 2) and for 10 elements 42.6 % (data set 1), 40.4 % (data set 2) of all information objects used in a 15 minutes segment have been actually recommended.

Interesting results is the performance of MOU for data set 1 compared to the MOU performance for data set 2. While data set 1 reaches 69.3 % of accuracy for 20 minutes length and 20 recommendations, data set 2 only shows an accuracy of 44.7 %. A similar peculiarity is the performance of LRU which shows a good performance on data set 2 reaching an accuracy of 63.6 % for 15 minutes and 20 recommendations while for data set 1 only 49.6 % of accuracy are reached for the same value. The overall weak performance of TR (23.5 % is the highest reached accuracy value) is another notable result. The different performances and especially the peculiarities with respect to the specific characteristics of the data sets are discussed in the following.

### 6.6.4 Evaluation Discussion

The evaluation showed a good performance of PASTREM for both data sets. The only algorithm with comparable results for data set 1 is MOU which shows a less good performance on data set 2.

Discussion of LOU and TR: LOU shows stable results between 24 and 50 % recommendation successes which show that the usage duration indicates relevance while it is not very useful on its own. The TR recommender shows exceptionally weak results. The assumption is that considering topic relatedness fails to rank the information objects which belong to the relevant topics. Additional relevance indicators are required to rank the information objects of one topic, e.g. frequently

**Table 6.1** Data set 1: Accuracy of recommendations for PASTREM, LRU, MOU, LOU, TR for a short (15 min) and longer (20 min) real use time segment of recommendation validity with lists of 10, 15 and 20 elements

| | Number of recommendations | | |
|---|---|---|---|
| | 10 | 15 | 20 |
| PASTREM 15 minutes | 42.6 % | 58.1 % | 67.2 % |
| PASTREM 20 minutes | 35.6 % | 39.2 % | 68.1 % |
| LRU 15 minutes | 41.5 % | 42.2 % | 49.6 % |
| LRU 20 minutes | 40.1 % | 41.3 % | 49.2 % |
| MOU 15 minutes | 43.7 % | 64.7 % | 69.1 % |
| MOU 20 minutes | 43.2 % | 64.7 % | 69.3 % |
| LOU 15 minutes | 24.2 % | 37.5 % | 54.0 % |
| LOU 20 minutes | 24.3 % | 37.1 % | 54.7 % |
| TR 15 minutes | 13.6 % | 17.2 % | 23.5 % |
| TR 20 minutes | 12.7 % | 16.5 % | 22.4 % |

**Table 6.2** Data set 2: Accuracy of recommendations for PASTREM, LRU, MOU, LOU, TR for a short (15 min) and longer (20 min) real use time segment of recommendation validity with lists of 10, 15 and 20 elements

| | Number of recommendations | | |
|---|---|---|---|
| | 10 | 15 | 20 |
| PASTREM 15 minutes | 40.4 % | 54.7 % | 71.0 % |
| PASTREM 20 minutes | 36.0 % | 47.5 % | 59.6 % |
| LRU 15 minutes | 29.5 % | 47.7 % | 63.6 % |
| LRU 20 minutes | 25.3 % | 44.4 % | 60.3 % |
| MOU 15 minutes | 31.7 % | 41.5 % | 44.7 % |
| MOU 20 minutes | 28.3 % | 38.3 % | 40.3 % |
| LOU 15 minutes | 30.0 % | 40.0 % | 48.0 % |
| LOU 20 minutes | 27.5 % | 37.7 % | 44.9 % |
| TR 15 minutes | 16.0 % | 20.0 % | 20.0 % |
| TR 20 minutes | 14.5 % | 18.8 % | 18.8 % |

used for longer periods of time should be ranked higher than a resource which is only infrequently used for a short time. This is considered in PASTREM based on the integration of additional relevance factors which always influence the semantic relatedness based on an overall relevance ($ac$ and $ad$ are always bigger than 1).

PASTREM, MOU and LRU: A closer investigation of data set 1 showed a strong tendency of the user to switch between tasks. The good performance of MOU most likely results from the frequent task switches which are best supported by recommending resources of an overall relevance without paying much attention to the topic which will change only minutes later. The second data set shows a more focused work type, even including phases of several minutes without any switch of the focus application. The good performance of LRU results from the stable work provided with data set 2 which creates strong local contexts of a high return probability to earlier used resources. For PASTREM, this data set benefits from topic specific recommendations ranked by access count and access duration.

Overall, the combination of semantic relatedness and relevance within PASTREM shows promising results. Next to the accuracy, the type of recommendations is of relevance. LRU and MOU tend to propose elements which were recently and often used, therefore it is likely that the subject remembers those resources and the respective locations without help. In contrast, a review of the PASTREM recommendations showed that often elements not used for a longer period of time or with a medium access count (not the top 4 and not the last 4) were recommended. Those elements probably represent archived and ephemeral elements which is of specific benefit, as the recall of those elements is complex.

## 6.7 Conclusion

We have presented PASTREM, a recommender system to support information reuse in information work. PASTREM extends existing work on recommender systems for information work in several respects. The approach covers a broad range of different data types, is completely unsupervised and requires few user input. The use of the CWO ontology to structure the data integrates PASTREM into an existing infrastructure for information work support. A specific benefit of PASTREM is the modification of the algorithm for a more focused or a more multitasking oriented work execution. As the respective calculation is a "cheap" reordering of a list, this modification of recommendations can be triggered by the user during runtime. Another aspect of PASTREM is that it provides an entry point to an ontology based on the topic. The abstract nature of topics seem to be a valuable entry point for browsing and extension of the recommender by other, topic related elements.

PASTREM, TR, LRU, MOU and LOU were evaluated by comparing the recommendations to real information object usages in two collected interaction histories. PASTREM showed better results for both data sets, with a balanced influence of topic relatedness to duration and access count.

Future work will investigate into a user interface for PASTREM. A first implementation makes use of the jumplist in Windows 7. Further research will try to improve the accuracy and consider the automatic calibration of the algorithm to the preferred work style of the user. A calibration which is feasible by applying the technique used to evaluate the recommender performance.

## References

Adomavicius, G., & Tuzhilin, A. (2005). Toward the next generation of recommender systems: a survey of the state-of-the-art and possible extensions. *IEEE Transactions on Knowledge and Data Engineering, 33*(6), 81–749.

Aha, D. W., Kibler, D., & Albert, M. K. (1991). Instance-based learning algorithms. *Machine Learning, 6*(1), 37–66.

Aral, S., & Brynjolfsson, E. (2007). *Information, technology and information worker productivity: task level evidence*. Cambridge: National Bureau of Economic Research.

Austin, J. L. (1962). *How to do things with words*. Cambridge: Harvard University Press.

Barreau, D., & Nardi, B. (1995). Finding and reminding: file organization from the desktop. *ACM SIGCHI Bulletin, 27*(3), 39–43.

Bergman, O., & Whittaker, S. (2012). How do we find personal files?: the effect of OS, presentation & depth on file navigation. In *Proceedings of the 2012 ACM annual conference on human factors in computing systems*.

Bergman, O., Tucker, S., Beyth-marom, R., Cutrell, E., & Whittaker, S. (2009). *It's not that important: demoting personal information of low subjective importance using GrayArea*.

Blei, D. M., Ng, A. Y., & Jordan, M. I. (2003). Latent Dirichlet allocation. *Journal of Machine Learning Research, 3*(4–5), 993–1022.

Cheyer, A., Park, J., & Giuli, R. (2005). *IRIS: integrate, relate. infer. share*. DTIC Document.

Czerwinski, M., Horvitz, E., & Wilhite, S. (2004). A diary study of task switching and interruptions. In *Proceedings of the SIGCHI*.

Farhoomand, B. A. F., & Drury, D. H. (2002). Managerial information overload. *Communications of the ACM, 45*(10), 127–131.

Gallup and San Jose State University and Park, Institute for the Future in Menlo (1999). Managing corporate communications. In *The information age*. Stamford: Pitney Bowes.

Gangemi, A., Borgo, S., & Catenacci, C. (2004). Task taxonomies for knowledge content. *METOKIS deliverable D*.

Gangemi, A., Guarino, N., & Masolo, C. (2002). Sweetening ontologies with DOLCE. In *Knowledge engineering and knowledge management: ontologies and the semantic web* (pp. 223–233). Berlin: Springer.

González, V. M., & Mark, G. (2004). Constant, constant, multi-tasking craziness: managing multiple working spheres. In *Proceedings of the SIGCHI conference on human factors in computing systems* (Vol. 6, pp. 113–120). New York: ACM.

Heinrich, G. (2009). *Parameter estimation for text analysis* (Fraunhofer Technology Report).

Hussein, T., Westheide, D., & Ziegler, J. (2007). Context-adaptation based on ontologies and spreading activation. In *Proceedings of ABIS '07: 15th workshop on adaptivity and user modeling in interactive systems*.

Jensen, C., Lonsdale, H., Wynn, E., & Cao, J. (2010). The life and times of files and information: a study of desktop provenance. In *Proceedings of the 28th CHI* (pp. 767–776). New York: ACM.

Kaptelinin, V. (2003). UMEA: translating interaction histories into project contexts. In *Proceedings of the SIGCHI conference on human factors in computing systems* (Vol. 5, pp. 353–360). New York: ACM.

Link, H., Lane, T., & Magliano, J. (2005). Models and model biases for automatically learning task switching behavior. In *Foundations of augmented cognition* (Vol. 5, pp. 510–519). Hillsdale: Erlbaum.

Lokaiczyk, R., Faatz, A., Beckhaus, A., & Goertz, M. (2007). Enhancing just-in-time E-learning through machine learning on desktop context sensors. In *Modeling and using context* (pp. 330–341). Berlin: Springer.

Makolm, J. (2008). DYONIPOS: proactive knowledge management. In *BLED 2008 proceedings* (pp. 475–482).

Masolo, C., Borgo, S., Gangemi, A., Guarino, N., Oltramari, A., & Horrocks, I. (2001). *WonderWeb deliverable D18. Ontology library (final)*. WonderWeb project.

Middleton, S. E., Shadbolt, N. R., & Roure, D. C. D. E. (2004). Ontological user profiling in recommender systems. *ACM Transactions on Information Systems, 22*(1), 54–88.

Morteo, R., Gonzalez, V. M., Favela, J., & Mark, G. (2004). Sphere juggler: fast context retrieval in support of working spheres. In *Proceedings of the fifth Mexican international conference in computer science, 2004. ENC 2004* (pp. 361–367).

Nadkarni, P. M., Ohno-Machado, L., & Chapman, W. W. (2011). Natural language processing: an introduction. *Journal of the American Medical Informatics Association, 18*(5), 544–551.

Oberle, D., Lamparter, S., Grimm, S., & Vrande, D. (2006). Towards ontologies for formalizing modularization and communication in large software systems. In *Handbook on ontologies*. Berlin: Springer.

Polyanyi, M. (1966). *The tacit dimension*. London: Routledge & Kegan Paul.

Rath, A., & Weber, N. (2008). Context-aware knowledge services. In *Personal Information Management: PIM* (pp. 1–11).

Salvucci, D., & Taatgen, N. (2008). Threaded cognition: an integrated theory of concurrent multitasking. *Psychological Review, 115*(1), 101–130.

Schmidt, B., & Godehardt, E. (2011). Interaction data management. In *Knowledge-based and intelligent information and engineering systems*. Berlin: Springer.

Schmidt, B., Kastl, J., Stoitsev, T., & Mühlhäuser, M. (2011a). Hierarchical task instance mining in interaction histories. In *Proceedings of the 29th annual international conference on design of communication (SIGDOC)*. New York: ACM.

Schmidt, B., Paulheim, H., Stoitsev, T., & Mühlhäuser, M. (2011b). Towards a formalization of individual work execution at computer workplaces. In *Lecture notes in artificial intelligence. Conceptual structures for discovering knowledge* (pp. 270–284). Berlin: Springer.

Schmidt, B., Godehardt, E., & Pantel, B. (2012). Visualizing the work process—situation awareness for the knowledge worker. In *3rd IUI workshop on semantic models for adaptive interactive systems (SEMAIS 2012)*.

Shen, J., Li, L., Dieterich, T. G., & Herlocker, J. L. (2006). A hybrid learning system for recognizing user tasks from desktop activities and email messages. In *Proceedings of the 11th international conference on intelligent user interfaces—IUI '06* (pp. 86–92).

Sproull, L. S. (1984). The nature of managerial attention. In *Advances in information processing in organizations* (pp. 9–27). London: JAI Press.

# Chapter 7
# Visualizing Search Results of Linked Open Data

Christian Stab, Dirk Burkhardt, Matthias Breyer, and Kawa Nazemi

**Abstract** Finding accurate information of high quality is still a challenging task particularly with regards to the increasing amount of resources in current information systems. This is especially true if policy decisions that impact humans, economy or environment are based on the demanded information. For improving search result generation and analyzing user queries more and more information retrieval systems utilize Linked Open Data and other semantic knowledge bases. Nevertheless, the semantic information that is used during search result generation mostly remains hidden from the users although it significantly supports users in understanding and assessing search results. The presented approach combines information visualizations with semantic information for offering visual feedback about the reasons the results were retrieved. It visually represents the semantic interpretation and the relation between query terms and search results to offer more transparency in search result generation and allows users to unambiguously assess the relevance of the retrieved resources for their individual search. The approach also supports the common search strategies by providing visual feedback for query refinement and enhancement. Besides the detailed description of the search system, an evaluation of the approach shows that the use of semantic information considerably supports users in assessment and decision-making tasks.

## 7.1 Introduction

Assessing information is a common task for decision makers. Especially in the area of policy modeling, analysts have to consider different perspectives when designing a new policy that impacts humans, economy and the environment. So homogeneous access possibilities as well as adequate representations for distributed data plays a major role for providing adequate tools that facilitate decision making. Thereby, semantic technologies provide adequate tools for linking heterogeneous data sources and for generating broader contexts that facilitate information access and enables

C. Stab (✉) · D. Burkhardt · M. Breyer · K. Nazemi
Fraunhofer Institute for Computer Graphics Research (IGD), Darmstadt, Germany
e-mail: christian.stab@igd.fraunhofer.de

T. Hussein et al. (eds.), *Semantic Models for Adaptive Interactive Systems,*
Human–Computer Interaction Series, DOI 10.1007/978-1-4471-5301-6_7,
© Springer-Verlag London 2013

data exchange between different systems (Shadbolt et al. 2006). With the ongoing establishment of semantic technologies like the *Resource Description Framework* (RDF), the *Web Ontology Language* (OWL), semantic-oriented query languages like *SPARQL* and *Linked Open Data* (LOD) platforms like DBpedia (Auer et al. 2007) these developments are not only limited to specific domains but also adopted in daily search processes (Fernandez et al. 2008) and even for interlinking government data in so-called *Linked Government Data* (LGD) platforms (Ding et al. 2010; Wood 2011). For accessing these large amounts of interlinked data usually information retrieval methods are utilized that retrieve relevant resources by means of given search terms or keywords. The results of search processing are usually presented in sorted lists and in most cases the ordering of list entries represents the relevance of the results for the individual search according to various criteria (Cutrell et al. 2006). So the most relevant result is placed in the first row followed by less important ones. The semantic information of the resources that is used during the search result generation and the analysis of search terms remains hidden from the user in most cases, though this information considerably supports users in information-seeking tasks and selection of appropriate documents for further examination.

For designing search user interfaces efficient and informative feedback about the retrieved resources is critically important for the user to be able to assess the presented search results (Hearst 2009). In particular this includes feedback about query formulation and about reasons the results were retrieved from the information system. However, the use of additional relevance indicators in result lists besides relevance ordering such as numerical scores or special icons turned out to be not successful for supporting users in understanding the retrieved results because the meaning of the relevance score is opaque to the user (White et al. 2007). This is because the majority of existing relevance indicators only presents a single relevance per search result that summarizes all criteria instead of offering a more fine-grained insight to search result processing.

In contrast to common search result presentations the presented approach makes use of information visualizations for representing search results of semantically modeled data. In order to offer users an adequate tool for assessing the relevance of the retrieved search results the approach combines information visualization techniques with semantic information and different weights that emerge during the search process. The approach also visually supports the common search strategies by providing visual feedback for query evolution. The main contributions and benefits of the presented approach are:

- *Query-Result-Relations*: The semantic search processing of the approach analyzes the given queries and identifies relations between query terms and search results. The visualization of these relations offers a fine-grained overview of search result relevancies and facilitates information seeking and assessment tasks.
- *Relevance Assessment*: The inclusion of semantic information in search result presentation offers more transparency in search result generation and successfully supports user in assessing the relevance of the presented resources.
- *Visual Query Enhancement*: The visual recommendation of additional query terms related to the set of search results supports the common search strategy and

allows users to narrow current search results and to immediately receive visual feedback.

In the next section we give an overview of related work that influenced the development of our approach. Subsequently, we introduce our approach for processing and visualizing searches in semantic domains and give a detailed description of each component. We present the results of an evaluation comparing our approach to already existing solutions followed by an outlook of its application in the area of policy modeling.

## 7.2 Related Work

Semantic models are increasingly used for linking heterogeneous data sources as well as for generating broader contexts that facilitate information access (Shadbolt et al. 2006). Nowadays, these technologies are not only limited to specific domains but also adopted in daily search processes of web-based search engines (Fernandez et al. 2008). A commonly used and useful approach for representing search results is the term highlighting technique (Aula 2004) where the terms of a given query are highlighted in the surrogates of search result lists. This approach is also referred to as Keyword-In-Context (KWIC). For example the BioText System (Hearst et al. 2007) represents beside extracted figures from relevant articles, query terms highlighted in the title and boldfaced in the text excerpts for communicating reasons the particular results were retrieved. Even though term highlighting can be useful for improving search result list presentations, it does not reveal the semantic interpretation of search results and prevent users from scanning the whole result list for getting an overview.

Although the initial intention of semantic technologies was not focused on presenting semantics to end-users, there are several approaches that benefit thereby. SemaPlorer (Schenk et al. 2009) is an interactive application that makes use of multiple semantic data sources and allows users to visualize results of their search in various views. The user interface of SemaPlorer combines a geographic visualization and a media view for visualizing geospatially annotated data and picture galleries respectively. The approach also includes facetation of search results and focuses on combining search results from different heterogeneous knowledge bases. Another approach of presenting semantic information to the user is the Relfinder interface (Heim et al. 2010). It supports users in interactively discovering relations between resources in semantic knowledge spaces. Users can prompt two or more resources and the relations between them are shown in a graph-based visualization. Although this approach demonstrates the benefit of communicating semantic knowledge to users, it is strictly limited to relation discovery.

Other approaches utilize different information visualization techniques for improving search result presentations. To name only a few, the Microsoft Academic Search interface[1] incorporates geographic, graph-based and temporal visualization

---

[1] http://academic.research.microsoft.com.

techniques for searching and exploring publications or authors and offers also a stacked area chart for analyzing trends in the field of computer science. Skyline-Search (Stoyanovich et al. 2011) is a search interface that supports life science researchers in performing scientific literature search. It leverages semantic annotations to visualize search results in a scatterplot representing relevance against publication date. Even though semantic annotations are used for search processing and estimating relevance values, semantic knowledge is not directly presented to the user. The WebSearchViz (Nguyen and Zhang 2006) is an approach for visualizing web search results based on the metaphor of the solar system. It offers users the possibility to observe the relevance between a query and a web search result by the spatial proximity between objects. However, the system does not visualize semantic interpretations of search results or semantic structures.

The visual design of the presented visualization is based on a force-based visualization method similar to RadVis (Hoffman et al. 1997). Force-based visualization methods utilize physical laws (e.g. Hooke's Law) to locate each data record on a two dimensional screen by assigning different forces between the visual representations of each record. By adapting these forces in an iterative simulation, the physical system reaches a mechanical equilibrium resulting in an aesthetical layout of the given data. Originally, RadVis is a visualization technique for multivariate data. For each dimension this visualization locates an anchor point on a circle. Theses anchor points can be seen as fixed ends of springs. Each representation of a data record is attached to all related anchor points and the attraction force for each spring is weighted with the value of the record for the specific dimension. This results in different distances between the data records and the anchor points that represent the characteristics of each record according to the visualized dimensions. This approach is especially useful for identifying outliers in the data and for recognizing clusters.

Although there are different approaches that make use of semantic information for improving search results or result presentation and approaches that utilize information visualization for representing search results, there is still a gap in combining semantic search processing, information visualization and search user interfaces. The approach presented in this chapter aims at combining these three technologies into an interactive search user interface that facilitates information access and relevance assessment.

## 7.3 Search Procedure

For visualizing search results, there are also additional requirements for the search procedure and in particular the result generation. In contrast to commonly used textual list presentations that are based on ordered result lists, for the visualization of search results structured data is needed. For instance these additional structures may include clusters, relations, or labeled taxonomies that can be exploited for providing meaningful visual representations. The semantic information provided e.g. in Linked Open Data databases provides a useful starting point for extracting this structural information.

**Fig. 7.1** Process for
retrieving search results,
query-result-relations and
recommendations from
semantic databases

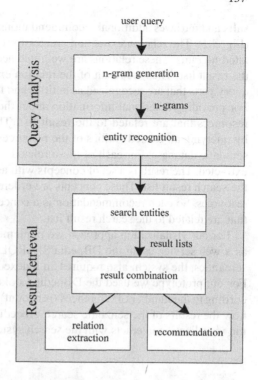

The procedure used for retrieving the needed result structures from a semantic database consists of several steps at two different stages (Fig. 7.1). In the first stage the given user query is analyzed and dissembled into n-grams. Each of these n-grams is then mapped to an instance in the semantic data base e.g. by using an entity recognition approach like that described in Paulheim and Fümkranz (2012). Additionally, the type label of each recognized entity is retrieved by identifying the most specific concept in the semantic structure. So the result of the query analysis is a set of n-grams related to an instance and its most specific concept. We also considered different filtering strategies for discarding incomplete results. In particular there are two different filters: (1) an entity filter that filters all n-grams that could not be mapped to an entity and (2) a type filter that removes all entities whose concepts could not be retrieved. The search system can be parameterized to use one, both or none of these filters.

In the second stage the results for each recognized entity are retrieved and extended with additional structural information. In the first step each recognized entity that meets the given filter condition is searched in the semantic data base using an indexed search. The result lists are combined using two sorting fields. The first sorting field refers to the number of occurrences for each retrieved resource in the retrieved lists and the second sort field is the number of references that each retrieved resource has in the underlying semantics data base. So the first element is the element that is retrieved for most of the recognized query terms. Based on the combined result list, the search system extracts relations between the recognized query terms and re-

sults and retrieves additional recommendations as resources related to the result list
(Fig. 7.1). The relation extraction creates for each resource a set of relations to related n-grams. These relations are weighted according to the rank of the resource in
the result list. Thus the result of the relation extraction is a set of relations between
query parts that are recognized as entities and the results in the combined result list.
For providing additional information about the search, the procedure retrieves also
resources that are related to the result list. These recommendations are extracted
by querying all related entities of the resources in the combined result list from the
semantic database. For each of these related resources the most specific concept is
extracted. The result is a set of concepts with associated resources that are related to
the search result list. These concepts are ordered according to the number of related
resources. So each recommendation is a concept with a set of associated resources
that are related to the search result list.

For our visualization approach we implemented the described search procedure
as a web service using the DBpedia SPARQL-Endpoint. Besides the access to the
semantics, the system also requires an indexed search for retrieving the result lists.
For our prototype we used the DBpedia Lookup Service[2] that ranks the results according to the number of references (refCount). In the following section we describe
how the results of the semantic search procedure are presented to the user and how
the visualization interacts with the search system.

## 7.4 Visualizing Semantic Search Results

Our visualization approach for representing search results in semantic domains is
based on the semantics visualization framework SemaVis[3] (Nazemi et al. 2013).
The Framework includes several aspect-oriented visualization techniques (e.g. sunburst visualizations (Stab et al. 2010b), timelines (Stab et al. 2010a), map-based approaches (Nazemi et al. 2009), etc.) that can be combined to an application-specific
visualization cockpit to represent different aspects of the underlying data (Nazemi
et al. 2010). Several data providers for common semantic file formats and service
APIs, a modular representation model for adapting the visual appearance (Nazemi
et al. 2011) as well as a script-based configuration language called *Semantics Visualization Markup Language* (SVML) (Nazemi et al. 2013) are also included in
the framework. In the following, we will first describe the basic concepts of the
visualization component before introducing the details in succeeding sections.

The approach for visualizing semantic search results distinguishes between two
different node types: (1) *Term Nodes* and (2) *Result Nodes*. Each node type is treated
by different layout algorithms in the visualization and used to represent different
information:

---

[2]For the prototype we use the DBpedia lookup service that is available at http://wiki.dbpedia.org/
lookup/.

[3]SemaVis Framework: http://www.semavis.net.

- *Term Nodes* represent the terms recognized by the described search process. These nodes are placed by a concentric layout algorithm at the startup of the visualization. Users are also able to freely move and order them on the surface according to their individual preferences.
- *Result Nodes* represent the hits in the combined result list that are found for the given user query. These nodes are visually connected to related term nodes with directed edges and are treated by a force-based layout algorithm according to their weights to the surrounding term nodes.

The placement of the result nodes in the center of the visualization is done by a force-based layout algorithm. The algorithm positions nodes in a two-dimensional space by assigning different forces to the edges and the nodes of a graph. These forces are adapted during the layout process in an iterative simulation until the physical system reaches a mechanical equilibrium. Due to this layout technique, the overlapping of nodes and edges is prevented as far as possible and an aesthetical layout of the graph is achieved. Another interesting characteristic of force-based layout methods is that the forces between the nodes can be weighted with different similarity values. As a result of the weighting, different distances between the nodes are derived and the placement of the nodes is affected. To exploit this feature we assign different values to the visualized result nodes and their edges and utilize a model based on the weights emerged during the semantic retrieval process. In the representation, a result node is then placed nearer to similar term nodes and further away from terms that are less related to it. So the placement of the result nodes indicates the relevance of the results to the surrounding terms and users are able to distinguish different characteristics of retrieved hits.

Figure 7.2 shows an example of the visualization approach[4] for the query term "apple computer steve jobs". The query analysis stage of the search process identified the six terms "apple computer", "steve jobs", "apple", "computer", "steve" and "jobs" and for 4 of these terms the most specific concepts "company", "person", "plant" and "given name". Each of these identified terms is represented in a term node and the retrieved result nodes are attached to them using the weights identified during the relation extraction step. In the next section, we describe how this visualization metaphor can be used for providing more transparency in search processing and how it can be utilized for fostering search result comprehension.

## 7.4.1 *Query-Result-Relations*

Semantic technologies enable information retrieval systems to "understand" on the one hand the query terms given by the user (Sect. 7.3) and on the other hand different properties of the underlying resources. Based on the occurrences of the query terms

---

[4]A version using the DBpedia database and the described search processing is available at http://semanticsearch.semavis.net.

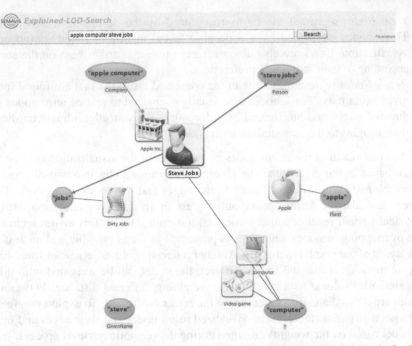

**Fig. 7.2** Semantic search result visualization presenting the six most relevant search results for the query "apple computer steve jobs". Each result is attached between the terms recognized during the semantic query analysis and according to the retrieved query-result-relations

either in the content, in the semantic properties or even in the semantic neighborhood, the underlying resources are filtered and ranked using information retrieval methods for presenting the result resource to the end user. In this process semantic information improves the retrieval process by providing an extended feature space for each resource as well as by offering methods for disambiguating and interpreting the query terms given by the user. However, the semantic information utilized during the retrieval process remains in most cases hidden from the user though it provides useful feedback about the reasons the results were retrieved. For example the query term "ford" might be interpreted as the name-property of a car manufacturer, as the surname-property of the famous inventor or the title-property of an activity for crossing rivers. Each of these interpretations will deliver a completely different result set. So it is not sufficient to only present the relations between recognized query terms and results, but it is also necessary to point out the semantic interpretation of the given query terms to allow an unambiguous assessment of retrieved results.

To meet these demands and to provide an adequate tool that allows users to unambiguously determine the most relevant result for their individual search, our approach visualizes both query-result-relations and the interpreted semantic meaning of query terms. Therefore, each term of the given query is presented in a term node of the visualization. The interpreted semantic meaning emerged during search

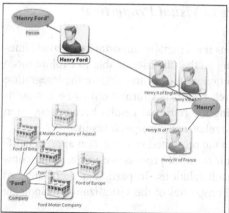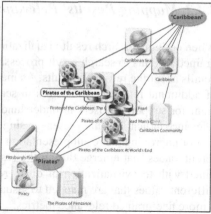

**Fig. 7.3** *Left*: The visualization of query-result-relations reveals that only one of the ten results is related to the requested person name. *Right*: The visual representation of the results avoids mistakes in result assessment tasks

processing (the label of the most specific concept) is visible in the label of the term node. So for every possible interpretation a new node is created that represents the query term and its retrieved interpretation. The relations between search results and the term nodes are depicted as directed and weighted edges between term nodes and result nodes. As mentioned above, the weighting of a query-result-relation is derived according to the rank of the result in the individual result list. As consequence of this weighting, the results are placed nearer to more relevant entities and term nodes respectively.

Figure 7.3 shows two examples of the visualization approach representing two different queries and in each case the first ten hits of the result set. For the sake of clarity, we limited the number of simultaneously visible results to a fixed number and added common paging functions for switching between pages. The left example shows the visualization of the results for the query "Henry Ford" where the term "Henry Ford" is identified as person and the term "Ford" as company. Additionally, the term "Henry" is recognized by the query analysis step of the search processing but there is no specific type other than owl:Thing available. So the type for this query part is not evident. However, the visualization of the results reveals that only one of the results is related to the queried person whereas other results are related to the recognized company (Fig. 7.3 left).

The second example shows the visualization of the results for the query "Pirates of the Caribbean" (Fig. 7.3 right). For the given query the system identifies two entities "Pirates" and "Caribbean". By visualizing the connections between search results and query terms, users are able to recognize the four movies that are related to both search terms.

## 7.4.2  Mapping Results' Relevance to Visual Properties

When designing search result visualizations it is crucially important to provide fine-grained insights to search result processing so that the user is able to explore more details about the retrieved results. As mentioned in the introduction, the integration of additional relevance indicators in search result lists turned out to be not sufficient for supporting users in understanding the retrieved results because common relevance indicators only presents a single relevance per search result.

For improving the result presentation in the presented visualization approach different values that emerge during the result retrieval process are utilized and combined with the visualization of query-result-relations. In particular there are two different values that are mapped to visual properties of the visualization to indicate a more fine-grained relevance metrics:

- *Relation Weights* indicate the relevance between a query term and a retrieved search result. These weights are the result of the relation extraction step described in Sect. 7.3. With respect to the presented visualization, these weights correspond to a relevance metric between the result nodes and related term nodes.
- *Result Rank* indicates the overall relevance of a search result according to the given query. The result rank is equivalent to the rank identified during the result combination step of the described search process.

In order to make the optimum use of these values, each of them is mapped to specific visual properties like length, color and size that can be preattentively perceived (Ward et al. 2010). Thanks to the characteristic of preattentive perception, these relevance indicators can be perceived faster and easier by the users compared to common indicators that are often represented as textual percentages. To take these advantages, the result rank is used to adjust the size and the intensity of the result nodes. Thereby the resource that has the highest overall rank for a specific search query is presented most conspicuous whereas resources with minor rank are visualized less notable (Fig. 7.2). On the other hand the relation weights are used to adapt the weighting of edges between results and term nodes. This results in different lengths of the visible connections and indicates the relevance between specific query terms and search results.

## 7.4.3  Visual Support for Query Evolution

A search process of common users includes various search requests and queries until the needed information is found. Usually such a process starts with a general query that is revised in consecutive search queries until some resources for further exploration are found in the result set. This kind of search strategy was also revealed in several studies which showed that it is a common strategy for the user to first issue a general query, then review a few results, and if the desired information is not found, to reformulate or to enhance the query (Hearst 2009; Jansen et al. 2005, 2007). To support this behavior of common users when searching for information in query-based information retrieval systems, we integrated several features that enable users to interactively change their queries in the visualization.

In the presented visualization approach the query terms of the user are visualized in term nodes that are arranged in a circular form around the result nodes. According to this characteristic, the state of these visible term nodes and the included terms reflect the current search intention of the user. Transferred to the visualization approach, the before mentioned strategy of query evolution corresponds to a substitution, reassignment, creation or removal of term nodes. Hence, the change of the current state of the term nodes results in a new search condition that in turn changes the visible result set or the visible relations between result and term nodes. On the one hand, the creation of further terms defines a more specific search condition and on the other hand, the removal of term nodes results in wider-ranged search spaces. In contrast to commonly used search user interfaces, the influence of changing search conditions is immediately visible in the visualization. The representation of query-result-relations reveals which of the current search results fulfill new conditions (Fig. 7.4) and provides an immediate visual feedback of the users' query evolution.

To ensure that users are aware of additional terms and resources respectively, the visualization also represents the recommendations retrieved by the semantic search process for supporting users in finding needed information. These recommendations are visualized as additional term nodes that are labeled with a question mark to encourage users to instantiate them for narrowing their search. The size of the recommended term nodes is mapped to their influence to the current result set. So term nodes whose instantiation will cause major changes of the result set are represented larger than term nodes whose instantiation will only affect smaller parts. By selecting a specific recommendation, users are able to select different resources for instantiating the term node and narrowing their retrieved results (Fig. 7.4).

## 7.5  Evaluation of the Visualization Approach

For assessing the effectiveness of the presented approach we performed a user study in which we compared the visualization approach with a common list view that includes the identical information for each result resource. The main focus of the evaluation was to answer the question whether the presented visualization approach can support users in assessing search results and if our approach satisfies the needs of searchers. For verifying our assumption we investigated the task completion time and formulated the following hypothesis:

- *H1: There is a difference in task completion time between the list view and the visualization in assessing search results.*

In addition to the task completion time we considered several subjective criteria that were collected with additional questionnaires for each task and participants. In

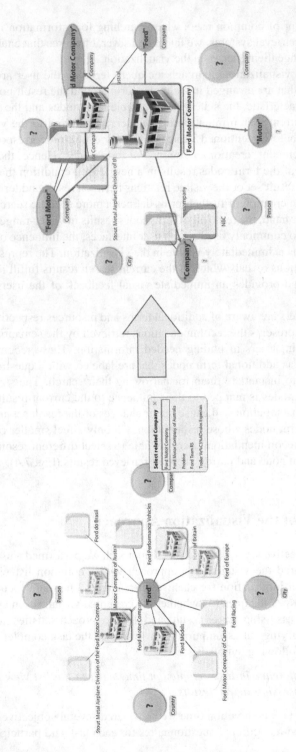

**Fig. 7.4** The recommendation of additional terms supports users in their common search strategy and provides a visual tool for query evolution and narrowing search results. The impact of query changes is immediately visible in the visualization

particular, we captured the user satisfaction and the following three additional items for getting an impression of the user experience:

- *Q1: With the help of the system, I was able to quickly and effectively solve the given task.*
- *Q2: The system presented the information needed for answering the question clear and unambiguous.*
- *Q3: Would you use the system in the future for similar search tasks?*

Each of these items was rated by the participants on a five point Likert scale from 1 (strongly disagree) to 5 (strongly agree).

### 7.5.1 Experimental Design

According to the hypothesis that contains one independent variable with two different conditions (list view and visualization) the design of our experiment is based on a basic design (Lazar et al. 2010). Additionally, we decided to use a within-group design for our experiment where each participant accomplishes the given tasks in each condition (in this case the different user interfaces). In contrast to between-group designed experiments, in within-group designs less participants are needed and individual differences between the participants are isolated more effectively (Lazar et al. 2010). Possible learn effects when switching between conditions are controlled by a systematic randomization of condition- and task-ordering. Furthermore, participants were advised to disregard the knowledge from previous conditions and to explicitly show the solution of tasks by means of elements in the user interface.

Altogether, the experiment contains three tasks that had to be accomplished from every participant with both conditions (list view and visualization). Because the focus of the evaluation is the comparison of two different user interfaces and not the investigation of the whole search process, we were able to pre-assign the query terms for every task. So every participant retrieves the same results for every task and thus also the same visual representation and the evaluation outcome is not influenced by other factors.

In the first task participants had to identify the relations between each search result and the recognized terms of the given query. The second task was of the same type as the first task with the difference that the result set contains more complex relations. In the third task participants had to identify the most relevant item for a specific search situation. To ensure that the solution could be found in each condition, we performed several pretests. We also ensured that each participant gets the same visual presentation for each task and condition. The time limit for each task was set to three minutes. If a wrong answer was given or a participant could not solve a task, the completion time of the task was also set to three minutes.

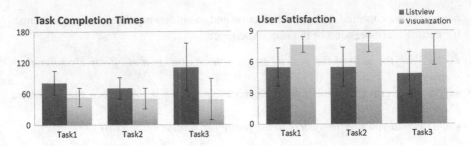

**Fig. 7.5** Task completion time and user satisfaction

## 7.5.2 Procedure

17 participants, mainly graduates and students attended the evaluation. The participants were between 24 and 29 years old and mainly involved in computer science (M = 4.65; SD = 0.6).[5] After a general introduction to the user study and an explanation of the procedure and tasks, participants got a brief introduction to both systems in systematically randomized ordering. Both systems were queried with a reference query and participants had the chance to ask questions about the systems. After each task, participants had to rate their overall satisfaction with the system on a scale from 1 to 9 and the three before mentioned items concerning their subjective opinion about the system on a Likert scale from 1 (strongly disagree) to 5 (strongly agree). After participants had completed all tasks, they had to answer a brief demographic questionnaire.

## 7.5.3 Results

Figure 7.5 shows the average task completion times for each of the three tasks and both conditions. The direct comparison of the average task completion times reveals that participants performed better with our visualization approach (avg($t$) = 51.3 s; SD = 25.8) compared to the list view (avg($t$) = 88.1 s; SD = 30.1).

A paired-samples t-test also suggests that there is a significant difference in the task completion time between the group who used the list view and the group who used our visualization approach ($t(50) = 7.8028$, $p < 0.05$). Hence, the null hypothesis is refuted and the alternative hypothesis confirmed. The comparison of means also indicates that users performed significantly faster with the visualization approach compared to the list presentation. So we can proceed from the assumption that visualizing search results taking semantic information into account has a positive effect on the efficiency when assessing the relevance of search results.

---

[5]Measured on a five point scale (5 = very much experience; 1 = very little experience) in the demographic part of the questionnaire.

**Table 7.1** Results of the
subjective ratings indicate
that users prefer the
visualization approach

| Presentation | Q1 | Q2 | Q3 |
|---|---|---|---|
| Visualization | 4.33 | 4.37 | 4.25 |
| Listview | 3.15 | 3.03 | 3.14 |

The evaluation of satisfaction ratings indicates that participants feel more comfortable with our visualization approach instead of the commonly used list view. The list view obtained an average rating of 5.31 with a standard deviation of 1.91 whereas the visualization obtained an average rating of 7.57 and a standard deviation of 1.10. Additionally, the result of the subjective ratings (Table 7.1) and in particular question "Would you use the system in the future for similar search tasks?" confirms the assumption that users prefer the visualization to the list presentation (list: M = 3.14; SD = 0.87; visualization: M = 4.25; SD = 0.77).

## 7.6  Visualizations and Linked Data in the Policy Modeling Process

Retrieving and accessing information is a challenging task and crucially important in many different domains. This is especially true in the area of policy modeling where decisions impact humans, economy or environment. The creation of novel policies is a very complex task that requires several process steps (Macintosh 2004) to ensure validity and positive effects. It is easy to imagine that an insufficient analysis of the underlying problem and the consideration of all impact factors will result in a policy that fails the intended goals. Accurate decision making in this domain not only requires the consideration of diverse impact factors but also the inclusion of increasingly complex and dynamic scenarios. For improving this process and the quality of the achieved policies respectively, recent initiatives, like Open Government Data or Linked Government Data aim at publishing and interlinking vast amounts of data for enabling accurate decision support and innovative ICT solutions for fostering political decision making. However, the amount of available data that contains implicit and hidden information relevant for specific policy decisions and scenarios continuously increases and the access gets more and more complicated.

To improve the retrieval tools, not only the interlinking of open administrative data gains enormous importance for policy modeling but also the development of novel result presentations and exploration tools. Present systems for searching and accessing this information are currently limited to textual result presentations and require comprehensive knowledge about the domain for finding the information that fits to the specific case. Approaches, like the presented visualization technique, will on the one hand provide a homogeneous access for distributed and interlinked data and on the other hand enable political decision makers to identify unknown and hidden information. In particular during the information foraging step of the policy modeling process (Kohlhammer et al. 2012), visualization techniques will enable an optimal analysis of the need for a policy and accurate assessment of issues relevant to a specific scenario. In order to further develop this idea, we investigate different visualization approaches along each step of the policy modeling process in the European project FUPOL 287119: Future Policy Modeling, partially supported by the European Commission. The FUPOL project proposes a comprehensive and new governance model to support the policy design lifecycle. The innovations are driven by the demand of citizens and political decision makers to support the policy domains in urban regions with appropriate ICT technologies.

# References

Auer, S., Bizer, C., Kobilarov, G., Lehmann, J., Cyganiak, R., & Ives, Z. (2007). DBpedia: a nucleus for a web of open data. In *Proceedings of the 6th international semantic web and 2nd Asian semantic web conference*, ISWC'07/ASWC'07, Busan, Korea (pp. 722–735).

Aula, A. (2004). Enhancing the readability of search result summaries. In *Proceedings of HCI 2004, the 18th British HCI group annual conference* (Vol. 2, pp. 1–4).

Cutrell, E., Robbins, D., Dumais, S., & Sarin, R. (2006). Fast, flexible filtering with phlat. In *Proceedings of the SIGCHI conference on human factors in computing systems*, CHI '06, Montreal, Quebec, Canada (pp. 261–270).

Ding, L., DiFranzo, D., Graves, A., Michaelis, J. R., Li, X., McGuinness, D. L., & Hendler, J. A. (2010). TWC data-gov corpus: incrementally generating linked government data from data.gov. In *Proceedings of the 19th international conference on world wide web*, WWW '10. Raleigh, North Carolina, USA (pp. 1383–1386).

Fernandez, M., Lopez, V., Sabou, M., Uren, V., Vallet, D., Motta, E., & Castells, P. (2008). Semantic search meets the web. In *2008 IEEE international conference on semantic computing* (pp. 253–260).

Hearst, M. A. (2009). *Search user interfaces* (1st ed.). New York: Cambridge University Press.

Hearst, M. A., Divoli, A., Guturu, H., Ksikes, A., Nakov, P., Wooldridge, M. A., & Ye, J. (2007). BioText search engine: beyond abstract search. *Bioinformatics*, 23(16), 2196–2197.

Heim, P., Lohmann, S., & Stegemann, T. (2010). Interactive relationship discovery via the semantic web. In *Proceedings of the 7th international conference on the semantic web: research and applications, Part I*, ESWC'10. Heraklion, Crete, Greece (pp. 303–317).

Hoffman, P., Grinstein, G., Marx, K., Grosse, I., & Stanley, E. (1997). DNA visual and analytic data mining. In *Visualization '97, proceedings* (pp. 437–441).

Jansen, B. J., Spink, A., & Pedersen, J. (2005). A temporal comparison of AltaVista web searching: research articles. *Journal of the American Society for Information Science and Technology*, 56(6), 559–570.

Jansen, B. J., Spink, A., & Koshman, S. (2007). Web searcher interaction with the dogpile.com metasearch engine. *Journal of the American Society for Information Science and Technology*, 58(5), 744–755.

Kohlhammer, J., Nazemi, K., Ruppert, T., & Burkhardt, D. (2012). Toward visualization in policy modeling. *IEEE Computer Graphics and Applications*, 32(5), 84–89.

Lazar, J., Feng, J. H., & Hochheiser, H. (2010). *Research methods in human-computer interaction*. New York: Wiley.

Macintosh, A. (2004). Characterizing e-participation in policy-making. In *Proceedings of the 37th annual Hawaii international conference on system sciences, 2004*.

Nazemi, K., Breyer, M., & Hornung, C. (2009). SEMAP: a concept for the visualization of semantics as maps. In C. Stephanidis (Ed.), *Lecture notes in computer science*: Vol. 7. *HCI* (pp. 83–91). Berlin: Springer.

Nazemi, K., Breyer, M., Burkhardt, D., & Fellner, D. W. (2010). Visualization cockpit: orchestration of multiple visualizations for knowledge-exploration. *International Journal of Advanced Corporate Learning*, *3*(4), 26–34.

Nazemi, K., Stab, C., & Kuijper, A. (2011). A reference model for adaptive visualization systems. In *Proceedings of the 14th international conference on human-computer interaction: design and development approaches, Part I*, HCII'11. Orlando, FL (pp. 480–489).

Nazemi, K., Breyer, M., Burkhardt, D., Stab, C., & Kohlhammer, J. (2013). SemaVis—a new approach for visualizing semantic information. *Towards the internet of services: the Theseus project*.

Nguyen, T., & Zhang, J. (2006). A novel visualization model for web search results. *IEEE Transactions on Visualization and Computer Graphics*, *12*(5), 981–988.

Paulheim, H., & Fümkranz, J. (2012). Unsupervised generation of data mining features from linked open data. In *Proceedings of the 2nd international conference on web intelligence, mining and semantics*, WIMS '12 (pp. 31:1–31:12).

Schenk, S., Saathoff, C., Staab, S., & Scherp, A. (2009). SemaPlorer—interactive semantic exploration of data and media based on a federated cloud infrastructure. *Journal of Web Semantics*, *7*(4), 298–304.

Shadbolt, N., Berners-Lee, T., & Hall, W. (2006). The semantic web revisited. *IEEE Intelligent Systems*, *21*(3), 96–101.

Stab, C., Nazemi, K., & Fellner, D. W. (2010a). SemaTime—timeline visualization of time-dependent relations and semantics. In *Proceedings of the 6th international conference on advances in visual computing, Part III*, ISVC'10. Las Vegas, NV, USA (pp. 514–523).

Stab, C., Breyer, M., Nazemi, K., Burkhardt, D., Hofmann, C. E., & Fellner, D. W. (2010b). SemaSun: visualization of semantic knowledge based on an improved sunburst visualization metaphor. In *ED-media 2010* (pp. 911–919). Chesapeake: AACE.

Stoyanovich, J., Lodha, M., Mee, W., & Ross, K. A. (2011). SkylineSearch: semantic ranking and result visualization for PubMed. In *Proceedings of the 2011 ACM SIGMOD international conference on management of data*, SIGMOD '11. Athens, Greece (pp. 1247–1250).

Ward, M., Grinstein, G., & Keim, D. (2010). *Interactive data visualization: foundations, techniques, and applications*. Natick: AK Peters.

White, R. W., Bilenko, M., & Cucerzan, S. (2007). Studying the use of popular destinations to enhance web search interaction. In *Proceedings of the 30th annual international ACM SIGIR conference on research and development in information retrieval*, SIGIR '07. Amsterdam, The Netherlands (pp. 159–166).

Wood, D. (2011). *Linking government data*. New York, Dordrecht, Heidelberg, London: Springer.

# Chapter 8
# A Context-Aware Shopping Portal Based on Semantic Models

Tim Hussein, Timm Linder, and Jürgen Ziegler

**Abstract** This chapter illustrates how semantic models can be used as a backend data source for both exploration and adaptation purposes. For a fictitious shopping portal, we implemented a faceted navigation approach that provides means for exploring the portal's content manually. In addition to that, we implemented an adaptation mechanism based on spreading activation that also exploits the semantic structure of the underlying data.

## 8.1 Introduction

The overwhelming amount of information contained in large web applications, such as online shops or news portals, can make these systems difficult to use. Finding the appropriate content within the flood of data can be challenging and may eventually even cause a user to reject the web application. Various approaches have been proposed to overcome these problems by using recommendation techniques for content adaptation, each with its particular advantages and drawbacks. In this chapter, we present Discovr, the prototype of a fictitious context-aware shopping portal based on semantic models. We show how a context-aware recommendation algorithm based on spreading activation can be used to adapt the web site to the user's situation and interest. In addition to that, we demonstrate how these models can also be used to automatically create widgets for manually navigating the content.

We start this chapter by giving a short overview of recent research in the areas of exploration and recommendation in Sect. 8.2, including content-based recommendation algorithms based upon semantic models like spreading activation-based approaches. After that, we introduce Discovr in Sect. 8.3 and explain in detail how

T. Hussein (✉) · T. Linder · J. Ziegler
University of Duisburg-Essen, Duisburg, Germany
e-mail: tim.hussein@uni-due.de

T. Linder
e-mail: timm.linder@uni-due.de

J. Ziegler
e-mail: juergen.ziegler@uni-due.de

T. Hussein et al. (eds.), *Semantic Models for Adaptive Interactive Systems*,
Human–Computer Interaction Series, DOI 10.1007/978-1-4471-5301-6_8,
© Springer-Verlag London 2013

context, products and users are modeled and how these models can be used for navigation purposes (Sect. 8.4). In addition to that, we illustrate how these models can be exploited for adaptation purposes (8.5). Finally, Sect. 8.6 summarizes our contributions in this chapter, and shortly discusses future plans for enhancement.

## 8.2 Exploration and Recommendation of Content

A major challenge of large web applications is to help the user find interesting content fast and with little effort. Often, the information flood is just overwhelming for the user—especially in environments with lots of items to choose from (which is very typical for online e-commerce portals or news sites). There are several ways to overcome this problem, each with its own benefits and drawbacks. This is usually done by either providing means for manual exploration or adapting the content automatically to his or her needs.

*Faceted browsing* is an approach of navigating structured data that has recently gained much attention (Yee et al. 2003). The basic idea is to filter items by attributes (e.g. shoes by size and color). If the items that are supposed to be explored can be classified by certain characteristic features, faceted browsing is a suitable way of narrowing alternatives. This is especially useful if the user does not look for a particular item, but for alternatives meeting certain requirements.

Adaptation, on the other hand, is often realized with the help of recommender systems (Ricci et al. 2010). A recommender system can be defined as a software system that attempts to identify a subset of items from a—typically large—information space that meet a user's interests and preferences best among all alternatives, and which subsequently presents those items to the user in a suitable manner. Formal definitions specifying this view more precisely can be found in, for instance (Adomavicius and Tuzhilin 2005). Recommender systems can be found in entirely different areas of application, such as e-commerce (Linden et al. 2003), education (Manouselis et al. 2010), news (Li et al. 2010), media libraries (Davidson et al. 2010), or social networks (Freyne et al. 2010).

### 8.2.1 Exploration Techniques

A relatively novel approach of navigating structured data is called faceted browsing (Plaisant et al. 1999; Gibbins et al. 2003). The basic idea is, to filter items by their attributes (e.g. shoes by size and color). If the items that are supposed to be explored can be classified by certain characteristic features, faceted browsing is a suitable way of narrowing alternatives. This is especially useful, if the user does not look for a particular item, but for alternatives meeting certain requirements.

Based on the facet theory (Ranganathan 1962), the information space is partitioned using conceptual dimensions of the data. Faceted browsing is used to narrow the search space gradually by means of so called facets, until the user finds what he or she is looking for. This theoretical concept has been adopted to the semantic web scenarios in the last years: There have been various approaches of browsing semantic data sets modeled in OWL or RDF (Yee et al. 2003; Quan et al. 2003; Hildebrand et al. 2006; Heim et al. 2008) by using facets.

Each facet is able to filter the relevant items in a different way (Oren et al. 2006). An important advantage of facets is the flexible exploration of the data space from various entry points reflecting the features of the items. The user does not have to know the underlying structure or the objects itself. Instead, he uses the navigation structure automatically generated from the objects and is able to narrow the search space until he finds what he is looking for. As a convenient side effect, the user implicitly learns about the items' features, which might help him to find them even more efficiently in the future.

In order to classify objects, we need some kind of metadata about them. Usually, the objects features are used for that purpose. We want to illustrate this technique by using the example of an electronic product catalog for books, CDs, DVDs, and other items. Each of these products can be described in a certain manner: A book has specific features such as title, author, publisher, year of publication and more. In this fashion, other products can be classified as well: DVDs by using actors, directors, and so on. These features then can be grouped to categories such as author, title, publisher, etc., which are used as facets. The user can use an arbitrary facet as the entry point for the navigation. After he or she selects a certain facet, for instance author, all possible values are listed for filtering the items. In this case, all authors of all books would be displayed.

### 8.2.2 Recommender Systems

Having their roots in various disciplines such as cognitive science (Rich 1979) and information retrieval (Salton and Buckley 1988), recommender systems have been established as an independent research area during the 1990s. Most techniques can be roughly divided into content-based (Mooney and Roy 2000), collaboration-based (Goldberg et al. 1992; Resnick et al. 1994) and hybrid approaches (Claypool et al. 1999; Burke 2002). Content-based (CB) systems incorporate features associated to the objects of interest. User ratings or transactions can be analyzed in order to find out his or her interests, to recommend items similar to those bought in the past or rated as positive. Neural networks, decision trees and vector-based representations can be used for that purpose for instance.

Collaborative filtering (CF) methods are probably the most widely implemented ones. They can be partitioned into classical user-based CF and Item-based CF. User-based techniques generate recommendations for a user by first identifying other users with similar purchase or rating patterns. These users are usually called "mentors" or "neighbors". Items that have been purchased or rated very positively by the mentors are then advertised as recommendations. These computations may be time-consuming and are often inappropriate for real-time recommendations with massive data sets and tens of millions of customers. Depending on the number of users and items that are supposed to use the system, item-based CF techniques (Sarwar et al. 2001; Linden et al. 2003) may be more appropriate in certain cases. For each product, a list of similar items is pre-computed regularly based on which products users tend to purchase together.

Different recommendation approaches are often combined into so called hybrid recommender systems (which may also incorporate information like social or demographic data for instance). The majority of hybrid recommender systems use collaborative filtering as the core method while content-based filtering offers solutions to the shortcomings of CF (Balabanovic and Shoham 1997; Pazzani 1999; Han and Karypis 2005). A systematic approach for classifying hybrid recommenders has been taken by Burke (2002, 2007). He identifies the following recurring patterns for hybrid recommendation generation.

### 8.2.3 Context-Aware Recommendations

Most recommender systems base their results only on the user and his or her interests independently of the usage context, which is sufficient in many cases. There are, however, situations in which including contextual information can be beneficial for producing meaningful recommendations. For instance, a tourist guide only based on user preferences might suggest outdoor venues even when it is raining. Examples like this create the motivation for investigating *context-aware recommender systems* (Adomavicius et al. 2005; Adomavicius and Tuzhilin 2010; Kaminskas and Ricci 2011). A typical field of application for context-aware recommendations are mobile guides (Abowd et al. 1997; Carmagnola et al. 2008). However, factors such as mood, company of other people, daytime, season, upcoming holidays, or others may be used for recommendation generation as well.

Context-aware recommending may also be influenced by factors that are not directly observable such as the user's task (although not all authors use the term *context* in this case). One of the first approaches that takes user tasks into consideration has been proposed by Herlocker and Konstan (2001). They use *task profiles* either specified manually or derived from user behavior to improve the recommendation process. Jin et al. (2005) model the behavior of web users based on task patterns and infer underlying interests or goals from those patterns (Jin et al. 2005). The task context then is exploited during the recommendation process. Anand and Mobasher (2007) suggest deriving contextual cues from a user's long-term profile that is generated from interaction (Anand and Mobasher 2007).

Different approaches have been proposed to address context-awareness in recommender systems. So-called "item-splitting" approaches have been presented by Baltrunas and Ricci (2013). The underlying idea is to record and incorporate the circumstances under which items are rated. If a certain item is rated significantly different under different contextual circumstances, it is split into virtual items that take the particular context into account. The modified 2-dimensional matrix can then be used as a basis for collaborative filtering. Finally, the recommendations are derived from the item ratings under the given context. Hussein et al. (2013) introduce a software framework for hybrid and context-aware recommendation generation (Hussein et al. 2013).[1]

## 8.2.4 Recommender Systems Based on Semantic Models

Recommender systems that use ontologies as a representation for user interests have been introduced, for instance, by Middleton et al. (2004), where the authors present two systems for the recommendation of academic research papers. The papers are divided into ontology classes based upon an existing research paper taxonomy, making it possible to build user interest profiles relating to these classes from browsing and rating behavior. Recommendations for potentially interesting research papers are then generated by ontological inference.

Sieg et al. (2010) use an ontology as the basis for their user profiles. For each user, the concepts in the ontology are weighted based upon the user's recent interests. The learning of new weights occurs via a spreading activation algorithm (explained below). Recommendations are then generated in a collaborative fashion, by comparing the weight vectors of individual users. Kim and Kwon (2007) describe a recommender system for a grocery store, based upon an ontology that is split into four parts: The products, location information (i.e. context), as well as consumers and their shopping records. In Loizou and Dasmahapatra (2006), not only items, user profiles or context are modeled in an ontology, but also different components of the recommender system such as clustering mechanisms or classifiers which can be dynamically selected at runtime. Mobasher et al. augment an item-based CF recommender with semantic attributes that are mined automatically from a web-based ontology, subsequently calculating item similarities as a linear combination of rating and semantic values to alleviate the cold start and new item problems (Mobasher et al. 2004).

## 8.2.5 Recommendations Based on Spreading Activation and Ontologies

The concept of Spreading Activation was first proposed by Collins and Loftus (1975), when they applied the corresponding networks in the fields of psycholinguistics and semantic priming (Anderson 1983). Later, the idea was adopted by computer scientists. The principles have successfully been used in several research areas in computer science, most notably in information retrieval (Cohen and Kjeldsen 1987; Crestani 1997; Berger et al. 2004). Spreading Activation has also been used by Pirolli and Card (1995) in their information foraging theory.

---

[1]The authors of this chapter co-authored that publication as well. Some of the ideas presented in this chapter have already been introduced in there.

**Fig. 8.1** The basic principle
of Spreading Activation:
*node A* receives an initial
activation of 1.0. This
activation is spread to
adjacent nodes with
decreasing activation

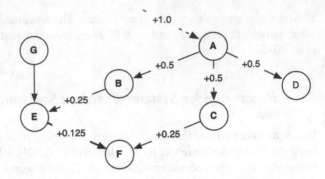

The basic concept behind Spreading Activation is that all relevant information is mapped onto a graph as nodes with a certain activation level. Relations between two concepts are represented by a link between the corresponding nodes. If, for any reason, one or more nodes are activated, their activation level rises and the activation is spread to adjacent nodes (and their neighbors, in turn, and so on) like water flowing through a river bed. While doing so, the flow of activation is reduced the more it strides away from the initially activated node(s). Eventually, several nodes are activated to a certain degree expressing how they semantically related to the concepts originally selected. Figure 8.1 illustrates the basic concept.

## 8.3 The Discovr Portal

We implemented a fictitious shopping and information portal *Discovr* to demonstrate the versatility of semantic models as a backend data source for web portals. Discovr presents information to the user about several hundreds of CDs, DVDs and books, as well as descriptions of concerts and sport events or venues such as restaurants or pubs. The user can browse through the content using a faceted navigation approach. Depending on the user's current context and previous interaction with the system, Discovr recommends potentially interesting items to the user at a number of different places within the portal. Figure 8.2 shows how Discovr looks like. A faceted navigation menu is located on the left side, while several areas display certain items that are supposed to meet the user's interests in the context at hand.

### 8.3.1 User, Product, and Context Modeling

Discovr comprises several semantic RDF/OWL models. First and foremost, all products offered in the shop are modeled in such a fashion. In addition to that, several context dimensions (time, weather, etc.) are modeled semantically as well. At runtime, all these models are aggregated (like the *Linked Data* cloud) and constitute the information backend for Discovr. As an example, Fig. 8.3 shows small excerpts

**Fig. 8.2** Screenshot of the fictitious Discovr shopping and information portal (reprinted from Hussein et al. 2013)

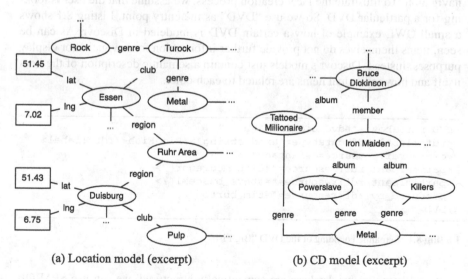

(a) Location model (excerpt)                    (b) CD model (excerpt)

**Fig. 8.3** Two of many models used in Discovr. At system start, the models are aggregated, so that relations across different models can be exploited. "*Metal*", for instance, is a concept that is used in both the location and the CD model

**Fig. 8.4** Facets for DVD
browsing (reprinted from
Hussein and Münter 2010)

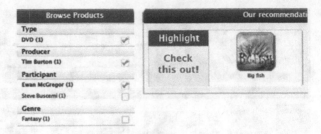

from the location model and the cd model both used in Discovr. In this particular
case, the node "Metal" would be an aggregation point for the models. OWL models
in Discovr are handcrafted, but in principle it is possible to use existing RDF Data
Sets or SPARQL endpoints such as http://www.dbpedia.org.

## 8.4 Exploring the Discovr Portal

In this section, we present a concept for the automated generation of faceted navigation widgets that was implemented in Discovr (Fig. 8.2 on the left or Fig. 8.4).
These navigation widgets are generated on-the-fly depending on the type of data at
hand, and are based upon the models used in Discovr. By applying generic SPARQL
queries, the generation of navigation structures can be made completely independent
from both content and structure of the underlying models.

One advantage of faceted browsing is that it supports multiple entry points for
navigation. To illustrate the facet creation process, we assume that the user is looking for a particular DVD. So we use "DVD" as the entry point. Listing 8.1 shows
a small OWL example of how a certain DVD is modeled in Discovr. As can be
seen, items themselves do not provide further information for navigation or display
purposes; instead, Discovr's models just contain a semantic description of the item
itself and how individual items are related to each other.

```
<DVD rdf:about="#dvd_big_fish">
 <rdfs:label rdf:datatype="&xsd;string"> Big Fish</rdfs:label>
 <genre rdf:resource="#fantasy"/>
 <participant rdf:resource="#ewan_mcgregor"/>
 <participant rdf:resource="#steve_buscemi"/>
 <produced_by rdf:resource="#tim_burton"/>
</DVD>
```

**Listing 8.1** Semantic encoding of the DVD "Big Fish"

As all items in our database are semantically structured, we can use SPARQL
queries to select a certain subset of those items. SPARQL is a SQL-like query language that can be used to filter OWL or RDF data by semantic queries. Listing 8.2

shows a simple example on how to select all DVDs from the entire data set. A query like this would be triggered to start the facet creation process.

```
SELECT DISTINCT ?item WHERE {
  ?item rdf:type domain:DVD .
}
```

**Listing 8.2**  SPARQL query to retrieve all DVDs

Clicking on a certain button or link triggers a filtering of the content—for instance, for retrieving all items of type "DVD". The request is encoded into SPARQL by the server-side back end, and that SPARQL request then gets applied to the underlying semantic model. The result of the query is converted into an HTML representation and delivered to the browser. The underlying process is relatively simple: All relations of all items returned by the query are examined and grouped by type, for instance "Producer" or "Participant", and a facet is created for each type of relation. Of course, most real web shops contain a very large amount of DVDs. This is a typical case where faceted browsing makes sense to further narrow down the results. Here, we can make use of the additional features that are encoded in the RDF data set. In this example, the user can browse a collection of DVDs by filtering by producer, genre, participating actors, etc. Upon each click on a certain element within a facet, the selection is further narrowed down. A typical workflow could look thus like this:

- The user clicks on a (statically predefined) "Browse all DVDs" button.
- This triggers a request like the one shown in Listing 8.2.
- A navigation structure like the one from Fig. 8.4 is created on-the-fly.
- The user can filter the content by selecting one or more options, in this case e.g. by selecting "Tim Burton" as a producer.
- The selected facet items are encoded into a SPARQL query that is then used to narrow down the result set. The process is similar to step 2.
- The original selection (all DVDs) is constrained to only those items that fulfill all conditions: They have to be DVDs and they have to be produced by Tim Burton.
- In a third step, the user could, for instance, select "Ewan McGregor" as an actor that has to appear in the movie, which is another constraint that is treated in the same way as above.
- At any time, the user can release a facet condition to expand the result set again.

In this way, the user is able to explore the item space in many different ways.

## 8.4.1  Widget Decoration

The example illustrated in the previous section entirely used *nominal* data, a form of categorical data where the order of the categories is not significant (Stevens 1946).

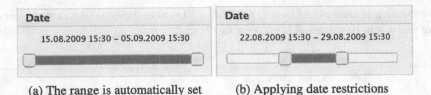

(a) The range is automatically set          (b) Applying date restrictions

**Fig. 8.5** An automatically generated facet for filtering by date. This facet uses a slider instead of a selection box. Depending on the type of data to be displayed, certain navigation widgets are more useful than others

The categories are, for instance "Movies with Ewan McGregor", "Movies with Matt Damon", and so on. A selection box like the one in Fig. 8.4 is a good form of representation. In our case, only the top *n* values are displayed with the option to show the other entries by using a "more"-button (or constraining the option by using other facets). Showing all possible alternatives, however, is not suitable in case of *ordinal* or *interval* data. Figure 8.5 is an example for an automatically generated facet based on dates.

As dates follow a certain order and can be restricted by intervals, a navigation widget using a slider is a better approach to restrict the selection. It therefore makes sense to always choose a meaningful display widget depending on the type of data. Fortunately, we can again use SPARQL for this purpose. Using a query like the one presented in Listing 8.3, the data type can be determined in order to select the appropriate widget as a representation.

```
SELECT DISTINCT ?facetType ?facetLabel
WHERE {
  ?individual rdf:type ?type ;
  ?facetType ?restriction .
  ?facetType rdfs:label ?facetLabel .
}
ORDER BY ?facetType
```

**Listing 8.3** Text

In 8.1, we used only one variable (*?item*). Now, we query the data that we want to create a facet for, and use two variables: *?facetType* and *?facetLabel*. We use the label just for sorting the elements within the facet. The *facetType*, on the other hand, is the key for the widget selection process. This type is expressed as an XML schema data type, such as *xsd:integer*, *xsd:string* or *xsd:date*. With that in mind, a mapping is created for all the possible types of facets to corresponding widget types: For example, string data can be mapped to selection boxes, and date values to slider widgets. We here make use of the *Decorator* design pattern (Gamma et al. 1993) to automatically create a suitable navigation widget that is intuitive to use for that kind of data.

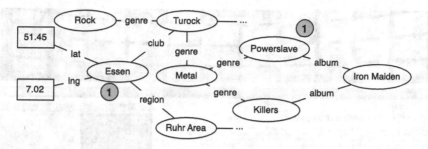

**Fig. 8.6** Individual weights are assigned to the semantic models to reflect the user's situation (reprinted from Hussein and Münter 2010)

## 8.5  Context-Aware Adaptation in Discovr

The semantic data structure that serves as an information backend (see Fig. 8.3) is identical for each user. In Discovr, we assign weights from 0 to 1 to the semantic entities and concepts to reflect the user's current interests and situation at hand. 1 means that a certain entity or concept is important for the user under the current circumstances, 0 means that it is not important. Weights between 0 and 1 indicate importance to a certain degree. If the user, for instance, is located in Duisburg and expresses interest in the album "Powerslave" by clicking on it, we assign 1 to both *Duisburg* and *Powerslave* (see Fig. 8.6).

This allows us to create individual weighted networks for each user that represent his or her personal interests and situation at hand. We will later describe how we use these weights to adapt the web site. While it relatively easy to keep track of the user's interests (simply interpreting each click on an entity as an expression of interest), identifying the user's current context is not so easy.

### 8.5.1  Determining Relevant Context Factors

Discovr uses a set of software-based sensors to identify the user's context at hand. For most context factors, this happens once when the user first accesses the portal. Figure 8.7 shows the home page of the Discovr portal, which displays a selection of the context factors at session start.

For each context factor, a particular *sensor* or *resolver* takes care of identifying its current value. A sensor determines its current value directly, whereas a resolver "post-processes" the output of another sensor or resolver to deduce additional knowledge. An example of a sensor might be a date or time sensor. A component which deduces the next upcoming holiday based upon a previously sensed date and time, possibly also taken a geographical position into account, however, is a resolver according to our definition. Context factors determined by resolvers, in general,

**Fig. 8.7** Home page of Discovr, which gives an overview of the external context factors that were detected at session start (except for date and time, which are updated during each request)

need to be updated once the particular inputs that they depend on have changed.[2] The following types of sensors and resolvers have been implemented in Discovr to showcase this functionality:

- *IP Sensor:* This sensor is particularly important because it provides the input for the following chain of resolvers. The IP address of the current user is extracted from the initial HTTP request, once an HTTP session has started.
- *Geo Resolver:* Determines the user's current geographical coordinates (latitude and longitude) and closest city, by providing the IP address sensed by the IP sensor to an external web service.
- *Time Resolver:* Determines the current time, season, time of day (morning, noon, afternoon, evening, night) and upcoming holidays. Because the time may vary with the user's position, the geo coordinates determined by the Geo resolver are taken into account. The holidays are modeled locally in an OWL model (only for Germany, for demonstration purposes).
- *Weather Resolver:* An external web service provides the current weather at the user's current location.

---

[2]Further information on the sensing mechanism applied in Discovr can be found in a different publication by the authors (Hussein et al. 2013).

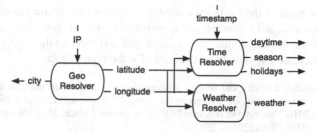

**Fig. 8.8** Resolvers used in Discovr and their respective input and output properties (the Time Resolver needs the user's location in order to correctly determine holidays and seasons: January, for instance is a winter month in Europa but summer in Australia. Upcoming holidays are derived from time and location information, but only for Germany in this use case)

Figure 8.8 depicts the flow of information between the resolvers implemented in Discovr.

### 8.5.2 Spreading-Activation-Based Adaptation

For adapting the web site to reflect the user's situation and interests, we use a spreading activation approach. Whenever a context factor is recognized/updated or a user clicks on a certain entity (a music album for instance), we assign a 1 to the respective node in the semantic model, call this input "activation" and "spread" this activation through the model following the principles illustrated in Fig. 8.1. Applying this approach to the example depicted in Fig. 8.6, the node "Turok", a metal club in Essen receives activation from both the user's location (Essen) as well as from an album, he/she expressed interest in ("Powerslave" by Iron Maiden).

We can use this information to generate context-aware recommendations for the user. In areas that show recommended clubs, we can use SPARQL queries in order to retrieve those clubs with the highest activation for a particular user. This principle can be extended to other types of recommendation as well (movie and music recommendations, events, etc.).

### 8.6 Conclusions

In this chapter we have presented Discovr, a prototype of a fictitious shopping portal, in which both item data (products, events, venues, etc.) and context dimensions are modeled in RDF/OWL. User preferences are expressed by assigning individual weights to the different concepts and instances in the ontology.

Although creating an extensive OWL model for the particular use case can be a time-consuming task, we have shown that these semantic models can successfully be exploited for a number of different purposes. We have discussed how semantic models can be used as the basis for a context-aware recommendation algorithm as well as for automatically generating faceted navigation widgets. This approach is independent from the actual items to be displayed and exploits the type of feature to automatically create a widget that is suitable for the type of data.

**Acknowledgements**   Discovr and several predecessors that have been implemented over the years, have been mentioned in publications by the authors: Hussein and Ziegler 2008, 2010, Hussein and Gaulke 2010, Hussein and Neuhaus 2010, Hussein and Münter 2010, Hussein 2010, Hussein et al. 2007, 2009, 2010a, 2010b, 2013.

# References

Abowd, G. D., Atkeson, C. G., Hong, J., Long, S., Kooper, R., & Pinkerton, M. (1997). Cyberguide: a mobile context-aware tour guide. *Wireless Networks, 3*(5), 421–433.

Adomavicius, G., & Tuzhilin, A. (2005). Toward the next generation of recommender systems: a survey of the state-of-the-art and possible extensions. *IEEE Transactions on Knowledge and Data Engineering, 17*(6), 734–749.

Adomavicius, G., & Tuzhilin, A. (2010). Context-aware recommender systems. In F. Ricci, L. Rokach, B. Shapira & P. B. Kantor (Eds.), *Recommender systems handbook* (pp. 217–253). Berlin: Springer.

Adomavicius, G., Sankaranarayanan, R., Sen, S., & Tuzhilin, A. (2005). Incorporating contextual information in recommender systems using a multidimensional approach. *ACM Transactions on Information Systems, 23*(1), 103–145.

Anand, S., & Mobasher, B. (2007). Contextual recommendation. In B. Berendt, A. Hotho, D. Mladenic & G. Semeraro (Eds.), *From web to social web: discovering and deploying user and content profiles* (pp. 142–160). Berlin: Springer.

Anderson, J. R. (1983). A spreading activation theory of memory. *Journal of Verbal Learning and Verbal Behavior, 22*, 261–295.

Balabanovic, M., & Shoham, Y. (1997). Combining content-based and collaborative recommendation. *Communications of the ACM, 40*, 66–72.

Baltrunas, L., & Ricci, F. (2013). Experimental evaluation of context-dependent collaborative filtering using item splitting. *User Modeling and User-Adapted Interaction*. doi:10.1007/s11257-012-9137-9.

Berger, H., Dittenbach, M., & Merkl, D. (2004). An adaptive information retrieval system based on associative networks. In *APCCM '04: proceedings of the 1st Asian-Pacific conference on conceptual modeling* (pp. 27–36). Darlinghurst: Australian Computer Society.

Burke, R. (2002). Hybrid recommender systems: survey and experiments. *User Modeling and User-Adapted Interaction, 12*(4), 331–370.

Burke, R. (2007). Hybrid web recommender systems. In P. Brusilovsky, A. Kobsa & W. Nejdl (Eds.), *Lecture notes in computer science: Vol. 4321. The adaptive web. Methods and strategies of web personalization* (pp. 377–408). Berlin: Springer.

Carmagnola, F., Cena, F., Console, L., Cortassa, O., Gena, C., Goy, A., et al. (2008). Tag-based user modeling for social multi-device adaptive guides. *User Modeling and User-Adapted Interaction, 18*(5), 497–538.

Claypool, M., Gokhale, A., Miranda, T., Murnikov, P., Netes, D., & Sartin, M. (1999). Combining content-based and collaborative filters in an online newspaper. In *Proceedings of ACM SIGIR workshop on recommender systems*. New York: ACM.

Cohen, P. R., & Kjeldsen, R. (1987). Information retrieval by constrained spreading activation in semantic networks. *Information Processing & Management, 23*(4), 255–268.

Collins, A. M., & Loftus, E. F. (1975). A spreading activation theory of semantic processing. *Psychological Review, 82*(6), 407–428.

Crestani, F. (1997). Application of spreading activation techniques in information retrieval. *Artificial Intelligence Review, 11*(6), 453–482.

Davidson, J., Liebald, B., Liu, J., Nandy, P., van Vleet, T., Gargi, U., et al. (2010). The YouTube video recommendation system. In *RecSys '10: proceedings of the 4th ACM conference on recommender systems* (pp. 293–296). New York: ACM.

Freyne, J., Berkovsky, S., Daly, E. M., & Geyer, W. (2010). Social networking feeds: recommending items of interest. In *RecSys '10: proceedings of the 4th ACM conference on recommender systems* (pp. 277–280). New York: ACM.

Gamma, E., Helm, R., Johnson, R., & Vlissides, J. (1993). Design patterns: abstraction and reuse in object-oriented designs. In *ECOOP '93: proceedings of the 7th European conference on object-oriented programming*. Berlin: Springer.

Gibbins, N., Harris, S., Dix, A., & Schraefel, M. C. (2003). *Electronics and computer science: Vol. 8639. Applying mSpace interfaces to the semantic web*. Southampton: University of Southampton.

Goldberg, D., Nichols, D., Oki, B. M., & Terry, D. (1992). Using collaborative filtering to weave an information tapestry. *Communications of the ACM, 35*(12), 61–70.

Han, E.-H., & Karypis, G. (2005). Feature-based recommendation system. In *CIKM '05: proceedings of the 14th ACM international conference on information and knowledge management* (pp. 446–452). New York: ACM. ISBN: 1-59593-140-6.

Heim, P., Ziegler, J., & Lohmann, S. (2008). Gfacet: a browser for the web of data. In S. Auer, S. Dietzold, S. Lohmann & J. Ziegler (Eds.), *IMC-SSW'08: proceedings of the international workshop on interacting with multimedia content in the social semantic web* (pp. 49–58).

Herlocker, J. L., & Konstan, J. A. (2001). Content-independent task-focused recommendation. *IEEE Internet Computing, 5*(6), 40–47.

Hildebrand, M., van Ossenbruggen, J. R., & Hardman, L. (2006). Gfacet: a browser for heterogeneous semantic web repositories. In *ISWC '06: proceedings of the 5th international semantic web conference* (pp. 272–285). Berlin: Springer.

Hussein, T. (2010). Interfaces and interaction design for learning and simulation environments. In N. Baloian, W. Luther, D. Söffker & Y. Urano (Eds.), *Context-aware recommendations*. Berlin: Logos.

Hussein, T., & Gaulke, W. (2010). Hybride, kontext-sensitive Generierung von Produktempfehlungen. *i-com. Zeitschrift für interaktive und kooperative Medien, 9*(2), 16–23.

Hussein, T., & Münter, D. (2010). Automated generation of a faceted navigation interface using semantic models. In T. Hussein, J. Ziegler, S. Lukosch & A. Dix (Eds.), *SEMAIS '10: proceedings of the 1st workshop on semantic models for adaptive interactive systems*.

Hussein, T., & Neuhaus, S. (2010). Explanation of spreading activation based recommendations. In T. Hussein, J. Ziegler, S. Lukosch & A. Dix (Eds.), *SEMAIS '10: proceedings of 1st workshop on semantic models for adaptive interactive systems*.

Hussein, T., & Ziegler, J. (2008). Adapting web sites by spreading activation in ontologies. *ReColl '08: proceedings of the international workshop on recommendation and collaboration*. New York: ACM.

Hussein, T., & Ziegler, J. (2010). Situationsgerechtes recommending. *Informatik Spektrum, 34*(2), 143–152.

Hussein, T., Westheide, D., & Ziegler, J. (2007). Context-adaptation based on ontologies and spreading activation. In I. Brunkhorst, D. Krause & W. Sitou (Eds.), *Proceedings of ABIS '07: 15th workshop on adaptivity and user modeling in interactive systems*.

Hussein, T., Linder, T., Gaulke, W., & Ziegler, J. (2009). Context-aware recommendations on rails. *CARS ' 09: proceedings of the 1st workshop on context-aware in recommender systems*. New York.

Hussein, T., Linder, T., Gaulke, W., & Ziegler, J. (2010a). A framework and an architecture for context-aware group recommendations. In G. Kolfschoten, T. Herrmann & S. Lukosch (Eds.), *Lecture notes in computer science: Vol. 6257. CRIWG '10: proceedings of the 16th conference on collaboration and technology* (pp. 121–128). Berlin: Springer.

Hussein, T., Gaulke, W., Linder, T., & Ziegler, J. (2010b). Improving collaboration by using context views. In *CAICOLL '10: proceedings of the 1st workshop on context-adaptive interaction for collaborative work.*

Hussein, T., Linder, T., Gaulke, W., & Ziegler, J. (2013). Hybreed: A software framework for developing context-aware hybrid recommender systems. *User Modeling and User-Adapted Interaction.* doi:10.1007/s11257-012-9134-z.

Jin, X., Zhou, Y., & Mobasher, B. (2005). Task-oriented web user modeling for recommendation. In *Lecture notes in computer science: Vol. 3538. UM '05: proceedings of the 10th international conference on user modeling* (pp. 109–118).

Kaminskas, M., & Ricci, F. (2011). Location-adapted music recommendation using tags. In J. A. Konstan, J. L. Marzo, R. Conejo & N. Oliver (Eds.), *UMAP '11: proceedings of the 19th international conference on user modeling, adaptation, and personalization* (pp. 183–194).

Kim, S., & Kwon, J. (2007). Effective context-aware recommendation on the semantic web. *International Journal of Computer Science and Network Security*, 7(8), 154–159.

Li, L., Chu, W., Langford, J., & Schapire, R. E. (2010). A contextual-bandit approach to personalized news article recommendation. In *WWW '10: proceedings of the 19th international conference on world wide web.*

Linden, G., Smith, B., & York, J. (2003). Amazon.com recommendations: item-to-item collaborative filtering. *IEEE Internet Computing*, 7(1), 76–80.

Loizou, A., & Dasmahapatra, S. (2006). Recommender systems for the semantic web. In *ECAI 06: recommender systems workshop.*

Manouselis, N., Drachsler, H., Vuorikari, R., Hummel, H., & Koper, R. (2010). Recommender systems in technology enhanced learning. In F. Ricci, L. Rokach, B. Shapira & P. B. Kantor (Eds.), *Recommender systems handbook* (pp. 387–415). Berlin: Springer.

Middleton, S. E., Shadbolt, N. R., & de Roure, D. C. (2004). Ontological user profiling in recommender systems. *ACM Transactions on Information Systems*, 22(1), 54–88.

Mobasher, B., Jin, X., & Zhou, Y. (2004). Semantically enhanced collaborative filtering on the web. In B. Berendt, A. Hotho, D. Mladenic, M. van Someren Myra Spiliopoulou & G. Stumme (Eds.), *Lecture notes in computer science: Vol. 3209. Web mining: from web to semantic web.* Berlin: Springer.

Mooney, R. J., & Roy, L. (2000). Content-based book recommending using learning for text categorization. In *Proceedings of the 5th ACM conference on digital libraries* (pp. 195–204). New York: ACM. ISBN: 1-58113-231-X.

Oren, E., Delbru, R., & Decker, S. (2006). Extended faceted navigation for RDF data. In *ISWC '06: proceedings of the 5th international semantic web conference* (pp. 559–572).

Pazzani, M. J. (1999). A framework for collaborative, content-based and demographic filtering. *Artificial Intelligence Review*, 13(5–6), 393–408.

Pirolli, P., & Card, S. (1995). Information foraging in information access environments. In I. R. Katz, R. Mack, L. Marks, M. B. Rosson & J. Nielsen (Eds.), *CHI '95: proceedings of the 1995 SIGCHI conference on human factors in computing systems* (pp. 51–58). Denver: ACM.

Plaisant, C., Shneiderman, B., Doan, K., & Bruns, T. (1999). Interface and data architecture for query preview in networked information systems. *ACM Transactions on Information Systems*, 17(3), 320–341.

Quan, D., Huynh, D., & Karger, D. R. (2003). Haystack: a platform for authoring end user semantic web applications. In *ICSW '06: proceedings of the 2nd international semantic web conference* (pp. 738–753). Berlin: Springer.

Ranganathan, S. R. (1962). *Elements of library classification.* Bombay: Asia Publishing House.

Resnick, P., Iacovou, N., Suchak, M., Bergstrom, P., & Riedl, J. (1994). GroupLens: an open architecture for collaborative filtering of netnews. In *CSCW '94: proceedings of the 1994 ACM conference on computer supported cooperative work* (pp. 175–186). New York: ACM. ISBN: 0-89791-689-1.

Ricci, F., Rokach, L., & Shapira, B. (2010). Introduction to recommender systems handbook. In F. Ricci, L. Rokach, B. Shapira & P. B. Kantor (Eds.), *Recommender systems handbook* (pp. 1–35). Berlin: Springer.

Rich, E. (1979). User modeling via stereotypes. *Cognitive Science, 3*(4), 329–354.

Salton, G., & Buckley, C. (1988). On the use of spreading activation methods in automatic information retrieval. In Y. Chiaramella (Ed.), *Proceedings of the 11th annual international ACM SIGIR conference on research and development in information retrieval* (pp. 147–160). New York: ACM.

Sarwar, B., Karypis, G., Konstan, J. A., & Riedl, J. (2001). Item-based collaborative filtering recommendation algorithms. In V. Y. Shen, N. Saito, M. R. Lyu & M. E. Zurko (Eds.), *WWW '11: proceedings of the 10th international conference on world wide web* (pp. 285–295). Hong Kong: ACM. ISBN: 1-58113-348-0.

Sieg, A., Mobasher, B., & Burke, R. (2010). Improving the effectiveness of collaborative recommendation with ontology-based user profiles. In *HetRec '10: proceedings of the 1st international workshop on information heterogeneity and fusion in recommender systems* (pp. 39–46). New York: ACM.

Stevens, S. S. (1946). On the theory of scales of measurement. *Science, 193*(2684), 677–680.

Yee, K.-P., Swearingen, K., Li, K., & Hearst, M. (2003). Faceted metadata for image search and browsing. In *CHI '03: proceedings of the 2003 SIGCHI conference on human factors in computing systems* (pp. 401–408). New York: ACM. ISBN: 1-58113-630-7.

# Chapter 9
# Semantic Models for Interactive Systems: The Case of Tagging and Folksonomies

Steffen Lohmann

**Abstract** Tagging, i.e. the annotation of resources with arbitrary text labels by users, has become a popular indexing method for interactive systems in the last few years. The linked vocabulary resulting from tagging is known as folksonomy and provides a valuable source for the exploration of digital resources. However, the interoperable use of folksonomies and related user interface components requires a consistent and comprehensive domain description. For this purpose, we developed a semantic model that describes the main concepts and relationships in the domain of tagging in a consistent and extensible way. It contributes to a better domain understanding and facilitates the development of interactive systems that use tagging as indexing method. By using the semantic model, folksonomies become independent from individual systems, which increases their interoperability and the reusability of related user interface components.

## 9.1 Introduction

Having its roots in social bookmarking and media sharing, *tagging* has become a popular indexing method in the last few years and can now be found in many interactive systems. In this indexing method, users annotate digital resources with arbitrary text labels, so-called *tags*, in order to organize the resources for themselves and/or others. What is considered a resource depends on the application context. It can be a web page *tagged* with social bookmarking services like Delicious, a photo or video on media sharing websites like Flickr or YouTube, or a mail in an email client. Even digital references of physical objects can be tagged, as long as they are uniquely addressable. For instance, books that are referenced in cataloging websites like LibraryThing or products in online shops like the one of Amazon are also subject to tagging.

In contrast to other keyword-based indexing methods, the people who perform the tagging are not professionals (e.g., authors, publishers, librarians, etc.) but common users. Furthermore, tagging breaks radically with most traditional forms of

S. Lohmann (✉)
University of Stuttgart, Stuttgart, Germany
e-mail: steffen.lohmann@vis.uni-stuttgart.de

T. Hussein et al. (eds.), *Semantic Models for Adaptive Interactive Systems*,
Human–Computer Interaction Series, DOI 10.1007/978-1-4471-5301-6_9,
© Springer-Verlag London 2013

indexing by using neither a controlled vocabulary nor a hierarchical structure for classification. Instead, a tag can be any character string a user considers helpful in organizing a resource. Even though many interactive systems recommend tags, no terms are 'forced' onto users but people are free to use their own vocabulary. This vocabulary of the people along with the many links resulting from tagging has come to be called *folksonomy*.

Tagging and folksonomies have also become popular research topics in the last few years. They have been analyzed and utilized in a number of works, resulting in several interesting findings, for example, on tag use and distribution (Peters 2009). However, they still lack a shared understanding and common conceptualization. Though several models and representations have been proposed (Kim et al. 2008; Lohmann et al. 2011), a consistent and comprehensive description of tagging is still missing. Such a consistent domain description is not only important for a better understanding of tagging and folksonomies but can also improve the interoperability and reusability of interactive systems that use tagging as indexing method. Especially reusable user interface components require a conceptual representation that is independent from individual systems.

In order to close this gap, we developed a semantic model that describes the main concepts and relationships in the domain of tagging. In the following, we present this model and illustrate its benefits for interactive systems. We start with a description of the core concepts and relationships in the domain of tagging and folksonomies in Sect. 9.2. In Sect. 9.4, we present an ontology that implements our semantic model. We illustrate its application by an example scenario in Sect. 9.5 and show how graph visualizations can be derived from it in Sect. 9.6. In Sect. 9.3, we discuss related work before we conclude this chapter in Sect. 9.7.

## 9.2 Concepts and Relationships

In order to create a semantic model for tagging and folksonomies, we first need to identify the core concepts and relationships in the domain. Apart from basic structures and elements, we must also consider related and more advanced concepts.

### 9.2.1 Basic Concepts and Relationships

Tagging consists of three sets of elements that form the basis for the semantic model (Mika 2005; Heymann and Garcia-Molina 2006; Smith 2008; Peters 2009, p. 157):

1. *Resources* that are being tagged. As mentioned in the introduction, these resources can be anything, as long as they are uniquely addressable by the interactive system.
2. *Users* who perform the tagging. In tagging contexts, the term 'user' denotes all people who use an interactive system for tagging, independently of their role and motivation.

3. *Tags* that are associated with the resources. Tags can be common words, slang, abbreviations, emoticons, star-ratings, or even individual text strings that are only meaningful to the person who assigns them, but not for others.

Though these elements are differently named in the literature, their semantics and relationships are always the same: One or more *users* (or people, actors, etc.) annotate *resources* (or objects, instances, etc.) with one or more *tags* (or keywords, labels, etc.). This fundamental principle of tagging can be defined as an axiom, as it has to be true for any folksonomy:

**Axiom 1** *Each tagging links exactly one resource with one user account and one or more tags.*

Apart from that, there are some additional principles that are key to tagging and that can also be defined as axioms:

**Axiom 2** *Each tag can be assigned at most once to each resource by each user account.*

**Axiom 3** *A tag has always exactly one label—otherwise it is not a tag.*

More formally, a semantic model for tagging and folksonomies consists of three finite and disjoint sets $R = \{r_1, r_2, \ldots, r_k\}$, $T = \{t_1, t_2, \ldots, t_l\}$, and $U = \{u_1, u_2, \ldots, u_m\}$ that represent the *resources, tags,* and *users*. They are interconnected by taggings, i.e. the set of annotations $A = \{a_1, a_2, \ldots, a_n\}$ that defines the relationships according to the axioms given above. A basic model for folksonomies can thus be described by the quadruple $F = (R, T, U, A)$ (Hotho et al. 2006; Lohmann and Díaz 2012).

## 9.2.2 Further Concepts and Relationships

However, there is more than the interlinked resources, tags, and users that must be considered in a comprehensive description of the domain of tagging and folksonomies. Another important piece of information is the date and time of tagging. Many interactive systems use this information to display taggings in reverse chronological order, while others enable users to define time intervals when browsing folksonomies (Li et al. 2007). This is why some consider *time* as another core element of folksonomies (Wu et al. 2006; Smith 2008, p. 101).

Others emphasize the source of tagging as an important piece of information (Gruber 2007). This is particularly true with regard to the interoperability of folksonomies: Source information is important if folksonomies leave the borders of one interactive system, for example, to be shared with other systems and/or merged with other folksonomies. In these cases, it may be relevant to know which parts of the folksonomy are from which system.

Examples of further concepts that need to be taken into account are comments added to taggings or hierarchical tag relations, as they can be defined in some interactive systems (e.g. Bibsonomy). Likewise, there can also be links between resources (e.g. hyperlinks) or users (e.g. group links). Though these relationships are not part of the folksonomy itself, they must be taken into account by the conceptualization.

A comprehensive semantic model must also consider more advanced forms of tagging. For instance, some systems (e.g. Flickr or Bibsonomy) support *group tagging* by enabling the creation of a group account that single user accounts can be linked to. Other systems (e.g. Faviki) offer features for *semantic tagging*, where the meaning of tags is disambiguated by linking them to well-defined entities, such as DBpedia resources (Bizer et al. 2009) or Wordnet terms (Miller 1995). Finally, *automatic tagging* denotes tagging with automatic tags, i.e. text labels that are automatically assigned to a resource by the interactive system. Strictly speaking, the latter is not really tagging, as there is no user involved. However, since automatic tagging is an important concept of the domain, it should also be taken into account by the semantic model.

A powerful way to formally describe all this information is an *ontology*. In computer science, an ontology is briefly defined as "an explicit specification of a conceptualization" (Gruber 1993). Ontologies gained much popularity with the rise of the Semantic Web as a way to give information well-defined meaning. They describe the concepts and relationships of a semantic model in a logic-based language that allows for machine interpretation and automated reasoning.

## 9.3 Existing Ontologies

Before starting to develop a new ontology, it is recommended to look for existing ontologies that describe the same or a similar domain and examine if they can reasonably be reused (Noy and McGuinness 2001). In case of tagging and folksonomies, there already exist several ontologies.

Early conceptualizations have been presented by Gruber (2007, 2005), Newman (2005) and Mika (2005). They do a good job in describing the basic concepts and relationships of tagging and folksonomies, as they were defined above. While Gruber's conceptualization is a rather informal description of ideas and Mika's model has only little explicit semantics, the conceptualization of Newman is already a well-defined ontology implemented in the *OWL Web Ontology Language*.

Newman's early ontology was followed by a number of other ontologies in the subsequent years. Table 9.1 lists nine ontologies we found in an extensive survey of the literature and web. It gives the main purpose of the ontologies along with the OWL sublanguage and OWL 2 profile they are compliant with. A detailed discussion of the ontologies can be found in Lohmann et al. (2011). An earlier review of a part of the ontologies is provided by Kim et al. (2008).

**Table 9.1** Related ontologies in the domain of tagging and folksonomies that our semantic model is based on

| Name | Authors | Release date (latest update) | Main purpose | OWL sublanguage | OWL 2 profile |
|------|---------|------------------------------|--------------|-----------------|---------------|
| Tag ontology | Newman et al. | 2005-03-23 (2005-12-21) | First tagging ontology | OWL Full | – |
| Tagging ontology | Kner | 2006 (2007-01-15) | Domain description | OWL Full | – |
| Ontology of folksonomy | Echarte et al. | 2007 (–) | Domain description | OWL DL | – |
| Social semantic cloud of tags | Kim et al. | 2007-03-23 (2008-06-13) | Tag clouds | OWL Full | – |
| Meaning of a tag | Passant & Laublet | 2008-01-15 (–) | Semantic tagging | OWL Full | – |
| Upper tag ontology | Ding et al. | 2008 (–) | Upper ontology | OWL Lite | OWL 2 RL |
| Common tag | Tori et al. | 2009-06-08 (–) | Minimal ontology | OWL Full | – |
| TAGora tagging ontology | Szomszor et al. | 2009 (2010) | Automatic disambiguation | OWL Lite | OWL 2 RL |
| NiceTag ontology | Limpens et al. | 2009-01-09 (2010-09-09) | Taggings as speech acts | OWL Full | – |

Though the ontologies describe many important aspects of tagging, none of them defines all of the aforementioned concepts and relationships needed for a comprehensive domain description. Taking one ontology and extending it is difficult due to various conceptual limitations. An integration and alignment of a part of the ontologies results in similar problems (Lohmann et al. 2011).

Hence, we finally decided to develop a new ontology that takes the best parts of the reviewed ontologies, adds missing pieces and combines all in one consistent conceptualization. To keep the ontology compact and understandable, we decided for a modular approach that separates rare and very specific concepts from the core ontology. Such a separation of concerns is well-known from ontologies and schemata like SIOC (with its access, types, and services modules) or RSS (with its dc, syndication, and content modules).[1] It also helps to keep the core ontology relatively stable with regard to future changes in the domain of tagging and folksonomies.

Certain concepts of the domain, such as the resources that are being tagged or the users who perform the tagging, are already well described in other contexts or more general ontologies. Therefore, we also surveyed ontologies of related domains.

---

[1]Ontologies and schemata are abbreviated by their common namespace prefixes in the following. The namespace prefixes and URIs of all referenced vocabularies are given in Table 9.2 at the end of this chapter.

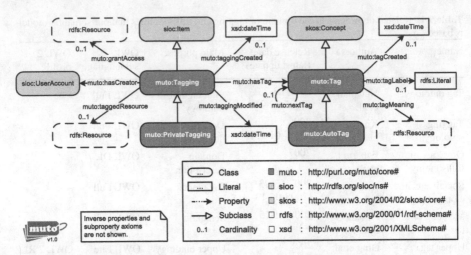

**Fig. 9.1** Core concepts and relationships of the Modular Unified Tagging Ontology (MUTO)

In particular, we considered ontologies that are widely used and investigated, such as SKOS or FOAF, as we can expect their conceptualizations to be comparatively mature and stable.

## 9.4  An Ontology for Tagging and Folksonomies

Based on the previous considerations, we developed the *Modular Unified Tagging Ontology (MUTO)* to formally describe the semantic model. Like the related tagging ontologies listed in Table 9.1, it is implemented in the OWL Web Ontology Language. This language is based on the *Resource Description Framework (RDF)* and closely related to *RDF Schema (RDFS)*. All three languages are recommendations of the *World Wide Web Consortium (W3C)*. With regard to the first version of OWL, MUTO is compliant to the sublanguage OWL Lite; with regard to the second OWL version, it is compliant with the OWL 2 RL profile. This profile fits particularly well in our case, as it is recommended for "relatively lightweight ontologies [that] are used to organize large numbers of individuals" and approaches "where it is useful or necessary to operate directly on data in the form of RDF triples" (W3C OWL Working Group 2012).

We presented an earlier version of MUTO in (Lohmann et al. 2011). In the following, we describe the core conceptualization of version 1.0 of the ontology, as it is depicted in Fig. 9.1. Note that inverse properties and subproperty axioms are not shown in this compact diagram. The complete specification is publicly available on the web at the persistent URL http://purl.org/muto.

The ontology defines two core classes, one for the taggings *A* (muto:Tagging) and one for the tags *T* (muto:Tag), which form the center of the ontology. They are both specializations of more general classes from the well-known SIOC and

SKOS vocabularies. The other two key concepts, the resources $R$ and users $U$, are not unique to tagging. We do not need to define new classes or specializations here, as we can directly reuse concepts from existing vocabularies, namely `sioc:UserAccount` and `rdfs:Resource`. Based on these four key concepts, we present the MUTO ontology in more detail in the following.

## 9.4.1 Taggings

The central `muto:Tagging` class describes the taggings, i.e. the set of annotations $A$. It contains the n-ary relations that link the resources, tags, and users. Using classes to represent n-ary relations is well-known from many modeling languages (e.g., UML with its *association class* construct) and common practice in OWL (Noy et al. 2006).

`muto:Tagging` is defined as a subclass of `sioc:Item`. We regard this as an adequate alignment, since `SIOC` has been designed to describe "user-generated content" from "online community sites" (Bojars et al. 2008). Apart from `sioc:Item`, there is a number of other concepts of the `SIOC` vocabulary that can be fruitfully reused in the domain of tagging. For instance, we do not need to create a new concept for comments assigned to taggings, as we can take `sioc:note`. Likewise, we can reuse concepts of `SIOC` to describe the source of tagging by first grouping taggings with `sioc:Container` and then linking them to a joined source with `sioc:has_space`.

## 9.4.2 Tags

The second core class of the MUTO ontology is `muto:Tag`. It describes the set of tags $T$. Each tag is an instance of this class with its own URI. Using class instances for tags instead of simple literals allows for the definition of tag properties, such as the later described `muto:tagMeaning` and `muto:nextTag`.

It is important to note that tags with the same label are not merged in MUTO, as this would not only affect the labels but also other tag properties. In our understanding, aggregations of tags with the same label (e.g. for the generation of *tag cloud* visualizations) are not a part of the semantic model but are rather performed by the interactive system. However, the MUTO core ontology can be extended by a module for aggregated tags if this information should be included in the semantic model.

Semantically, tags are very close to what is commonly represented by `skos:Concept`. We thus made `muto:Tag` a subclass of `skos:Concept`, which results in similar benefits to those described above for the subclassing of `sioc:Item`. For instance, it allows us to reuse SKOS concepts in MUTO, such as `skos:narrower` and `skos:broader` to represent hierarchical relations between tags. Likewise, `skos:related` can be used to describe tag relations of a more general nature. The description of other tag relations is not part of the MUTO core ontology, but could easily be integrated with a corresponding module if needed.

The only tag relation we explicitly defined in the MUTO core ontology is `muto:nextTag` (and its inverse counterpart `muto:previousTag`) to describe the sequential order in which tags are entered by the users during the act of tagging. Usually, people enter more than one tag per tagging (Halpin et al. 2007) and they expect the ordering of the tags to remain the same whenever they access a tagging. Using property relations to represent sequences is common practice in OWL (Drummond et al. 2006).

MUTO strictly distinguishes between tags (which have exactly one label according to Axiom 3) and concepts (which can have more than one label). However, it supports the mapping between tags and concepts with the property `muto:tagMeaning`. This is particularly useful in the aforementioned case of *semantic tagging* where the meaning of tags is made explicit by linking them to well-defined entities, such as DBpedia resources (see Sect. 9.2.2 and the example in Sect. 9.5). `muto:tagMeaning` can also be used to indicate synonym tags, simply by linking all tags with identical meaning to the same resource. This includes different tags that are variations of the same term (e.g. if one tag has an underscore as delimiter and the other a hyphen).

### 9.4.3 Users

MUTO reuses `sioc:UserAccount` to represent the accounts of the users who created the taggings (i.e. the set of users $U$). Linking users by their accounts is more accurate and flexible than linking them directly (e.g. by using `foaf:Person`), as it allows one user to have several accounts (e.g. one for work-related and one for personal taggings).

An alternative to `sioc:UserAccount` would have been the semantically closely related class `foaf:OnlineAccount`. We decided for the SIOC variant because we also used other concepts of this vocabulary along with `muto:Tagging` and can thus stay in one namespace. Moreover, it provides flexible support for group tagging (see Sect. 9.2.2) with its class `sioc:Usergroup` that `sioc:UserAccount` can be linked to. Yet, since `sioc:UserAccount` is a subclass of `foaf:OnlineAccount`, concepts from the FOAF vocabulary can also be used to describe users and user-related information.

### 9.4.4 Resources

Resources are linked to taggings by the property `muto:taggedResource`. Like `muto:tagMeaning` and `muto:grantAccess`, the property has no explicit range and can thus be linked to all instances of `rdfs:Resource`, as indicated in Fig. 9.1. Since `rdfs:Resource` is "the class of everything" and "all other classes are subclasses of this class" in RDF (Brickley and Guha 2004), it means that taggings can be linked to any kind of resource. This is in line with the general idea of tagging, where the interactive system determines what is considered a resource.

### 9.4.5 Further Concepts

In addition, we reused concepts from the Dublin Core vocabulary (DCMI Usage Board 2012) to enrich the instances of both `muto:Tagging` and `muto:Tag` with date and time information. Instead of directly linking Dublin Core properties, we defined own subproperties in order to equip them with exact domain and range axioms. We defined two such properties for `muto:Tagging`, one describing the creation date and time (`muto:taggingCreated`) and the other one tracking every single edit (`muto:taggingModified`). The latter can be useful, for instance, to sort taggings by date of last modification.

The date and time information of tags (`muto:tagCreated`) is conceptually separated from that of taggings. This is useful if certain tags of a tagging are added at a later time. Omitting the separate date and time information in these cases can result in biased tag statistics and wrong conclusions about the evolution of the folksonomy. However, since the creation dates and times of tags are usually the same as the creation dates and times of the associated taggings, we defined `muto:tagCreated` as an optional property to prevent a redundant representation of this information. If no separate date and time information is given for a tag, it is assumed that the tag has been created at the same date and time as the associated tagging (i.e., `muto:tagCreated = muto:taggingCreated`). The ranges of all three subproperties `muto:tagCreated`, `muto:taggingCreated`, and `muto:taggingModified` are given with `xsd:dateTime` in order to force a standardized format and improve interoperability.

Finally, the MUTO core ontology includes the domain-specific concepts of *private* and *automatic* tagging (see Sect. 9.2.2). They are defined as specializations of the central `muto:Tagging` and `muto:Tag` classes. A private tagging is only visible to its creator, unless the creator has not explicitly granted access to it by others, as expressed by the `muto:grantAccess` property. Note that the ontology can only provide a description of the concept; the correct implementation of privacy constraints remains the duty of the interactive system.

As automatic tagging denotes tagging with automatic tags, `muto:AutoTag` is a subclass of `muto:Tag`. Describing manual and automatic tagging in the same ontology makes sense, as it avoids redundant modeling and allows for an easier transformation of automatic tags into manual (i.e. user validated) ones. In addition, it allows to associate both types of tags with the same tagging instance, which is conceptually consistent with how automatic tags are often applied, namely as a complement to the tags entered by the user.

Note that there is no need to define the 'counterpart' concepts of public and manual tagging, as these are the default modes, i.e. the usual case is public tagging with user-assigned tags. Therefore, taggings that are not instances of muto:PrivateTagging are public by default. Likewise, all tags that are not instances of muto:AutoTag are assumed to be manually entered.

### 9.4.6 Cardinality Constraints

We equipped the MUTO ontology with cardinality constraints to ensure that the fundamental principles of tagging (as defined by the axioms in Sect. 9.2.1) are not violated. Since these fundamental principles are important for the interoperability and processability of folksonomies, we decided to define them globally. That is, we used functional properties (owl:FunctionalProperty) instead of property restrictions (owl:Restriction), what is different from earlier versions of MUTO which used property restrictions exclusively (Lohmann et al. 2011). This decision was also motivated by the fact that the maximum cardinality is one for all properties that need to be constrained in MUTO. Furthermore, functional properties do not force their use but can be omitted, keeping MUTO flexible despite all constraints.

Taggings and tags are linked by the property muto:hasTag. The cardinality of this property is not restricted, as there is no restriction on the number of tags that a tagging may consist of (see Axiom 1). MUTO even allows for taggings without tags to support cases where users first simply index a resource and add tags later, as possible in some systems (e.g. Delicious).

In contrast, we defined muto:taggedResource to be functional, since each tagging is uniquely linked to a single resource according to Axiom 1. The axiom states the same for the user account, i.e. each tagging is created by one user. Hence, muto:hasCreator is also a functional property in MUTO.

As tags have always exactly one label (Axiom 3), muto:tagLabel has also a cardinality of one. Finally, muto:taggingCreated, muto:tagCreated, and muto:nextTag have a cardinality of one, since multiple definitions of these properties for the same instance would not make sense. Apart from these cardinality constraints we have avoided to overly specify the ontology. In particular, we did not use OWL constructs that are not part of OWL Lite, such as owl:disjointWith or owl:unionOf, to not unnecessarily increase the formal complexity of the ontology.

## 9.5 Application Example

Figure 9.2 depicts a sample scenario of using the MUTO ontology with the social bookmarking system Example.org. It shows the RDF graph of user Alice who an-

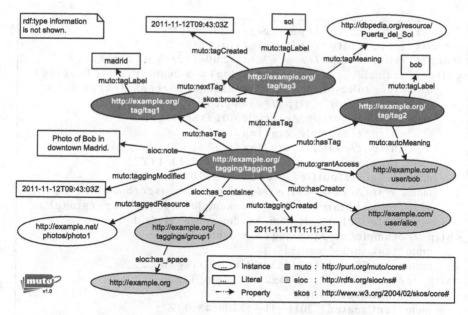

**Fig. 9.2**  Example RDF graph depicting a private tagging of a photo by user Alice

notated a photo from the website Example.net. Assume that Alice interacts with a well-designed user interface. She does not get in touch with the ontology but it is rather used for the design and internal representation in the interactive system and/or for sharing the folksonomy with other systems. Listing 9.1 provides the OWL code of the example in RDF/Turtle format.

### 9.5.1 Scenario

Imagine the following scenario that led to the creation of the tagging instance:[2] Alice logs into her account of the social networking service Example.com (`sioc:hasCreator`). From there, she uses the social bookmarking system Example.org to annotate a photo she uploaded to the media sharing website Example.net (`muto:taggedResource`). As the photo shows her friend Bob in downtown Madrid, she starts tagging with entering the tag 'madrid' (`muto:Tag`). Then, she recognizes that the system has automatically identified Bob on the photo and added his name as a tag (`muto:AutoTag`). The system got his name (and further information) from the social networking service Example.com, of which Bob is also a member. In addition, the system links Bob's name to his account (`muto:autoMeaning`, a subproperty of `muto:tagMeaning`). Though Alice

---

[2]In brackets, we give the ontology classes and properties used to represent the information.

```
@prefix muto: <http://purl.org/muto/core#> .
@prefix sioc: <http://rdfs.org/sioc/ns#> .
@prefix skos: <http://www.w3.org/2004/02/skos/core#> .
<http://example.org/tagging/tagging1> a muto:PrivateTagging;
    muto:taggedResource <http://example.net/photos/photo1>;
    muto:hasCreator <http://example.com/user/alice>;
    muto:hasTag <http://example.org/tag/tag1>,
        <http://example.org/tag/tag2>,
        <http://example.org/tag/tag3>;
    muto:taggingCreated "2011-11-11T11:11:11Z";
    muto:taggingModified "2011-11-12T09:43:03Z";
    muto:grantAccess <http://example.com/user/bob>;
    sioc:has_container <http://example.org/taggings/group1>;
    sioc:note "Photo of Bob in downtown Madrid." .
<http://example.org/tag/tag1> a muto:Tag;
    muto:tagLabel "madrid" ;
    muto:nextTag <http://example.org/tag/tag2> .
<http://example.org/tag/tag2> a muto:Tag;
    muto:tagLabel "sol";
    muto:tagCreated "2011-11-12T09:43:03Z";
    muto:tagMeaning <http://dbpedia.org/resource/
        Puerta_del_Sol>;
    skos:broader <http://example.org/tag/tag1> .
<http://example.org/tag/tag3> a muto:AutoTag;
    muto:tagLabel "bob";
    muto:autoMeaning <http://example.com/user/bob> .
<http://example.org/taggings/group1> a sioc:Container;
    sioc:has_space <http://example.org> .
```

**Listing 9.1** OWL code of the example in RDF/Turtle format ('a' = rdf:type)

marked the tagging as private (muto:PrivateTagging), she decides to share it with Bob and grants him access (muto:grantAccess). She also adds a comment to the tagging describing the contents of the photo (sioc:note).

One day later, Alice looks at the photo again and recognizes that it was taken at Puerta del Sol, a central square in Madrid. She opens the tagging and adds the tag 'sol' (muto:Tag) to the previously assigned tags 'madrid' and 'bob'. Furthermore, she decides to 'semantify' the tag so that she will later remember what 'sol' means. First, she makes 'sol' a subtag of 'madrid' (skos:broader) to indicate that it is a specific location in Madrid. Second, she gives the tag explicit meaning by linking it to the corresponding DBpedia resource (muto:tagMeaning).

The information that the tag 'sol' was added at a later time than the other two tags is given by its property muto:tagCreated. This property would not be necessary if the tag would have been entered along with the others. Accordingly, the timestamp of muto:tagCreated is the same as of muto:taggingModified but different from the one of `muto:taggingCreated`. Source information is linked with `sioc:has_space` after the tagging has been assigned to a container with `sioc:has_container`.

### 9.5.2 Discussion

The example illustrates an advanced case of tagging that uses many of the concepts from the semantic model. The most basic variant of tagging—a list of tags without disambiguations, hierarchical relations, comments, or automatic tags—can be described with much fewer concepts. This capability of supporting different levels of tagging, from simple to semantic, from manual to automatic, and from public to private, was one of the main goals in the development of the semantic model. On the other hand, we avoided to make the semantic model unnecessary complex but kept it understandable to people who use it. Finding a good balance between comprehensiveness and compactness was thus another major goal in the development of the semantic model.

The example also indicates the benefits of a precise domain description for the development of interactive systems. There would be many different ways to represent the information from the scenario; having one common conceptualization helps to create a joint understanding among the developers of an interactive system. More importantly, the semantic model can also increase the interoperability between different interactive systems, as illustrated by the scenario: It links taggings of a social bookmarking system with photos from a media sharing website and user profiles of a social networking service.

### 9.6 Visualization

If folksonomies are based on the semantic model, they become independent from individual interactive systems. This opens up possibilities for developing user interface components that can be used in multiple systems. In the following, we illustrate these possibilities on the example of graph visualizations. Such visualizations nicely depict the core structure of folksonomies, as described by the annotations $A$ which link the resources $R$, tags $T$, and users $U$. If we consider the MUTO ontology, these sets are represented by the classes `rdfs:Resource`, `muto:Tag`, `sioc:UserAccount`, and `muto:Tagging`.

This core structure forms a hypergraph that can be split into several subgraphs representing specific parts of the folksonomy (Mika 2005). In particular, we derive three bipartite graphs $G(RT)$, $G(TU)$, and $G(UR)$ that describe the relations between each two of the basic element sets.

An example for the graph $G(RT)$ with $V = R \cup T$ is shown in Fig. 9.3a. The nodes represent the resources and tags, i.e. instances of `rdfs:Resource`

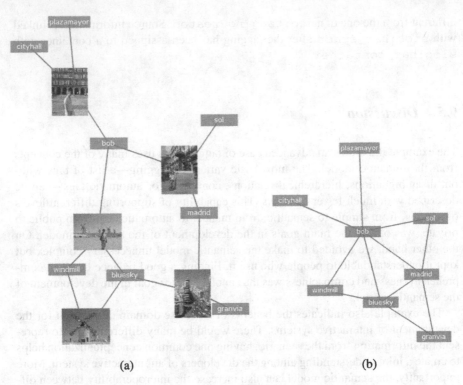

**Fig. 9.3** Graph visualizations: (**a**) photos linked by tags, (**b**) links between tags without photos

(or some more specific subclass) and `muto:Tag`, while the edges represent the links between them. These links are given by the `muto:hasTag` and `muto:taggedResource` property relations. Unlike in the semantic model, we merged tags with same labels in the graph visualization.

Continuing from the above scenario, assume that the graph was generated from the taggings of user Alice. The resources are a selection of photos which Alice uploaded to the media sharing website Example.net and which she annotated with tags. The graph visualization helps to explore relationships between the photos. We see, for instance, that there are other photos also showing Bob. These photos can then be selected and viewed in detail.

All three bipartite graphs $G(RT)$, $G(TU)$, and $G(UR)$ derived from the basic folksonomy structure can be further reduced, depending on what the user is interested in. If we split $G(RT)$ again, we get two graphs showing the set of resources and the set of tags, respectively. An example of the latter is shown in Fig. 9.3b. It visualizes the same tags as graph $G(RT)$ from Fig. 9.3a but without the resources, i.e. the tagged photos. Instead, it shows only the links that result from the tagging of the photos. This kind of visualization is sometimes called *tag graph*, as it is related to tag cloud visualizations but additionally displays the links between the tags based on their co-use (Lohmann and Díaz 2012). It can be extended in various directions, e.g. by weighting the font sizes of the tags like in tag clouds or by weighting the tag relations.

Apart from that, a large number of other graph visualizations can be derived from folksonomies; in particular, if we consider not only the basic folksonomy tuple $F = (R, T, U, A)$ but also other concepts of the semantic model, such as time information (`muto:taggingCreated`). Generally speaking, we are free to create all kinds of user interfaces, as long as they are consistent with the semantic model. This allows even for adaptable user interface components where users select the parts of the folksonomy they are interested in (e.g. choose from a selection of different graph visualizations). Thus, not only the folksonomies become independent from individual interactive system but also the related user interface components.

## 9.7 Conclusions and Future Work

In this chapter, we have presented a semantic model for the domain of tagging and folksonomies. It not only contributes to a better domain understanding but also improves the interoperability of folksonomies and the reusability of related user interface components. It is formally described in an OWL ontology allowing for machine interpretation and automated reasoning. We have illustrated how the model can support the graph-based representation and visualization of folksonomies. If folksonomies are based on it, they can be shared among interactive systems and the same program code (e.g. SPARQL queries) can be used to access and visualize parts of the folksonomies. This allows for the development of reusable and adaptable user interface components which offer different perspectives on folksonomies depending on the interests of the users.

Our goal was to develop a compact yet comprehensive semantic model that considers all important concepts and relationships in the domain of tagging and folksonomies. Furthermore, we wanted to keep it as understandable as possible for the people who use it. If we compare it with existing conceptualizations, it is most closely related to the "Tag Ontology" developed by Newman (2005) and the "Bookmark Schema" of the Annotea project (Koivunen 2006). However, it additionally considers several concepts that are missing in these approaches, such as some advanced tagging concepts described in the ontologies of Echarte et al. (2007) as well as Passant and Laublet (2008).

Two major challenges in the application of semantic models are performance and scalability. In this work, we have focused on a precise conceptualization rather than on a technical optimization for large folksonomies. In such cases, other representations that allow for a fast processing and efficient storage of the folksonomy might be more useful. Furthermore, specific modules may be integrated into the MUTO ontology that speed up processing, such as properties that directly link the resources, tags, and users in order to avoid the indirection via taggings. However, such pragmatic extensions should be used with care as they may lead to conceptual inconsistencies (e.g. direct relations between tags and resources can conflict with the concept of private tagging).

**Table 9.2** Alphabetical list of the names, namespace prefixes, and URIs of the referenced vocabularies

| Vocabulary name | Prefix | URI reference |
| --- | --- | --- |
| Common tag | CTAG | http://commontag.org/ns# |
| Friend of a friend | FOAF | http://xmlns.com/foaf/0.1/ |
| Meaning of a tag | MOAT | http://moat-project.org/ns# |
| Modular unified tagging ontology | MUTO | http://purl.org/muto/core# |
| NiceTag ontology | NT | http://ns.inria.fr/nicetag/2010/09/09/voc |
| Ontology of folksonomy | OF | http://www.eslomas.com/tagontology-1.owl |
| RDF schema | RDFS | http://www.w3.org/2000/01/rdf-schema# |
| RDF site summary | RSS | http://purl.org/rss/1.0/ |
| Semantically-interlinked online communities | SIOC | http://rdfs.org/sioc/ns# |
| Simple knowledge organization system | SKOS | http://www.w3.org/2004/02/skos/core |
| Social semantic cloud of tags | SCOT | http://scot-project.org/scot/ns# |
| Tag ontology | TAGS | http://www.holygoat.co.uk/owl/redwood/0.1/tags/ |
| Tagging ontology | TO | http://bubb.ghb.fh-furtwangen.de/TagOnt/tagont.owl |
| TAGora tagging ontology | TT | http://tagora.ecs.soton.ac.uk/schemas/tagging |
| Upper tag ontology | UTO | http://info.slis.indiana.edu/dingying/uto.owl |
| XML schema | XSD | http://www.w3.org/2001/XMLSchema# |

Future work includes the application and extension of the semantic model in various contexts. In particular, we are interested in ontology modules that add advanced tagging concepts to represent, for instance, specific types of tags (geotags, star ratings, etc.) or tag relations (synonymy, part-of, etc.). Furthermore, we plan to test the semantic model with different interactive systems to evaluate its general applicability and identify issues for improvement.

# References

Bizer, C., Lehmann, J., Kobilarov, G., Auer, S., Becker, C., Cyganiak, R., et al. (2009). DBpedia—a crystallization point for the web of data. *Journal of Web Semantics, 7*(3), 154–165.

Bojars, U., Breslin, J. G., Peristeras, V., Tummarello, G., & Decker, S. (2008). Interlinking the social web with semantics. *IEEE Intelligent Systems, 23*(3), 29–40.

Brickley, D., & Guha, R. V. (2004). *RDF vocabulary description language 1.0: RDF schema.* http://www.w3.org/TR/rdf-schema/.

DCMI Usage Board (2012). *DCMI metadata terms.* http://dublincore.org/documents/dcmi-terms/.

Drummond, N., Rector, A., Stevens, R., Moulton, G., Horridge, M., Wang, H., et al. (2006). Putting OWL in order: patterns for sequences in OWL. In *CEUR-WS.org: Vol. 216. Proceedings of the OWLED '06 workshop on OWL: experiences and directions.*

Echarte, F., Astrain, J. J., Córdoba, A., & Villadangos, J. E. (2007). Ontology of folksonomy: a new modelling method. In *CEUR-WS.org: Vol. 289. Proceedings of the semantic authoring, annotation and knowledge markup workshop (SAAKM '07)*.

Gruber, T. (1993). A translation approach to portable ontology specifications. *Knowledge Acquisition, 5*(2), 199–220.

Gruber, T. (2005). *TagOntology—a way to agree on the semantics of tagging data.* http://tomgruber.org/writing/tagontology.htm.

Gruber, T. (2007). Ontology of folksonomy: a mash-up of apples and oranges. In *Proceedings of the 1st conference on metadata and semantics research (MTSR '05). International Journal on Semantic Web and Information Systems, 3*(2), 1–11.

Halpin, H., Robu, V., & Shepherd, H. (2007). The complex dynamics of collaborative tagging. In *Proceedings of the 16th international conference on world wide web (WWW '07)* (pp. 211–220). New York: ACM.

Heymann, P., & Garcia-Molina, H. (2006). *Collaborative creation of communal hierarchical taxonomies in social tagging systems* (Technical Report No. 2006-10). Stanford InfoLab.

Hotho, A., Jäschke, R., Schmitz, C., & Stumme, G. (2006). Information retrieval in folksonomies: search and ranking. In *LNCS: Vol. 4011. Proceedings of the 3rd European semantic web conference (ESWC '06)* (pp. 411–426). Berlin: Springer.

Kim, H. L., Scerri, S., Breslin, J. G., Decker, S., & Kim, H. G. (2008). The state of the art in tag ontologies: a semantic model for tagging and folksonomies. In *Proceedings of the international conference on Dublin core and metadata applications (DC '08)* (pp. 128–137). Dublin: DCMI.

Koivunen, M.-R. (2006). Semantic authoring by tagging with annotea social bookmarks and topics. In *CEUR-WS.org: Vol. 209. Proceedings of the 1st semantic authoring and annotation workshop (SAAW '06)*.

Li, R., Bao, S., Yu, Y., Fei, B., & Su, Z. (2007). Towards effective browsing of large scale social annotations. In *Proceedings of the 16th international conference on world wide web (WWW '07)* (pp. 943–952). New York: ACM.

Lohmann, S., & Díaz, P. (2012). Representing and visualizing folksonomies as graphs: a reference model. In *Proceedings of the international working conference on advanced visual interfaces (AVI '12)* (pp. 729–732). New York: ACM.

Lohmann, S., Díaz, P., & Aedo, I. (2011). MUTO: the modular unified tagging ontology. In *Proceedings of the 7th international conference on semantic systems (I-SEMANTICS '11)* (pp. 95–104). New York: ACM.

Mika, P. (2005). Ontologies are us: a unified model of social networks and semantics. In *LNCS: Vol. 3729. Proceedings of the 4th international semantic web conference 2005 (ISWC '05)* (pp. 522–536). Berlin: Springer.

Miller, G. A. (1995). Wordnet: a lexical database for English. *Communications of the ACM, 38*, 39–41.

Newman, R. (2005). *Tag ontology design.* http://www.holygoat.co.uk/projects/tags.

Noy, N., & McGuinness, D. (2001). *Ontology development 101: a guide to creating your first ontology* (Technical Report No. SMI-2001-0880). Stanford Medical Informatics.

Noy, N., Rector, A., Hayes, P., & Welty, C. (2006). *Defining N-ary relations on the semantic web.* http://www.w3.org/TR/swbp-n-aryRelations/.

Passant, A., & Laublet, P. (2008). Meaning of a tag: a collaborative approach to bridge the gap between tagging and linked data. In *CEUR-WS.org: Vol. 369. Proceedings of the WWW2008 workshop on linked data on the web (LDOW '08)*.

Peters, I. (2009). *Folksonomies: indexing and retrieval in web 2.0.* Berlin: de Gruyter.

Smith, G. (2008). *Tagging: people-powered metadata for the social web.* Berkeley: New Riders.

W3C OWL Working Group (2012). *OWL 2 web ontology language document overview* (2nd ed.). http://www.w3.org/TR/owl2-overview/.

Wu, X., Zhang, L., & Yu, Y. (2006). Exploring social annotations for the semantic web. In *Proceedings of the 15th international conference on world wide web (WWW '06)* (pp. 417–426). New York: ACM.

# Chapter 10
# User Interaction Templates for the Design of Lifelogging Systems

Frank Hopfgartner, Yang Yang, Lijuan Marissa Zhou, and Cathal Gurrin

**Abstract** A variety of life-tracking devices are being created to give opportunity to track our daily lives accurately and automatically through the application of sensing technologies. Technology allows us to automatically and passively record life activities in previously unimaginable detail, in a process called lifelogging. Captured materials may include text, photos/video, audio, location, Bluetooth logs and information from many other sensing modalities, all captured automatically by wearable sensors. Experience suggests that it can be overwhelming and impractical to manually scan through the full contents of these lifelogs. A promising approach is to apply visualization to large-scale data-driven lifelogs as a means of abstracting and summarizing information. In this chapter, we outline various UI templates that support different visualization schemes.

## 10.1 Introduction

Traditionally, in terms of us remembering important events and activities of our own lives, the written diary has been the first choice. But with modern technology, the diary recording of our lives is now digital. Emails sent and received, web pages viewed and interacted with, photos and videos taken, viewed and shared, blog postings and tweets written, on-line social network activities, calendars, goods purchased and so on. These represent our present day. Through advances in wearable

F. Hopfgartner (✉)
TU Berlin, Berlin, Germany
e-mail: frank.hopfgartner@tu-berlin.de

Y. Yang · L.M. Zhou · C. Gurrin
Dublin City University, Dublin, Ireland

Y. Yang
e-mail: yyang@computing.dcu.ie

L.M. Zhou
e-mail: mzhou@computing.dcu.ie

C. Gurrin
e-mail: cgurrin@computing.dcu.ie

T. Hussein et al. (eds.), *Semantic Models for Adaptive Interactive Systems*,
Human–Computer Interaction Series, DOI 10.1007/978-1-4471-5301-6_10,
© Springer-Verlag London 2013

sensors, we now have the capability to automatically record at large–scale the places that we have been to, things we have seen, people we encountered and how active we are. Almost everything we do these days, on-line and physically, is in some way monitored, sensed and logged. Further, with the introduction of Facebook's Timeline (Sittig and Zuckerberg 2010), we have come to accept, or maybe we just ignore, this massive surveillance of our lives from a variety of sensors. This can be our smartphones, e.g. Reddy et al. (2007), Qiu et al. (2012), intelligent devices like TVs and cars but also the surveillance cameras, recording of travel data at subways and buses and purchases with credit cards. The creation of such multi-modal human media archives, or lifelogs, will be commonplace.

In 2011, the European Union agency ENISA[1] evaluated the risks, threats and vulnerabilities of lifelogging applications with respect to central topics such as privacy and trust issues. In their final report, they highlight that lifelogging itself is still in its infancy but nevertheless will play an important role in the near future (Daskala et al. 2011). Therefore, they recommend further research in order to influence its evolution to "be better prepared to mitigate the risks and [to] maximize the benefits of these technologies". Various researchers have worked on handling lifelogs, starting from identifying important events in the data stream, analyzing the sensor data to generating semantically meaningful annotations that describe these events and the implications on privacy (O'Hara et al. 2008; Gedik and Liu 2008).

Due to the characteristics of the capturing devices, we know that these lifelogs can be large and contain chronological ordered data. Captured materials may include text, photos/video, audio, location, Bluetooth logs and information from many other sensing modalities, all captured automatically by wearable sensors. Experience suggests that it can be overwhelming and impractical to manually scan through the full contents of these lifelogs. A promising approach is to apply visualization to large-scale data-driven lifelogs, as a means of abstracting and summarizing information.

Data visualization supports representation of abstract information, which facilitates further exploration (Shneiderman 1996). Previous studies mainly focused on plain numerical data, often in the form of charts, tables, figures, diagrams, etc. However, in the case of lifelogging, data generated from multiple sensor sources are more complex, requiring careful consideration of how to summarize and represent this information. In visual lifelogging, it is common for the sensing devices to automatically capture thousands of photos and tens of thousands of sensor readings per day (Kalnikaite and Whittaker 2012).

We argue that lifelog visualization should be capable of displaying the sheer quantity of mixed multimedia content in a meaningful way, taking into consideration user behaviors and needs. It requires incorporating domain knowledge into the data aggregation, compression and rendering process. Through different means of

---

[1]The objective of the European Network and Information Security Agency (ENISA) is to advise European institutions and Member states to improve network and information security for the benefit of all citizens and organizations in the union. More details can be found on their website at http://www.enisa.europa.eu/.

interaction, the visualizations should provide an insight to help users improve self-awareness, support retrospective memory access, and furthermore, discover their own stories and life events. Hence, lifelogging provides a new domain for the development of adaptive interactive systems.

In this chapter, we discuss the use of context-based HCI design templates, which support a more systematic approach in exploring the match between user needs and interaction provision. Template-based user interface development aims at providing a systematic approach to specify the user interface by means of models. It helps us to design for maximum usability. We will focus on different user scenarios, including (a) the creation of personal lifelogging legacies, (b) energy expenditure measurements, (c) reminiscence therapy and (d) social activity capturing. These UI templates serve as guidelines towards increasing the use of HCI design patterns for lifelogging devices.

The chapter is structured as follows. In Sect. 10.2, we provide a brief overview over existing lifelogging technology. Section 10.3 introduces use cases that demonstrate the application of these technologies, In Sect. 10.4, we introduce different interaction patterns for different lifelogging scenarios. Section 10.5 concludes this chapter.

## 10.2  Lifelogging Devices

Digital lifelogging is an ubiquitous concept and exists in various forms. As mentioned above, it includes any digital document one creates every day, e.g., letters that are typed on a personal computer, pictures taken with a digital camera or mobile phone, posts in the Internet, etc. Further, it can be automatically captured data such as GPS records, personal health information or ambient living awareness systems in an intelligent housing system. As the prevalence of digital logging devices, we now have the ability to gather and store large volumes of personal data under a meticulous concern of privacy. Furthermore, people have always collected mementos over lifetime. Besides, sharing digital information is already commonplace, through emails, mobile phones and social network. Focusing on an individual (i.e., the lifelogger), various lifelogging devices provide a constant stream of personal data. The functionality of lifelogging devices is as diverse as the data that is recorded by these devices. We classify these devices into four categories: (1) Portable Cameras, (2) Biometric Devices, (3) Other Portable Devices and (4) Networked Systems. All devices allow users to record some part of their daily life (GPS tracking, environmental surroundings, our body metrical information, etc.). The categories are introduced in the remainder of this section.

### 10.2.1  Portable Cameras

The most advanced application of personal lifelogs is the storage of pictures and videos that depict people's life. Various devices have been introduced that can be used to achieve this task.

An early product is Microsoft's SenseCam (Hodges et al. 2006), a camera with fisheye lens and various additional sensors which is worn around the neck. Sense-Cam has been used extensively in the MyLifeBits project (Gemmell et al. 2006), a research project aimed at creating lifetime storage databases. SenseCam is a small lightweight wearable camera used to passively capture photos and other sensor data (temperature, accelerometer, magnitude, infrared ray etc.). A similar product will soon be launched by the Swedish startup company Memoto,[2] who successfully raised money via crowdsourcing to start the production of a small lifelogging camera. Their funding campaign attracted world-wide media attention (e.g., by Wired Magazine, Wall Street Journal, The Guardian, The Huffington Post, BBC, Die Zeit, and others), indicating the growing attention that lifelogging receives nowadays. Other potential lifelogging cameras are Google's Project Glass, an augmented reality head-mounted display (Olsson 2012) and Looxcie (Boland and Pereira 2011), a mobile-connected, handsfree, streaming video camera.

A collection consisting of over 10.5 million personal lifelogging images (Doherty et al. 2009) has been used for the development and testing of various algorithms to automatically categorize image content. For example, researchers studied techniques to automatically segment the stream of daily lifelogging pictures into semantically coherent events and to group them in categories such as socializing, eating, travel behaviour, environments that people experience, or movements (Doherty 2009; Byrne et al. 2008; Doherty et al. 2008; Li et al. 2013). Doherty et al. (2012) introduce a browser that allows users to view of summary of daily events instead of watching all pictures of a day.

Apart from focusing on the technical handling of this big data, various research has been performed to study the potentials of lifelogging images in medical and other settings. For example, studies have shown (e.g., Berry et al.2007) that the process of reviewing lifelogging pictures has a positive effect on memory recall, with even better effects than the more traditional personal diary. The authors report that enabling patients with limbic encephalitis to relieve their day by exploring lifelogging images has a positive impact on the patients' confidence, stress level and their ability to cope with their impairment. Further, neuroscientists observed that viewing personal lifelogging images triggers activity in parts of the brain that is associated with normal autobiographical remembering (Berry et al. 2009). Similar results are reported by Piasek et al. (2011), Pauly-Takacs et al. (2011), who asked memory impaired patients to include lifelogging technologies in their daily lives.

### 10.2.2 Biometric Devices

Another popular domain where users rely on sensors to record aspects of their life is the health market. As shown in a recent survey (Zhou and Gurrin 2012), many

---

[2]http://www.memoto.com/.

sports enthusiasts are keen to record their sports life. There are a bundle of biometric devices that are capable of logging biometric information such as Galvanic skin response, skin temperature, heart rate or increased sweat production, sympathetic nervous activities, etc. These devices are mainly used to interpret physiological responses that provide evidence for the personal well being. Commercial products include ReadiBand from Fatigue Science,[3] a tiny device that has to be worn around the wrist and Bodymedia,[4] which is designed to determine energy expenditure and other biometric information. Targeting the amateur sports market, devices such a Fit-Bit[5] and Nike+iPod[6] promise fitness monitoring facilities based on internal sensor data. Both devices have in common that they are rather small and are comfortable to wear. Given their small size, these small devices play an essential role in the evaluation of sports and health related studies (e.g. Cole et al. 2004). Consequently, the underlying technology, i.e., the analysis of sensor data such as accelerometer data to determine energy expenditure has been studied extensively, e.g., by Albinali et al. (2010), Swartz et al. (2000), Montoye et al. (1983). Further related research includes the analysis of sensor data to determine biometric features include device-independent gesture recognition (Kratz et al. 2011) and the continuous and non-intrusive user identity verification in real-time environments (Messerman et al. 2011).

## 10.2.3 Other Portable Devices

Apart from devices that record visual or biometric data, various other portable devices exist that can be used for logging parts of our lives. For example, GPS data trackers constantly create time-annotated location points that allow tracking movements. These devices are often used to track animals, (e.g. Weimerskirch et al. 2002; Schofield et al. 2007), vehicles, employees, children and/or elderly people. Further, GPS sensors are used to geotag pictures and record travel, hiking, cycling, flying or racing routes, thus revealing information such as individual travel behavior (Clements et al. 2010) or general places of interest (Kennedy and Naaman 2008). Rekimoto et al. (2007) rely on WiFi signals to create such patterns. Further, Miyaki and Rekimoto introduce a mobile sensor which measures ambient air environment (Miyaki and Rekimoto 2008). By plugging the sensor on a mobile phone, a detailed record of air quality will be created, thus revealing details about one's personal ecological environment.

A promising portable device that comes with various internal sensors is the smartphone. A standard smartphone contains a wealth of sensors: a camera, a GPS

---

[3]http://www.fatiguescience.com/products/readiband.

[4]http://www.bodymedia.com/.

[5]http://www.fitbit.com/.

[6]http://www.apple.com/ipod/nike/.

chip, an audio recorder, a 3-axis accelerometer, an ambient light sensor and a digital compass. In essence, a standard smartphone contains the full specification for recording the entire physical and digital environment that a user is experiencing. Additionally, Bluetooth headsets that can record, store and upload 5+ hours of medium quality video are already available for less than EUR 200.

Hence, we have the ability to gather and store large volumes of personal data (location, photos, motion, orientation, etc.) in a very cheap manner. Exploiting the idea of using a smartphone as the primary tool for gathering lifelogging data, MIT's Media-Lab introduced the Funf Open Sensing Framework[7] which creates a snapshot of the user's life by recording data from over 30 sensors, including Wifi signals, locations, usage of apps on the phone, and others. Data will automatically be uploaded to the cloud and can then be analyzed by the user (Aharony et al. 2011). A similar framework has been presented by Rawassizadeh et al. (2011). Further, a framework is currently developed within the SenseSeer project.[8] The aim of this project is to develop a software platform that will automatically record, annotate and interpret a user's life activities, based upon the sensor data that they gather unobtrusively as part of daily life. Using a smartphone, the system can recognize activities like actions (sitting, eating, driving), people (who is nearby), places (physical locations, indoor/outdoor, office/home) or nearby objects (screen, steering wheel, people). In addition, the SenseSeer application supports automatically taking pictures, thus emulating the functionalities of a SenseCam (Qiu et al. 2012).

### 10.2.4 Networked Systems

The vast majority of devices that are used to record parts of our life are used to monitor the environment (e.g. CCTV cameras, digital time sheets) or to provide some customer-oriented services (e.g. ATM machines, Online web services, etc.). Combining all personal data streams that have been recorded by these networked systems can result in a detailed description of our every day activities. Elliott et al. (2009) propose a framework for capturing all personal data in a personal archive. However, the data that is recorded using these devices is often beyond our control. Besides, these systems are often networked with other systems and services, hence distributing this personal data. Therefore, combining personal data under these conditions should be examined with caution.

Recently, the European Commission funded the Dem@Care[9] project via its FP7 funding scheme. The aim of Dem@Care is to provide multi-parametric remote monitoring and enabling for persons with dementia, allowing them to live an independent life in their community. The analysis of multi-parametric sensor data has also

---

[7]http://funf.org/.

[8]http://senseseer.com/.

[9]http://www.demcare.eu/.

been studied within the context of the SmartSenior[10] project. The aim of this project was to improve life quality of elderly people at home, e.g., by enabling them to sustain mobility, safety and independence.

## 10.3  Use Cases

As shown in the previous section, various devices exist that can be used to record aspects of our lives. Bell and Gemmell (2009) argue that this is just the beginning of a "total recall revolution". The authors researched digital lifelogging for several years, concluding that technology is developed (or might be developed soon) that allows us to remember everything. In this section, we provide four use cases that illustrate the motivation that users of lifelogging technologies might have to create such digital memories.

### 10.3.1  Personal Lifelogging Legacy

**Scenario**

"John Doe is a technology enthusiast. Hence, it did not take much to convince him to buy one of those lifelogging devices that everyone was speaking about these days. *Buy one of our devices*, their marketing slogan said. *Leave a legacy behind that really represents you: A record of your every-day activities.* This promise fascinated him. Wearing a lifelogging device, he could record everything he did, day by day. People he met, places he had been to, … everything! The longer he would use the device, the more of his data would be available, leaving a "digital fingerprint" of his life. In a way, this data would keep a record of his life, the essence of his experiences. Of course it would not make him immortal, but still, with conscientious data storage, he would leave something behind that those about to follow could get back to …."

**Comment**

With the rise of Facebook, Twitter and other social network services, we already have access to technologies that allow us to share certain moments of our lives online. Nadkarni and Hofmann (2012) argue that social network services satisfy two primary human needs: (1) the need to belong and (2) the need for self-presentation. Thus, we argue that above scenario is very close to real life. John could be anyone, his need to share life moments drives many users of social network services to post aspects of their lives (pictures, videos, text, …) online.

---

[10]http://www.smart-senior.de/.

Above scenario has been addressed by Bluepatch Productions and Floating World Productions in their theatre play *Oh look, hummingbirds*, which premiered at the 2012 Dublin Fringe Festival. In this play, a journalist is given the experience to view the memories of a loved-one who passed away. This service is provided by a futuristic company that specializes on keeping one's lifelogging legacy and enabling selected persons to access this data. Although the play is set in the future, the technology to record such lifelogging databases already exist and indeed, early adopters already created their own personal lifelogs covering several years of life experience (Doherty et al. 2009).

### 10.3.2 Energy Expenditure Measurement

**Scenario**

"Mandy never was a very disciplined person. Therefore, it probably is no big surprise that every diet she tried so far was meant to fail. Although she initially manages to lose some weight by changing her food consumption habits, she eventually breaks in and eats that extra piece of cake again … Following up on her medical doctor's advise, she finally decides to get more physically active, hence losing weight by burning more calories rather than just reducing food intake. Knowing about her weak discipline, she joins a supervised fitness programme in her local gym where she is asked to monitor her physical activities and to discuss this activity log with her coach and other members of the training programme."

**Comment**

As argued in Sect. 10.2.2, various biometric devices exist that can be used to measure physical activities. Further, weight losing programmes as offered by Weight-watchers rely on recording, sharing and discussing food consumption habits with members of a self-help group. A discussion on the psychological impact of sharing and discussing such information with members of a group is discussed by Weiner (1998).

### 10.3.3 Reminiscence Therapy

**Scenario**

"Alzheimer! It hit him like a ton of bricks. When Pete started to forget things, he first blamed it on the stress he faced every day. But the more he forgot, the less he felt that it was due to stress. He finally decided to go to a specialist to have his memory checked. Then, the verdict came: *We are sorry to inform you that you suffer from an early form of Alzheimer's disease.* Alzheimer! It effects concentration, memory, judgement, rendering its victims helpless over the years. He did not want to forget! He wanted to remember his life! If only there was a way to help him remember his life . . . ."

## Comment

Reminiscence enables us to relive events from our past. The American Psychological Association defines reminiscence therapy as "the use of life histories—written or oral, or both—to improve psychological well-being" (VandenBos 2006). It is one of the most popular therapies in dementia care (Woods et al. 2009; Pittiglio 2000). Lifelogging technology has been successfully used to support such reminiscence sessions (Piasek et al. 2011; Bharoucha et al. 2009). The authors of these studies conclude that lifelogging material such as personal pictures can be used as memory trigger to help Alzheimer patients to remember certain events of their life and thus helps to improve their quality of life.

### 10.3.4 Social Activity Capturing

#### Scenario

"Carina was about to experience the time of her life. Months ago, she received the confirmation that she was selected to participate in the Erasmus programme, i.e., she would be allowed to go abroad and study at another university in Europe for a year. From what she has heard from previous participants of this programme, an Erasmus year was all about exploring the host nation's country and culture, meeting new people from all over the world and, most of all, party, party, party. Willing to share this experience with her friends at home, she installs a novel lifelogging application on her mobile phone which creates a daily log of her activities, locations and people she meets."

#### Comment

Technologies, e.g., mobile phone apps, that allow to capture various aspects of the life logger's life have been presented in Sect. 2.3. Various patents have been granted that lay ground for technology that enable tracking of activity and location (Haner 2002; Olmassakian 1999). A discussion on ethical issues regarding human centric GPS tracking and monitoring is provided by Michael et al. (2006).

The danger of sharing social activity data online is illustrated by Friedland and Sommer (2010), who present an algorithm that can be used to identify potential burglary targets based on the geo-location of videos and pictures that have been shared online by the potential victims. They refer to this as cybercasing, i.e., the method of "using online tools to check out details, make inferences from related data, and speculate about a location in the real world for questionable purposes".

## 10.4 Visualization Use Cases

As stated, personal lifelogs are voluminous and complex. Thus, visualization of the lifelog collection should be intuitive, logical and comprehensible. In this chapter, we discuss three use cases of lifelogs visualization. In each subsection talking about each pattern, we give some examples of this pattern. We demonstrate examples of our context-based visualization and hope that this research may invoke further research interest and efforts towards better visualizations for lifelogging content/information.

### 10.4.1 Visual Diary

A wearable camera passively captures thousands of photos per day. For example, SenseCam takes approximately 5500 images per day. Hence, grouping sequences of related images into *events* is necessary in order to reduce complexity (Doherty et al. 2008). This event recognition involves the segmentation of all photos into distinct groups, or events, e.g., having breakfast, talking to a work colleague, meeting a friend at a restaurant, etc. To achieve this goal, context-based sensor analysis is required in conjunction with content-based image analysis. Further, representative photos for each event have to be selected, namely a single photo from within an event which represents the event's content.

We observed that the user interest in visual logs is twofold: to gain an overview, and to find important events of interest. In this section, we present different visualization techniques to best display this information back to the user. Hence, this pattern addresses Use Cases 3.1 (Personal Lifelogging Legacy), 3.3 (Reminiscence therapy) and 3.4 (Social Activity Capturing) where a summary of the lifelogger's day/week/life is required. The different approaches are introduced in the remainder of this section.

#### Comic-Book Style Visual Diary

A Comic-book style interface requires least space when the screen space is limited. The design is inspired by the Squarified treemap (Bruls et al. 2000) pattern. In order to better utilize the limited screen space, compact view of the visual lifelog is displayed to fit full screen. As shown in Fig. 10.1, it provides a summary of user's daily

**Fig. 10.1** Interactive visual diary generated for one day, showing event segmentation (reprinted from Jung et al. 2013)

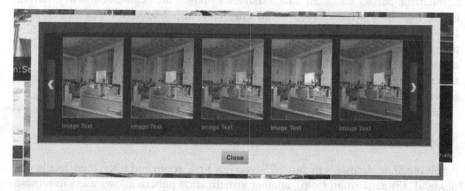

**Fig. 10.2** Each event has multiple images that allows further interaction on demand (reprinted from Jung et al. 2013)

visual log on one single page, with emphasis placed on more important events. Each grid represents an event (typically, about 20–25 events are detected for a normal day). The size of the grid provides an immediate visual cue to the events importance level, which offers users a clear entry point for exploration. The position of the grid depicts the time sequence.

Each picture that is displayed in this comic-style visual diary represents multiple similar images that depict the same event. At the same time, users are allowed to drill down (full photo stream and sensor log) inside each event. By clicking on one of the pictures, a user can view these additional pictures, together with a textual description as complementary information. Users tap on other view options to see lifelog data over a different timespan (week/month/year). An example is shown in Fig. 10.2.

**Fig. 10.3** Visualization of an interactive timeline

## Timeline (Relive the Day)

While the previous visualization focuses on highlighting important events, the following visualization theme allows users to browse through the entire collection chronologically. It is referred to as "timeline", i.e., users can see what they have done on a specific day. It can help users to see the relationship between events and comparison across historical data. Firstly, all images are segmented in to different event, then they are displayed on an interactive timeline series. For example, in Fig. 10.3, a list of events is displayed on a timeline for further exploration. For further exploration, users are allowed to access details by clicking or hovering over an event, i.e., users can see what they have done on a specific day. A short text description is generated automatically for each event, which acts as memory for better user experience.

## Master-Detailed

Applying Shneiderman's mantra of "overview first, zoom and filter, then details-on-demand" (Shneiderman 1996), another visualization pattern allows users to browse a large archive collection in one single place. The visual log is summarized in a master-list (thumbnail) of events and a text abstract representation of each event is shown. This example illustrate a thumbnail gallery to navigate visual life logs. This pattern displays visual lifelogs as a series of thumbnails of grids that users can hover over and zoom in to find more details. Drill-down is supported to reveal a detailed view. An example is shown in Fig. 10.4.

### 10.4.2 Social Interaction Radar Graph

Our goal is to build a visualization that users could use to facilitate discovery and increased awareness of their social activities. Sensor data from Bluetooth, Wi-Fi, and phone call logs, instant message logs, etc. can be used to gather users' social interaction information. This social context data is potentially valuable to life memories. Hence, the pattern can be applied in Use Case 3.4 (Social Activity Capturing).

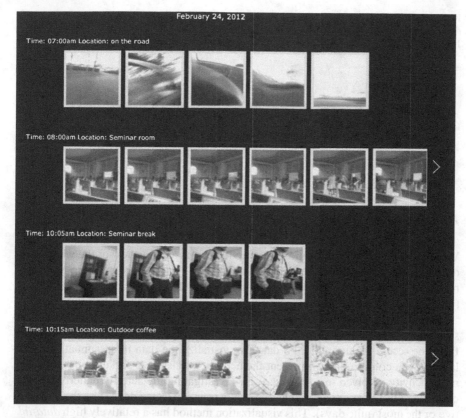

**Fig. 10.4** Master detailed view of visual log

Displaying one type of data along only reflects one aspect of social interaction activity. Aggregating all related sensors together can provide an informative and complete presentation to end-users.

This visual representation, Fig. 10.5, utilizes three embedded sensors' loggings (i.e., Bluetooth, Wi-Fi, GPS) to automatically identify social context data of individual users over the course of a whole year. Each concentric circle represents one type of sensor data. This radar graph has three dimensions: (1) type of sensor (different color been used), (2) social activity level (length of each area), (3) time (circular radar graph divided into 12 sections, one month per section). Scrolling around the circle enable rapid exploration and comparison between different months. The combination of visual attributes (length and coloring) leverages pre attentive processing to facilitate easy detection of trends or patterns over a year. For example, we can quickly perceive large clumps of gray sections in March, May and October, which tell us that the user experienced higher social activities during these months.

**Fig. 10.5** Social interaction radar graph (reprinted from Jung et al. 2013)

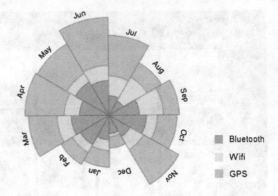

### 10.4.3 Activity Yearly Calendar

We want to design a visualization that provides users an overview of the whole year on user's activities, thus addressing Use Case 3.2 (Energy Expenditure Measurement). We focus on the accelerometer and GPS in this visualization because these two types of data are essential to reveal physical movement level directly.

Figure 10.6 shows the Activity view, which allows users gain a detailed understanding of their physical activities. The level of physical activity can be derived from the accelerometer and GPS data. We visualize the data in an annual calendar layout, with color-coding to present the activity intensity. A darker color indicates more activity involved in a given day. By investigating the activity pattern over the course of a full year, it is possible to detect a user's extreme days (i.e., the most active or the most quite days). This visualization method has a relatively high *data-ink ratio*, a concept defined by Tufte (1983). For example, in this graph, we can quickly see that the darker green grids are more heavily distributed towards beginning of April, May, July and August, indicating that more activities happened during that time.

### 10.5 Conclusion

Most existing approaches to the presentation of lifelog data use a generic type of user interface (UI) to present all their life-log collection. Given the fact that users may access their lifelogging data under different contexts and goals, we argue that the efficiency and accuracy or user interaction may suffer by relying on a single interface type. In this chapter, we have introduced different HCI design patterns that can be used as guidelines for the development of different lifelogging visualization tools. Therefore, we first introduce different lifelogging technologies that illustrate how this domain has already reached our every-day life. Further, we introduced different use cases that demonstrate different lifelogging scenarios. Based on these scenarios, we then outlined UI templates. We argue that applying these templates can ease the development of lifelogging visualization tools. As future research, we

**Fig. 10.6** Activity Calendar
View (reprinted from Jung et
al. 2013)

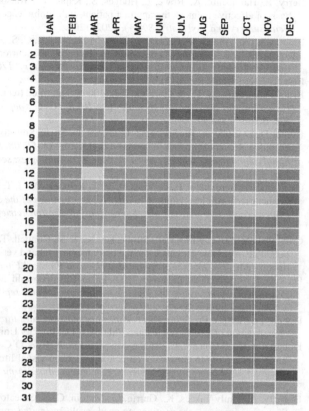

will develop various demonstrator systems based on these templates and aim to design common UI design pattern solutions for the visualization of lifelogging data.

**Acknowledgements**   This research was supported by the Norwegian Research Council (CRI number: 174867) and Science Foundation Ireland under Grant No. 07/CE/I1147.

# References

Aharony, N., Pan, W., Ip, C., Khayal, I., & Pentland, A. (2011). Social fMRI: investigating and shaping social mechanisms in the real world. *Pervasive and Mobile Computing*, 7(6), 643–659.

Albinali, F., Intille, S., Haskell, W., & Rosenberger, M. (2010). Using wearable activity type detection to improve physical activity energy expenditure estimation. In *UbiComp '10. Proceedings of the 12th ACM international conference on Ubiquitous computing* (pp. 311–320). New York: ACM.

Bell, G., & Gemmell, J. (2009). *Total recall*. New York: Dutton.

Berry, E., Kapur, N., Williams, L., Hodges, S., Watson, P., Smyth, G., et al. (2007). The use of a wearable camera, SenseCam, as a pictorial diary to improve autobiographical memory in a patient with limbic encephalitis: a preliminary report. *Neuropsychological Rehabilitation*, 17(4–5), 582–601.

Berry, E., Hampshire, A., Rowe, J., Hodges, S., Kapur, N., Watson, P., et al. (2009). The neural basis of effective memory therapy in a patient with limbic encephalitis. *Journal of Neurology, Neurosurgery and Psychiatry, 80*(11), 1202–1205.

Bharoucha, A., Anand, V., Forlizzi, J., Dew, M., Reynolds, C. S. S., & Wactlar, H. (2009). Intelligent assistive technology applications to dementia care: current capabilities, limitations, and future challenges. *American Journal of Geriatric Psychiatry, 17*(2), 88–104.

Boland, J., & Pereira, R. (2011). *Wireless headset camera lens.*

Bruls, D. M., Huizing, C., & van Wijk, J. J. (2000). Squarified treemaps. In *Data visualization '00. Proceedings of the joint Eurographics and IEEE TCVG symposium on visualization* (pp. 33–42). Berlin: Springer.

Byrne, D., Doherty, A. R., Snoek, C. G., Jones, G. G., & Smeaton, A. F. (2008). Validating the detection of everyday concepts in visual lifelogs. In *SAMT '08. Proceedings of the 3rd international conference on semantic and digital media technologies: semantic multimedia* (pp. 15–30). Berlin, Heidelberg: Springer.

Clements, M., Serdyukov, P., de Vries, A. P., & Reinders, M. J. T. (2010). Using flickr geotags to predict user travel behaviour. In *SIGIR '10. Proceedings of the 33rd international ACM SIGIR conference on research and development in information retrieval* (pp. 851–852). New York: ACM.

Cole, P., LeMura, L., Klinger, T., Strohecker, K., & McConnell, T. (2004). Measuring energy expenditure in cardiac patients using the body media armband versus indirect calorimetry. A validation study. *The Journal of Sports Medicine and Physical Fitness, 44*(3), 262–271.

Daskala, B., Askoxylakis, I., Brown, I., Dickman, P., Friedewald, M., Irion, K., et al. (2011). *Risks and benefits of emerging life-logging applications (Final report).* Iraklio, Greece: European Network and Information Security Agency (ENISA).

Doherty, A. (2009). *Providing effective memory retrieval cues through automatic structuring and augmentation of a lifelog of images.* PhD diss., Dublin City University.

Doherty, A. R., Ó Conaire, C., Blighe, M., Smeaton, A. F., & O'Connor, N. E. (2008). Combining image descriptors to effectively retrieve events from visual lifelogs. In *MIR '08. Proceedings of the 1st ACM international conference on multimedia information retrieval* (pp. 10–17). New York: ACM.

Doherty, A., Pauly-Takacs, K., Gurrin, C., Moulin, C., & Smeaton, A. F. (2009). Three years of SenseCam images—observations on cued recall. In *Invited speech at SenseCam 2009 symposium at the 39th annual meeting of the society for neuroscience.*

Doherty, A., Pauly-Takacs, K., Capriani, N., Gurrin, C., Moulin, C., O'Connor, N., & Smeaton, A. F. (2012). Experiences of aiding autobiographical memory using the SenseCam. *Human-Computer Interaction, 27*(1–2), 151–174.

Elliott, D., Hopfgartner, F., Leelanupab, T., Moshfeghi, Y., & Jose, J. M. (2009). An architecture for life-long user modelling. In *LLUM '09* (pp. 9–16).

Friedland, G., & Sommer, R. (2010). Cybercasing the joint: on the privacy implications of geotagging. In *Usenix security conference.*

Gedik, B., & Liu, L. (2008). Protecting location privacy with personalized k-anonymity: Architecture and algorithms. *IEEE Transactions on Mobile Computing, 7*(1), 1–18.

Gemmell, J., Bell, G., & Lueder, R. (2006). MyLifeBits: a personal database for everything. *Communications of the ACM, 49*(1), 88–95.

Haner, L. (2002). *Child monitoring system.*

Hodges, S., Williams, L., Berry, E., Izadi, S., Srinivasan, J., Butler, A., et al. (2006). SenseCam: a retrospective memory aid. In *UbiComp '06. Proceedings of the 8th international conference on ubiquitous computing* (pp. 177–193). Berlin: Springer.

Jung, H., Kim, T., Yang, Y., Carli, L., Carnesecchi, M., Rizzo, A., & Gurrin, C. (2013, to appear). Aesthetics in data visualization: case studies and design issues. In Huang, M. & Huang, W. (eds.), *Innovative approaches of data visualization and visual analytics.* Hershey: IGI Global.

Kalnikaite, V., & Whittaker, S. (2012). Synergetic recollection: how to design lifelogging tools that help locate the right information. In *Studies in computational intelligence: Vol. 396. Human-computer interaction: the agency perspective* (pp. 329–348). Berlin: Springer.

Kennedy, L. S., & Naaman, M. (2008). Generating diverse and representative image search results for landmarks. In *WWW* (pp. 297–306).

Kratz, S., Rohs, M., Wolf, K., Müller, J., Wilhelm, M., Johansson, C., et al. (2011). Body, movement, gesture & tactility in interaction with mobile devices. In *MobileHCI '11. Proceedings of the 13th international conference on human computer interaction with mobile devices and services* (pp. 757–759). New York: ACM.

Li, N., Crane, M., Ruskin, H., & Gurrin, C. (2013). Multiscaled cross-correlation dynamics on SenseCam lifelogged data. In *MMM '13. Proceedings of the 19th international conference on multimedia modeling, Part I* (pp. 490–501). Berlin: Springer.

Messerman, A., Mustafić, T., Camtepe, S. A., & Albayrak, S. (2011). Continuous and non-intrusive identity verification in real-time environments based on free-text keystroke dynamics. In *IEEE international joint conference on biometrics (IJCB 11): international conference on biometrics (ICB) and the biometrics theory, application and systems (BTAS)*.

Michael, K., McNamee, A., & Michael, M. (2006). The emerging ethics of humancentric GPS tracking and monitoring. In *ICMB '06: Proceedings of the international conference on mobile business* (p. 34).

Miyaki, T., & Rekimoto, J. (2008). Sensonomy: envisioning folksonomic urban sensing. In *UbiComp 2008 workshop programs* (pp. 187–190).

Montoye, H. J., Washburn, R., Servais, S., Ertl, A., Webster, J. G., & Nagle, F. J. (1983). Estimation of energy expenditure by a portable accelerometer. *Medicine and Science in Sports and Exercise, 15*(5), 403–407.

Nadkarni, A., & Hofmann, S. G. (2012). Why do people use Facebook? *Personality and Individual Differences, 52*(3), 243–249.

O'Hara, K., Tuffield, M. M., & Shadbolt, N. (2008). Lifelogging: privacy and empowerment with memories for life. *Identity in the Information Society, 1*(1), 155–172.

Olmassakian, V. (1999). *Child monitoring system.*

Olsson, M. I. (2012). *Wearable display device.*

Pauly-Takacs, K., Moulin, C. J. A., & Estlin, E. J. (2011). SenseCam as a rehabilitation tool in a child with anterograde amnesia. *Memory, 19*(7), 705–712.

Piasek, P., Irving, K., & Smeaton, A. F. (2011). SenseCam intervention based on cognitive stimulation therapy framework for early-stage dementia. In *PervasiveHealth* (pp. 522–525).

Pittiglio, L. (2000). Use of reminiscence therapy in patients with Alzheimer's disease. *Lippincott's Case Management, 5*(6), 216–220.

Qiu, Z., Gurrin, C., Doherty, A. R., & Smeaton, A. F. (2012). A real-time life experience logging tool. In *MMM'12* (pp. 636–638).

Rawassizadeh, R., Anjomshoaa, A., & Tomitsch, M. (2011). A framework for long-term archiving of pervasive device information. *MoMM '11. Proceedings of the 9th international conference on advances in mobile computing and multimedia* (pp. 244–247). New York: ACM.

Reddy, S., Burke, J., Estrin, D., Hansen, M. H., & Srivastava, M. B. (2007). A framework for data quality and feedback in participatory sensing. In *SenSys'07: Proceedings of the 5th international conference on embedded networked sensor systems* (pp. 417–418).

Rekimoto, J., Miyaki, T., & Ishizawa, T. (2007). LifeTag: a WiFi-based location life-logging device. In *ACM symposium on user interface and software technology.*

Schofield, G., Bishop, C. M., MacLean, G., Brown, P., Baker, M., Katselidis, K. A., et al. (2007). Novel GPS tracking of sea turtles as a tool for conservation management. *Journal of Experimental Marine Biology and Ecology, 347*(1–2), 58–68.

Shneiderman, B. (1996). The eyes have it: a task by data type taxonomy for information visualizations. In *VL '96. Proceedings of the 1996 IEEE symposium on visual languages* (p. 336). Washington: IEEE Comput. Soc..

Sittig, A., & Zuckerberg, M. (2010). *Managing information about relationships in a social network via a social timeline.*

Swartz, A. M., Strath, S. J., Bassett, D. R., Obrien, W. L., King, G. A., & Ainsworth, B. E. (2000). Estimation of energy expenditure using CSA accelerometers at hip and wrist sites. *Medicine and Science in Sports and Exercise, 32*, 450–456.

Tufte, E. (1983). *The visual display of quantitative information*. Cheshire: Graphics Press.

VandenBos, G. (Ed.) (2006). *APA dictionary of psychology* (1st ed.). Washington: American Psychol. Assoc.

Weimerskirch, H., Bonadonna, F., Bailleul, F., Mabille, G., Dell'Omo, G., & Lipp, H.-P. (2002). GPS tracking of foraging albatrosses. *Science, 295*(5558), 1259.

Weiner, S. (1998). The addiction of overeating: self-help groups as treatment models. *Journal of Clinical Psychology, 54*(2), 163–167.

Woods, B., Spector, A., Jones, C., Orrell, M., & Davies, S. (2009). Reminiscence therapy for dementia. In *Cochrane Database of Systematic Reviews 2005*.

Zhou, M., & Gurrin, C. (2012). A survey on life logging data capture. In *SenseCam '12*.

Printed in the United States
By Bookmasters

Printed in the United States
By Bookmasters